PENGUIN

JOURNEYMAN

SEAN PRONGER (yes, Chris's brother) grew up in Dryden, Ontario, and was drafted fifty-first overall by Vancouver in 1991. From 1995 to 2004 he played in the NHL for the Anaheim Mighty Ducks, the Pittsburgh Penguins, the New York Rangers, the Los Angeles Kings, the Boston Bruins, the Columbus Blue Jackets, and the Vancouver Canucks. He played in 260 regular-season games, earning 23 goals and 36 assists for 59 points, picking up 159 penalty minutes. Today he lives with his long-suffering wife, Mrs. Journeyman, in Newport Beach, California, where he has started a sportswear company: www.jrnymnwear.com.

DAN MURPHY is the host of Vancouver Canucks hockey on Sportsnet and has been (un)lucky enough to know the Pronger brothers since the late 80s.

JOURNEYMAN

THE MANY TRIUMPHS
(AND EVEN MORE NUMEROUS DEFEATS)
OF A GUY WHO'S SEEN JUST ABOUT EVERYTHING IN THE GAME OF HOCKEY

SEAN PRONGER

WITH DAN MURPHY

PENGUIN

an imprint of Penguin Canada Books Inc.

Published by the Penguin Group

Penguin Canada Books Inc., 90 Eglinton Avenue East, Suite 700, Toronto, Ontario, Canada M4P 2Y3

Penguin Group (USA) Inc., 375 Hudson Street, New York, New York 10014, U.S.A.

Penguin Books Ltd, 80 Strand, London WC2R 0RL, England

Penguin Ireland, 25 St Stephen's Green, Dublin 2, Ireland (a division of Penguin Books Ltd)

Penguin Group (Australia), 707 Collins Street, Melbourne, Victoria 3008, Australia
(a division of Pearson Australia Group Pty Ltd)

Penguin Books India Pvt Ltd, 11 Community Centre, Panchsheel Park, New Delhi – 110 017, India

Penguin Group (NZ), 67 Apollo Drive, Rosedale, Auckland 0632, New Zealand
(a division of Pearson New Zealand Ltd)

Penguin Books (South Africa) (Pty) Ltd, 24 Sturdee Avenue, Rosebank, Johannesburg 2196, South Africa

Penguin Books Ltd, Registered Offices: 80 Strand, London WC2R 0RL, England

First published in Viking hardcover by Penguin Canada, 2012
Published in this edition, 2013

2 3 4 5 6 7 8 9 10 (WEB)

Manufactured in Canada.

ISBN: 978-0-14-318102-6

Library and Archives Canada Cataloguing in Publication data available upon request to the publisher.

Visit the Penguin Canada website at **www.penguin.ca**

Special and corporate bulk purchase rates available; please see
www.penguin.ca/corporatesales or call 1-800-810-3104, ext. 2477.

THIS BOOK IS DEDICATED TO
ALL THE JOURNEYMEN EVERYWHERE.
KEEP FIGHTING THE GOOD FIGHT.

CONTENTS

FOREWORD

By Brian Burke

I was pleased when Sean asked me to write a foreword for his book. I was involved in drafting both Sean (in 1991 with Vancouver) and Chris (in 1993 with Hartford). As I said in a speech in Winnipeg years ago, this makes me "one for two"! Maybe in terms of talent, but not in terms of character or brains.

Sean was a great organizational player. He was smart positionally, versatile, and hard-nosed. He did many small things extremely well, which is the mark of a thoughtful player. Our coaches never had to tell Sean anything more than once. Not only that, Sean was able to pass much of this instruction on to other players.

Scouting description: extremely intelligent player with a high hockey I.Q. Excellent work habits in games and in practice. Very intense, utilized in every manpower and clock situation. Physical on every inch of the ice surface. Team-centred and coachable. So it's no surprise to me that Sean's post-hockey career has also been marked with distinction.

Reading Sean's book brings back a *lot* of memories, from my days as a Springfield Indian and Maine Mariner. (That is, getting paid almost no money, taking endless bus trips, and having no job security.) In fact, I had so much fun in the AHL I applied to Harvard and got in to their law school as soon as I could. For those of you fortunate enough to know Sean, obviously, this was not an option for him. We read every day about pro athletes who turn down multi-million dollar contracts. This book is written by a guy who scraped for every cent.

Reporters often ask me why I tend to draft guys with a good work ethic on the ice. Sean's book shows us why hard workers succeed: they are always learning and improving. I'm glad he wrote this book; it should be required reading for every person who is thinking of making a living from pro sports.

PRESS BOX EPISTLES

By Chris Pronger

Some may see the glamorous life of a professional hockey player and wish it were theirs. The thing is, they always envision themselves as the star player. Trust me, it's great and I wouldn't trade it for anything—but there is another side of life in the NHL that we never think about or see. I've been lucky in many respects; while having been traded four times in my career, I have always been wanted. I have been well-compensated for my play in the NHL and am very grateful for it. But Sean's book is all about that guy you don't hear about much—the one struggling for a spot on the fourth line, or hoping to be the seventh defenceman. These people do NOT make big money, especially if they are sent down to the minors, as they often are.

Don't believe me?

How many times have you read about the player who signs late or the last player cut at training camp? We see this happen all the time yet we don't seem to think much about it. But the media tend to ignore or forget the guy playing in Abbotsford for $35K a year. There are dairy clerks at your local grocery store who make more, while the guy in Abbotsford is living out his dream. My point? I think my brother's book is funny, self-deprecating, and full of stuff the average fan might not know. That's because the journeymen know how lucky we are, all of us, to be getting paid to play the most exciting game in the world. In fact, the journeymen are probably paying more attention than the guys who play the big minutes. They probably work harder than anyone else and they may even enjoy it more than anyone else, because every shift means something to them. They also know how lucky they are to be where they are. Other people start their shift in a factory at 5 a.m., or drive city buses till 2 a.m. We, on the other hand, fly first-class charters, stay at the best hotels, eat gourmet food, and then work about sixty to sixty-five minutes a night, three or four times a week. Journeymen never forget that. Ever.

Reading this book reminds me of long winter nights in Dryden—my brother the captain of team A, me the captain of team B, the whole ten of us freezing, but none of us caring. We would play the game we loved as long as we could, no matter the wind or cold. As we used to say, "It's for the love of the game." Well, when you're a journeyman, it's not only for the love of the game. It's also to keep the dream alive.

1

BLACKOUT

Where am I? How did I get here?

Before you jump to conclusions, let me clarify. No, I don't have a concussion. And no, I'm not in jail (though getting out of here won't be easy). Where I am is sitting on rented furniture in a room with a slanted floor and peeling walls, trying to figure out exactly how my dream of becoming a professional hockey player has turned into a nightmare.

Is it my black eye and broken nose? Maybe.

Is it the $500 a week I'm raking in playing in the East Coast Hockey League? Maybe.

Is it the unheated farmhouse on the outskirts of the hockey hotbed known as Knoxville, Tennessee, that I currently call home? Maybe.

Is it the eight-hour bus rides to go play a bunch of thugs who don't even realize there's a puck on the ice? Maybe.

Does the reason even matter?

I'm in a tailspin and I seriously don't know if it's worth the energy to try to pull out of it. Maybe it would be best if I just let my career (if you can call it that) go down in flames and take a different path.

I guess that mentality, more than anything, tells you just how bad it was. If a guy who's spent his whole life either playing hockey or wishing he were playing hockey suddenly thinks he might be better off doing something else—well, things are *bad*.

You see, while I was growing up playing road hockey on the frozen streets of Dryden, Ontario, my dreams didn't include the East Coast Hockey League. A biography of my early years could be written using nothing but sports clichés. A bunch of kids playing their hearts out on an outdoor rink. Early mornings and long drives to old rinks in surrounding small towns. Lying in bed at night, fantasizing about lifting my team to victory. The thing is, I pretended I was Wayne Gretzky scoring big goals for the Oilers, not Shawn Snesar mucking it up with the Hampton Road Admirals. It was the Stanley Cup I hoisted over my head, not the Patrick J. Kelly Cup or the Riley Cup or whatever the hell they call it this week. I was your average Canadian hockey-loving kid from a northern town who believed he could make it to the big league.

Other people must have believed in me, too. I wore a "C" on the sweater of my small-town team. I scored a lot of goals. I went on to play in the NCAA—collegiate sports—and I wore a "C" there too, so clearly at least a few people at a big hockey university believed in me. OK, no one ever thought I had magic hands, but there were guys in the NHL who believed in me—one of them named Brian Burke drafted me in the third round. Belief had never been a problem. I was always one of the best players on my team. There was never really a doubt in my mind that I would make it to the NHL. Everything had been going according to plan.

I put in the work. I listened to my coaches. I didn't cut corners. I did everything the right way. I loved the game and it had always loved me back.

But now, hockey seemed to be having second thoughts about me. Hockey was beginning to act like things might not be working out. Hockey was hinting it wanted to see other people.

After four years at Bowling Green State University (in the CCHA—the Central Collegiate Hockey Association) and being drafted, I figured I would sign a contract, play a year on the farm, and then follow that up with a long, successful stint in the NHL.

I got the first part right. It was the autumn of 1994, and I was definitely on the farm. But the thing is, nobody in the minors is interested in being some small-town boy's stepping stone to the big league. They're more than happy to put you in your place, and when you're a tall college kid in his first year with a younger brother playing in the NHL (did I mention I have a younger brother?), you better be ready to defend yourself both verbally and physically. My test came pretty early. In the first game, actually.

We were playing an exhibition in lovely Huntsville, Alabama. (I believe it's formally referred to as *Hockeytown, Ala-frickin-bama.* Or something like that.) A lot of people don't realize how physical U.S. college hockey is. Players are forced to wear cages, which is a big reason why some people consider it a soft league. But think about it. When your face is protected, there's not much of a fear factor when you're zeroing in to hit someone. The thought that the guy might get his stick up or stuff his elbow down your throat to defend himself doesn't even cross your mind. Why be cautious? You're wearing a cage, right? Now, factor in the lack of interference (that is, no one's holding you as you line up your guy), and the fact that NCAA players are generally older and stronger than the ones in major junior, and you have a recipe for some high-speed collisions.

In my first ECHL game I was running around like I was still in college. At one point, an opposing defenceman was coming around the net with his head down. Forecheckers live for this moment. I went charging in and absolutely crushed him. I couldn't believe how hard I hit him. It felt great. The ref gave me a penalty for charging but I didn't care. As far as I was concerned, it was a beautiful hit and my teammates were going to love it. That's what hockey is all about.

Strangely, while I was congratulating myself on how awesome that hit was, I forgot to take into account what the guys on the other bench might think. As I headed to the penalty box, one of the meatheads on the other team skated up beside me and growled, "You better keep your head up, rook, because you got a fight coming."

Was he talking to me? What did I do?

I sat in the box and ran the hit—and the comment—through my head for the two minutes, and then skated over to our bench to ask one of our grizzled veterans if he thought my hit was dirty.

"No," he said.

"Then why does that guy want to fight me?"

"It doesn't matter if it's dirty. You got the better of one of their players. They're not going to allow us to think we can hammer anyone we want. They're just letting you know you can't run around like that."

"Oh, OK. I'll try to take it easy. Does that mean he probably won't want to fight?"

"No, he's going to fight you."

His name was Todd Harris, and we did fight. And I didn't get knocked out. It felt good to get it out of the way.

But the bruises on my face and fists were an unambiguous message that I was a long way from the glamorous world of NCAA sports. (Another message from my aching hands: Punching people in the helmet may hurt you more than them.) Now, sitting on this couch—with no cable—I can't help looking back fondly on the good old days … of last year.

I remember playing in front of sold-out crowds in some of college hockey's legendary cathedrals. Places like Munn Ice Arena at Michigan State University or Yost Ice Arena at the University of Michigan. Now I get to play in front of friends and family in Birmingham, Alabama. I'm sure you can imagine the atmosphere on a Wednesday night in December. Unless they're giving away free trucker hats and six packs of PBR for every power-play goal, it can be depressingly quiet.

Don't get me wrong, now. The East Coast Hockey League is not all bad. In fact, the level of play is much higher than I expected. I'm sure it's because the 1994 NHL lockout has caused a ripple effect by pushing better players down a league. It's also not as violent as I thought it would be. Again, an influx of more skilled players from the AHL and IHL has taken some jobs away from the goons, so we're not reenacting a scene from *Slap Shot* every night. But that's not to say that things don't get ugly from time to time.

And when you're a kid, you're not looking around and seeing things for what they are. All you see is how they're not what you were hoping for.

In college, I had aspirations of big-time hockey with bright lights in major cities. Now, it's line brawls in Deliverance, Tennessee.

In college, we had pre-game meals at a high-end Italian restaurant. Now, it's the world famous Country Buffet—$4.99 all-you-can-eat for the regular folk, but we get it for free. And even that I usually pass up for some mac and cheese with a can of tuna on top back at the farmhouse.

In college, my teammates and I had hope. We would sit in the locker room and talk about opportunities, goals, and the path to success. We were going to make it, dammit! Come hell or high water. Now, I'd take an Al MacInnis slapshot in the mouth just to have a home with *hot* water.

I can't help thinking how fast things have changed over the course of a year, or six months for that matter. I went from living large as a varsity athlete—big man on campus, captain of an NCAA Division One hockey team—to just scraping by in the bowels of professional hockey while roughing it in a farmhouse in Knoxville. Why the farmhouse? That's a great question. (Back in '94 it wasn't all in anticipation of an "on the farm" metaphor for this book, believe it or not.)

It's common knowledge that players in the East Coast Hockey League aren't rewarded with million-dollar contracts. You could make more as a waiter. So Sean Brown (not *that* Sean Brown—this one didn't play a single career NHL game), Chris Fess (also zero career NHL games), and I had a great idea to try to stretch our money a little farther. We found a farmhouse thirty minutes out of town in the backcountry of Tennessee (cue "Dueling Banjos"). The owner was going to tear it down and build a mansion in the summer. He said if we wanted to stay in it, we could. RENT FREE! Whaaat?! And pocket an extra $300 a month? Done. The place was classic. We had a barn, a horseshoe pit, and, of course, the farmhouse. When we moved in, our to-do list read something like this:

1. Buy horseshoes.
2. Throw party in barn.

It should have included checking for cable, heat, and signs of rodents. What's that old saying? "If it seems too good to be true...."

Anyway, free is free, and he didn't charge extra for the mice, either. A couple hundred dollars in mousetraps later, we had only a cable and heat problem. I thought it never got cold in Tennessee.

But it does, my friend. Come December and guess whose pipes froze? For four days we showered at the rink and tried not to have a "movement" after 2 p.m. For those of us who weren't that regular, there was a truck stop a couple miles down the road. At least it was clean, right?

When a decent shower seems like a distant dream, making it to the NHL feels all but impossible. Doubt was creeping in. Maybe, I had begun to think, just maybe, I don't have what it takes to make it to the highest level of my sport. And that's a scary thought when you really haven't planned to do anything with your life. Anything *else* with your life, that is. I figured I had a plan: play in the NHL. Why would I try to picture any other future?

If you've never tried to make it to the NHL, then not making it probably doesn't sound all that bad. But imagine spending an entire afternoon on a project—baking a cake, tiling the kitchen floor, whatever—and finding out at the end of the day that you did it wrong and would have to start over. Pretty frustrating. Now imagine it was a whole month you'd spent on the project, or a whole year. What if you spent a year building a house, only to have it condemned on the day you're supposed to move in because you built it on unstable ground—and you don't have unstable-ground insurance? Devastating, right?

Well, then. Imagine investing your whole life and seeing all that you'd worked for begin to slip through your fingers. That's how I felt as I sat on a couch in Tennessee trying to figure out how things had gone so wrong.

Of course, that was a younger Sean Pronger. Since I've learned a few things over the years, he was also a stupider Sean Pronger. It's strange to think my life was in the hands of that kid. If the guy sitting on the couch with a beer in his hand and feeling sorry for himself had made different decisions, I might not be here writing this book.

I can't help wondering what Young Sean would have done if he'd known then what the future had in store. If only a fortune-teller had been in the room with me that day—sitting on a milk crate, with flowing robes, long press-on nails, and makeup that would make a clown proud. With the flip of each tarot card her face would go from amusement to shock to horror.

"Sean, the cards have spoken. And yes, an NHL contract is in your not-too-distant future."

"I knew it! I have to say, I'm relieved."

"Well, you'll actually start with their IHL affiliate and, oh dear, be back on the East Coast not too much longer after that."

"Wow, that doesn't seem all that promising."

"Just wait. I also see a painful injury killing your first professional season!"

"Injury?"

"Hush, Sean, the cards are just beginning to tell me your story. You will begin your second season at an NHL training camp, and I see an exhibition game against a team wearing blue shirts."

"Really? The Rangers? That sounds great. And...."

"Hold on ... yes, you will indeed play your first National Hockey League game just before you turn twenty-three years of age."

"What? I'll make the NHL before I'm twenty-three? That's fantastic!"

"Not quite. I don't see a lengthy stay. Maybe a week or two and then it will be back to bus rides for you."

"For how long?"

"The remainder of that season and the first half of the next season. But then you'll make your way back to the big leagues. And you're not sent down again."

"OK, that's a start."

"But I do see something of an address change in March."

"A trade?"

"Perhaps. I sense happiness the following summer, thanks to a contract with only one salary on it."

"A one-way deal? Finally, I made it!"

"Does a one-way deal mean you get a one-way ticket to the minors for the beginning of October?"

"You're joking."

"It's not me, it's the cards. And it appears that your lifeline makes many twists and turns at this point. I do see games in an NHL jersey. And then some games in another NHL jersey. And then some more games in yet another NHL jersey."

"Wait, slow down. All this happens in one season?"

"Yes. Would you like me to continue?"

"Might as well, because it can't get any worse."

"Actually, according to the tarot, it can."

"You've got to be kidding. How many death cards are in that deck?"

"Seems to be more for you than for others. You will play most of the season in the minors, but you'll be recalled and eventually dress in what will be your last NHL game. Without ruining the surprise, this will be a game that won't soon be forgotten."

Maybe it's lucky for me no fortune-teller was nearby that day. Her reading of the future would have crushed the spirit of that younger Sean. If you play to win, finding out you'll manage to *get by* doesn't seem all that inspiring. When you're used to being the guy the team looks to when they need a big play, the assurance that you'll do a half-decent job for the next decade or so would feel like a total defeat.

If Young Sean had access to that information, he'd have said "Screw it."

Fortunately, Young Sean was too short-sighted to see what may lie ahead. What's that old saying? Ignorance is bliss? It couldn't be more true in this case. I thank Young Sean every day for blindly following his dream. If he didn't, I'd be sitting on a barstool somewhere explaining to the man behind the wood how good I was and that I surely could have made it to the NHL if I'd wanted to. Inside, however, it would kill me that I never gave it a shot.

Young Sean didn't know a lot of things that Slightly Older Sean still doesn't know. (I still can't play Brahms' Second Piano Concerto, for example.) But I've learned a thing or two about dreams, and about realizing them. The way I see it now, not winning the Conn Smythe Trophy doesn't mean I didn't have a great career. After all, I doubt that the men and women who climb Mount Everest spend the rest of their lives wishing they'd done it a few minutes faster. In the end, those few minutes mean little beside the sheer feat of getting to the top at all.

I dreamed of getting to the top, and I got there. I was never a superstar, as much as I would have liked to have been. But being a journeyman is a pretty special thing, too. To be a journeyman means making it to the top, and making a living once you get there. Even that is a pretty rare accomplishment.

Does that sound like rationalization? Like I'm patting myself on the back for getting my name on a hockey card that features some pretty mediocre stats? That's not it at all. I'll be the first guy to bring myself down to Earth if I ever get too full of myself. (Just read on—you'll see.) But I do get to tell my kids about how their dad played in the best league in the world with and against some of the greatest to ever lace them up. I was good enough to beat Hall of Famers in the faceoff circle. I was good enough to beat NHL goalies from time to time. For all the gory details, however, they'll have to read this book. And so will you.

2

THE BEGINNING

When people talk about what Eric Lindros and I have in common, the same thing keeps coming up: We both were drafted on June 22, 1991. After that the conversation usually turns to something else.

Joking aside, I can tell you that draft day means everything to a kid who has spent his whole life working to make it to the NHL. I still love watching the draft, maybe because I have some sense of what's going on behind the scenes. Not just the scouting reports and the GMs' fretting. I mean what's going on as families sit around the kitchen table the night before and talk it all through for the thousandth time, weighing the questions of which team it's going to be, and which round, and maybe whether it's going to happen at all. If you want reality TV, that's about as real as it gets, watching young men and their families live through the experience of having their dreams weighed and pronounced upon in public.

The draft that year was held at The Aud in Buffalo. My dad and I made the trek from Dryden to New York State, so we had a long time to talk about what might happen.

And to be honest, we didn't have a clue what that might be. Since no one from my hometown had ever been drafted into the

NHL, we had no reference point. No framework we could use to better prepare ourselves. I could tell my dad was a little nervous, though. Big Jim is not a big talker to begin with (nowadays he can't hear jack shit, so he's not much of a listener either), but he was eerily quiet on the flight to Toronto, and likewise he didn't offer up much in the rental car from Toronto to Buffalo. Dad surely didn't want to see me disappointed, so perhaps he was silent to avoid saying something that would get my hopes up. Whatever the reason, he wasn't talking. I was, and still am, the exact opposite. When I'm nervous I'll chatter your ear off like we're a fivesome at ladies' twilight. My Dad got an earful that day. I can't remember what I was saying to him, but you can be sure it was just constant, useless ramblings. I can tell you that I was more excited than nervous. We were a couple of Dryden pioneers heading into the great unknown. Ready to pave the way for future NHLers from our little mill town. Or maybe we were just a couple of idiots driving to Buffalo.

I think I was ranked somewhere in the third or fourth round. But considering I lit up the CCHA for a monstrous three goals in my freshman year as a member of the Bowling Green Falcons, I wasn't holding my breath. Usually, if a guy is going to be drafted it happens before he gets to college. That's because just about everyone in the draft is eighteen—major junior players and guys about to go off to play NCAA. But since my birthday is in November, I was ineligible to be drafted before my first year of school. That means I would have been scouted as a seventeen-year-old playing against twenty-one-year-olds, and I didn't exactly dominate. I don't know that I would have been any better off playing in the OHL, though. In fact, I was so sure I wanted to go the college route that I told the OHL not to bother drafting me out of Midget—and every team seemed happy to respect my wishes. (Ever eager to follow in his big brother's footsteps, Chris too told the league he wouldn't report to an OHL team that drafted him. The Peterborough Petes seemed not to get the memo.)

Anyway, in college you get a lot more practice and far fewer games than you do in major junior, and I figured that kind of development would suit me better. (I would have been OK with scoring a few more goals, though.) Scouts are looking more for potential than for NHL-ready talent when they're making their notes on a bunch of kids. Still, I'd have liked to think that three goals didn't give a great sense of my potential.

Teams set up meetings with players before they invest in them—obviously, they want to get some sense of what kind of kid they're bringing into the club. And, even more obviously, the more interesting you are as a player, the more interviews you get (unless you're guaranteed to go with one of the top picks—then teams choosing lower won't bother interviewing you). When I arrived in Buffalo I had a grand total of one meeting lined up. The Vancouver Canucks were the only ones bright enough to try to learn a little more about the man behind the man. I can still remember sitting in that hotel room with the brass from the Canucks—Pat Quinn, Brian Burke, and Mike Penny. At six-foot-three and 205 pounds, I was by far the smallest person in that room.

You'd think that since I had only one meeting I would remember the conversation that took place. Nope. I can say that it was a lot less formal than I had envisioned. For some reason I'd pictured it being more of an interview with the three of them on one side of the table and me all by myself on the other side. They'd show me flash cards, I'd provide an insightful answer, and they'd look at each other, nod, and pretend to write something down. As it turned out, it was a very relaxed setting. We sat in a circle around a coffee table having a casual conversation. It was nice and civilized, but I couldn't help being intimidated by all three of them. Brian Burke was rocking his now-patented look of undone dress shirt with tie looking more like a scarf and a wad of chew in his mouth. Pat Quinn and Mike Penny were gnawing on a couple of foot-long stogies. They asked me things like, "What kind of player are you?" and "Why should we draft you?" As a relatively young player I didn't find those to be easy questions to answer. If only I'd had the balls to come back with, "like Wayne Gretzky, and because I'm awesome." The one thing that does stand out from that meeting was Brian Burke commenting on my sportcoat and tie. He said he knew I had just arrived and he appreciated the effort to look half decent for the interview. I thought that was pretty cool of him to notice. (And, for the record, my sportcoat was green. This detail will come back to bite me in the ass, as you'll hear later in the book.)

When Big Jim and I arrived at the draft we looked like a couple of tourists. We were wide-eyed, our heads on swivels, and we clearly had no idea where to go. Most of the players in attendance had agents who had been through this a hundred times before. Big Jim and I had only seen it on TV. Not knowing where to go, we just sat with the spectators. As the players were drafted it became easy to figure out where most of the picks were sitting. And it was nowhere near the two of us. (Author's note: In life, it's always the older brother paving the way for the younger one. Because of my draft experience, things ran a little more smoothly for Chris a couple years later. By the way, Snaggletooth—you're welcome.)

It didn't really matter much where we sat, because all eyes at the '91 draft were fixed upon the "Big E." Eric Lindros was already labelled the Next One. He had the size and skill to dominate the NHL for the next two decades. The only question was whether he'd be doing this dominating in a Quebec Nordiques jersey. It was all the pundits talked about leading up to the draft. And sure enough, when the Nordiques made Lindros the number one pick it was almost as if the draft were over. He walked up to the stage (which, I'm told, is where the first-round picks go), grabbed his sweater but didn't put it on, shook hands with Nordiques GM Pierre Page, smiled for the cameras, and left the stage. As he walked away the entire press section followed. Most of them returned about twenty minutes later. It's a good thing they came back, otherwise they would've missed seeing some pretty good players get picked—Scott Niedermayer, Peter Forsberg, and Alexei Kovalev, to name a few.

There was some discussion about who would go second. When the San Jose Sharks called out Pat Falloon's name I had to smile. I'd played against him in the Manitoba Midget AAA hockey league a few years back. (For a small-town kid like me it always makes for great barstool chit-chat when you can say you played against someone when you were a kid. "Hey, can you pass me a beer? Did I tell you about the time I played against Pat Falloon? I did? Are you sure? Anyway, he was playing for Shoal Lake and I….") The fifth pick in the draft was Aaron Ward. You young kids out there know him as a TV star now. I had played against him the previous year when he was a freshman at Michigan and I was a freshman at Bowling Green. Was I envious watching guys I had competed against go so high in the draft? Not at all. I was thinking that these guys are good hockey players—but they're not *that* great. If I could play with them, maybe I had a shot.

Considering I had met with only one team prior to the draft I was fairly certain I wasn't going in the first round. But part of me got a little nervous when Vancouver was about to make the seventh overall pick. Teams had taken a flyer on a player before, hadn't they?

"With the seventh pick in the 1991 entry draft the Vancouver Canucks are happy to select [wait for it…] Alek Stojanov." Stojanov turned out to be a great pick for the Canucks. He played only sixty-two games for the franchise and scored exactly zero goals, *but* he was eventually flipped for another struggling first-round pick from '91 named Markus Naslund, who went on to score 346 goals in a Canucks uniform. That's the thing about a high pick. You could get a guy who never plays a game in the league, or you could end up with M. Naslund. Or you *could* get S. Pronger. But the Canucks didn't, at least not then.

No problem, on to round two.

When Brian Burke and company stood up for their second-round pick about 20 percent of me started to get excited. They went with Jassen Cullimore. I guess three goals didn't warrant a second-round pick. Now it didn't matter that I hadn't allowed myself to get my hopes up too far. It's not a great feeling to have the team you're hoping for basically announce to a rink full of media, fans, agents, hockey players and their families that they would rather have someone else.

Still, I had to put it in perspective. I was sitting with my dad at the NHL entry draft and there was a good chance I would eventually be selected. How many kids would love to trade places with me? OK, I can tell you at least one who wouldn't have. But while he was smiling for the cameras, my dad gave me a tap on the knee and told me that the Canucks wouldn't pass me over again. I'm not sure I believed him. After the Cullimore pick I began to think that anyone could take me. Even though I tried to keep myself in check, I realized I was going through an agonizing cycle of hope and despair with each pick. I figured I could be taken anywhere from the third round to (gulp) not at all. It could have been a long day. Luckily, it wasn't.

I went through twenty-one ups and downs after the Canucks' second pick. Jamie McLennan, Dmitri Filimonov, Yanick Dupre ...

were these guys better than me? Somebody thought so. Somebody who was paid to know how to judge a hockey player. (I scored more goals in the NHL than all these guys, by the way. But then, McLennan was a goalie.) No dose of humility is quite like sitting through a couple rounds of the draft and being given a list of all the players your age that the NHL's general managers would rather have on their team.

But my trajectory toward humiliation eventually came to an end.

"With the fifty-first pick the Vancouver Canucks select Sean Pronger from Bowling Green State University."

I hugged my dad (if by "hugged" I mean "squeezed the crap out of"), and told him "We did it!" I wish I could tell you that I thanked him for all he had done for me. Thanked him for all the early morning practice sessions, the new equipment, the pep talks, the sacrifices, for everything—but I didn't. I was too stunned. I really hadn't prepared myself for what it would feel like to *actually* be drafted. I had talked and daydreamed about the moment a million times but I guess I never thought about what I would do if and when my name was called. It felt great, though, and I could tell my dad was proud. And, as every kid knows, there is nothing better than making your father proud.

After our brief celebration, I turned to Big Jim. "How in hell do we get down to the arena floor?" (Reminder to self for the next time I'm drafted: sit in the lower bowl.)

Eventually, we managed to talk our way down to the arena floor where the teams were assembled. It took us so long that guys drafted four or five picks after me were already in line for draft pictures. As we made our way onto the draft floor, I could see Steve Tambellini, from the Vancouver management team, peering up into the stands with a look of "I know he's here somewhere, what the hell is he doing?" Steve congratulated me on being drafted and becoming a member of the Canucks organization, and escorted me over to the Canucks table to meet the rest of the management team as well as most of the scouting staff. From there it was on to pictures. They gave me a Canucks jersey and snapped photos of me in front of the NHL logo. That was pretty cool. Then they had Dad step in for some pictures. The photo of Big Jim and I standing there together is one of my favourites to this day.

Part one of the dream was now complete. I was happy to have a path to NHL glory, a franchise to lead to the Promised Land. The Vancouver Canucks were going to look like geniuses for stealing me in the third round. I was going to make all those other franchises look like fools for drafting the likes of Niedermayer, Forsberg, and Kovalev ahead of me. (Looking back, that was a ridiculously strong draft year—even without including Lindros, who of course went first overall to the Quebec Nordiques and subsequently shunned an entire province. We didn't realize it as we were sitting there, but what we saw unfolding was the beginning of the process of Quebec City getting screwed—losing a guy who would dominate the league for years, losing their franchise only to watch it win in Denver. All we knew for sure was that we were watching a kid announce to the world that his dream was a lot bigger than playing in the NHL.) On the other hand, if any Vancouver Canucks fans are looking back, they're probably not pleased that the likes of Michael Nylander, Mike Knuble, and Sean O'Donnell were selected after me. (I have to say, though, that twenty-two guys picked ahead of me played fewer games in the NHL than I did. Not that I'm counting.) Whatever. A Pronger had been drafted into the NHL, and it was a big day for the family.

When the draft wrapped up, Big Jim and I were invited back to the Canucks hospitality suite to mingle with the other picks and Vancouver's hockey operations staff. It was a relaxed event and everyone seemed to be in a good mood. The draft is a stressful time for all involved. Owners, general managers, scouts, coaches, support staff, players, parents, siblings—once it's over, people want to let their hair down. Or so I thought. Since there were some cold brews in my vicinity I grabbed one and headed over for a conversation with Stojanov and Cullimore. After pretty much shotgunning my first beer I glanced down and noticed the two other guys were sipping on Cokes. I put down my empty can right before a scout came over and told the three of us it would be OK if we wanted to have a beer. Really? Don't mind if I do.

3

JOURNEYROOKIE

BOWLING GREEN, 1994

I remember my last college hockey game like it was yesterday. We were in Detroit playing the Michigan State Spartans in the Final Five, the CCHA's playoff weekend to anoint its champion. I was in my fourth year, and if we lost, this game would be my last in college. If we won, we'd be off to the semifinals. We'd had a fairly average year but still managed to qualify for the tournament. We did have some legit players on our team. Anchoring our defence was All-American Jeff Wells and current Pittsburgh Penguins assistant coach Todd Reirden. Up front we had future Hobey Baker winner and NHLer Brian Holzinger. Also up front was another future NHLer, Mike Johnson. Oh yeah—and yours truly.

Even though the Spartans finished ahead of us in the standings I thought we had a shot. On the other side of the red line was a trio of future NHL players (and fellow Canadians)—Rem Murray, Dancin' Anson Carter, and Steve Guolla. Now is not the time for the play by play, but suffice it to say that the barn was packed, and both teams went at it with everything we had. Naturally, we ended up tied at the end of regulation. Awesome, let's up the ante a little.

Well, Guolla scored the OT winner, effectively putting an end to my varsity career. I should've suckered him in the handshake line.

I recall sitting in the locker room, stunned. Now what to do? For the first time in my life I had no idea what my hockey future looked like. I knew what I wanted it to look like, but there was no sense daydreaming. In any case, from that moment on I was no longer a Falcon. I was the property of the Vancouver Canucks.

However, it had been three years since they drafted me. Brian Burke was gone. I had been watching their depth chart all that time, appraising my prospects of making it in Vancouver. Dan Kesa, Mike Peca, Dixon Ward, Libor Polasek, Alek Stojanov. (Strangely, the highest draft pick on that list is the guy who never made it. Libor Polasek never played a game in the NHL. Dixon Ward, though, went in the seventh round and played more than 500 games. Of course, I couldn't know that then. I just wanted to beat them both.)

There was nothing in the world I wanted more than to be on that team, but when the hockey operations guys in Vancouver looked at my file, this is what they saw.

- Freshman Year: three goals. Just getting my feet wet. But then, they already knew that when they drafted me.
- Sophomore Year: nine goals. Even though I tripled my total it was a disappointment.
- Junior Year: twenty-three goals. Now we're moving in the right direction.
- Senior Year: seventeen goals. Anything less than twenty-three was going to be a disappointment. For me, and for the people I wanted to think of as my new employers.

There were a couple of highlights to my final year, including being named a team captain by the legendary college hockey coach Jerry York. I won the Coaches' Award. I know this is typically given to the "little engine that could," but I needed to take something positive away from that season. Looking back on my pro career (excluding the NHL), I may have won that award for every team I played on. I'm surprised they don't call it the Sean Pronger Award.

After we made our way back to Bowling Green a few of us decided it was time to experience how most college kids live. *Spring break time, baby!* That's right: A. J. Plaskey, Tom Glantz, Will Clarke, Todd Reirden, and I rented an RV to make the journey south to sunny FLA.

Before we hit the road, I spoke with my "family adviser," Pat Morris. (Pat's name may be familiar as a notable player agent with very high-profile clients—like Chris Pronger, for example. But college players can't have agents, so instead they have "advisers." Interestingly, many of those advisers magically transform into agents once the players they advise turn pro.) I was calling Pat to see if any possibility existed of signing a contract with Vancouver. Pat informed me the chance could only be described as slim, and that I should go have a good time with my teammates. By "slim" I think he meant to say "none," but he had to give me a reason to not kill myself with the other college crazies on spring break. He did say I should check in with him just in case Vancouver wanted to sign me after all and send me to the Canucks farm team in Hamilton for the remainder of the season. Of course, this was all before cell phones—so to check in with him, I had to call from a pay phone. I wish I had a snapshot of that call, with me standing in a beachside 7-11 parking lot sporting a cowboy hat, Speedo, and greased up with Hawaiian Tropic oil. Too bad we didn't have Skype back then! Needless to say, after the first call I knew there was no need for a second call. Can you imagine if they had signed me, fresh off the beach in Panama City? I'm sure the boys in Hamilton would have appreciated the hungover college kid with the sunburn!

When the term was over, the time had come to begin my life as a professional athlete. As it turned out, my new life was depressingly like my old one. Sometimes playing hockey and earning a degree can be tough to accomplish at the same time, and there I was, at the beginning of a Midwestern summer, a couple of credits short—the only professional hockey player in summer school at BGSU.

It was not pleasant. But I thank my lucky stars that I made the decision to stick around for one more term. It allowed me to graduate in August and be only slightly behind schedule. Giving up a summer of fishing and golfing back home may have been torture at the time but it was also one of the best decisions I've ever made. Lord knows there is NO way I would've gone back to school once I left the campus.

At the time, though, I wasn't happy. If you've never experienced a Midwestern summer, I can assure you that the term "hot and humid" does not begin to describe the soul-melting torment of plodding through a summer day in Ohio. So I was already in a perpetually bad mood. Then one day, as I was getting ready for a business writing class, sulking about my situation, and thinking that things couldn't get much worse, my agent called. Turns out things *could* get worse. Pat informed me that Vancouver didn't think I had what it took to make their team in the next couple of years. With the lockout of '94 looming they didn't want any extra baggage. (They couldn't just release me; they had to give the reason!) Missing out on fishing became the least of my worries.

Unrestricted free agency is not necessarily a good thing before you've played a game in the league. Still, all was not lost. In July,

Pat called me to say the Detroit Red Wings were interested in my services.

What? Steve Yzerman's team? Me and Stevie Y? OK, I'm listening.

He said nothing was in writing, but their assistant general manager Doug MacLean wanted to talk contract. I remember giving Pat very specific instructions: "Whatever he writes down on paper, SIGN IT!"

A couple days later, Pat followed up on his earlier shot in the arm with a shot to the groin.

"Doug got fired."

"Are you kidding me? Let me guess. They don't want to sign me now."

"Good guess. Sorry, Sean. We'll figure something out."

That second blow, along with the blistering heat, did not deter me from academic glory. In August 1994, with a grade point average slightly higher than my IQ, I graduated from Bowling Green State University.

One thing I've found in life—and you may have noticed it, too—is that beer often can make things seem better. I'm not sure why this is, but it's a phenomenon I've observed enough times that I can confidently declare it to be true. In a fantastic twist of fate my graduation was on the same weekend as Bowling Green's Hockey Old Timer's Golf Outing, better known as the HOGO. It's the annual golf tournament for BG Hockey Alumni. One of BG's greatest alums, Dave Ellet (who was still in the NHL at the time), was attending. The drinks started flowing early that Saturday afternoon. I had just graduated and had no idea what the fuck I was going to do with my life, but I couldn't care less at that moment. At about six o'clock (or four hours into the shift) Ellet decided to call his good buddy Garry Galley. Galley (another BG alum who was in the midst of his NHL career) was in Ottawa at the time. Ellet told Galley about all who were in attendance and requested his presence at the party. That night! I will save you the trouble of googling the distance between the two cities and tell you that it's at least a seven-hour car ride. And, I can assure you, there are no direct flights. After Ellet hung up, he said, "Galley's coming!" Of course no one believed him. Who in their right mind would jump in a car at 6 p.m. on a Saturday night to drive seven hours to go to a party? Especially given the fact that everyone there was leaving the next day. Ellet was so convinced his good buddy would show up that he passed around a hat to take bets. He said he would match any amount thrown in. If I'd had any money I would've bet it all he wouldn't show. Yet at precisely 1:30 a.m., guess who kicks in the door? Garry freaking Galley.

Ellet hugged him like they both had just been freed by hostage-takers, then started cackling about the money he'd just made. From there the party really took off. My convocation was the next day, and I barely managed to lurch to the ceremony.

After the epic graduation weekend I had a couple weeks to myself, and went home to Dryden for a little R&R with family and friends. I felt I deserved it after spending three months in summer school while all my buddies were golfing, fishing, and not living in 120-degree humidity. The time back home gave me an opportunity to think about my options. With no teams calling, I guess these options were few—and one of them was to pack it in. But at the age of twenty-one, that didn't seem right. So quitting was an option I didn't consider.

I decided to head back to Bowling Green to skate and train with some of the pros who were down there. I had about three weeks before training camps opened, so there was a little time before I ran out of time.

I'll never forget the morning I left Dryden. My only plan was to make the twenty-hour drive to Toronto to see my girlfriend (now Mrs. Journeyman), spend a day or two there, and then head to Bowling Green. Outside of that, I had no idea where I was going or what I would be doing. My mom and dad were in the driveway in their housecoats, my mom was crying, and they both gave me the biggest hug ever. Being young and stupid I just kind of smiled at them and told them not to worry. I'd be OK, I said. Now that I have my own kids, I know what those tears and hugs were about. Watching your kid drive off with nothing more than hope and ignorance couldn't have been easy.

My three weeks of September skating with the likes of Chris Tamer, David Roberts, Denny Felsner, Pat Neaton, and Brett and Todd Harkins, to name a few, must have given super-agent Ari just enough time to call in all of his favours. After muddling through all of my one tryout invitations, I decided to attend the Las Vegas Thunder training camp. Looking back, it may not have been the best opportunity for an unproven rookie fresh out of college. The following players were already signed to a contract with the Thunder: Jarrod Skalde (100+ NHL games), James Black (350+ NHL games), Alex Hicks (250+ NHL games), Andrew McBain (600+ NHL games), Marc Habscheid (340+ NHL games), Bob Joyce (150+ NHL games), and Darcy Loewen (130+ NHL games).

Imagine what it's like for a kid fresh out of school to walk into a dressing room full of men. Even if I had just been there to play some pickup, I'd have been respectful to a room full of guys who were bigger, hairier, and certainly more covered in scars than anyone I'd ever played with. Add to this the fact that these guys aren't playing for their school jackets—they're playing to pay their bills. You walk into a room like that, and suddenly your choice of careers seems a lot more real. Job number one, though, is just to figure out where to sit.

Still, I realized right away there was no point in overthinking things. If I had really run the numbers, and calculated that I'd staked absolutely everything on beating a bunch of seasoned professional hockey players out of their jobs, I probably would have turned around and left the rink. But all I could think about was playing hockey, so that's what I did. And a week in, the young, tall, slow, skinny kid fresh out of college was having a pretty good camp. I think I scored in every scrimmage we had. Even with the abundance of NHL experience there still were one or two spots open on their roster, and even though the team was located in Vegas (there is more than a little gamble in my DNA), I was managing to show up on time, compete hard, and catch the coach's eye.

(Side note: We stayed at the Imperial Palace for training camp, and every morning the fine folks at the IP gave out a free ace with the all-you-can-eat breakfast buffet. That's right—a playing card with your Cheerios. So, why not sit down on the way to practice and let the ace play a few hands? A no-brainer, right?)

Anyway, back to training camp. Things were going pretty well and I liked my chances of making the squad. If I were a betting man (OK, back then I *was* a betting man), I would have set the odds at three to two that I would be on the opening-day roster.

Good thing the casino wasn't taking bets.

You see, a little thing called the '94 NHL lockout happened. Obviously, throughout the summer I had followed the progress of the negotiations (as closely as one could when reading the Bowling Green, Ohio, sports page). However, since I wasn't under an NHL contract at the time I underestimated the impact the lockout would have on me if they couldn't reach an agreement. As you can imagine, Vegas was a popular spot for a lot of NHLers to go to keep their "game" sharp. Let's give a great big Las Vegas Thunder welcome to Ottawa Senators thirty-goal scorer Alexei Yashin, and to 1994 third-overall pick Radek Bonk. (But hey, I'm hardly the only hockey player in the world who's lost a roster spot when Alexei Yashin swans in at the end of camp.) Let's give a big Las Vegas Thunder goodbye to Sean "Do Some Research before Attending Training Camp" Pronger!

Still, I kept plugging away until the last day of camp when they finally put me out of my misery with "the tap." GM Bob Strumm and coach Chris McSorley read to me a script I would come to learn all too well: "Sean, you had a great camp, but your flight leaves at 6 a.m." Is there a worse flight in the world than the 6 a.m. flight out of Vegas? As a matter of fact, yes: it's the 6 a.m. flight out of Vegas after you've just been kicked in the balls.

Since I managed to do just enough for Vegas management to keep me around for the entire month of September, I missed everybody else's training camp. Over the next two weeks I did the best I could to work out every day AND stay off the bottle while I waited for all the offers to pour in. All two of them. Again, I did have a third option—but as you'll read time and time again, I was just too stupid to quit.

So. I could play in England with my old Midget coach, or play in Knoxville, Tennessee.

My first question was, "Knoxville has a team?"

(Yeah! We have uniforms and everything.)

After conferring with my trusted adviser Mr. Canadian (Molson, to those of us close to him), I decided it was not time to head overseas just yet. I wanted to give it a try in North America. Looking back, I have to question whether Mr. Canadian had any clue what he was talking about. But he was a damn fine companion, and one hell of a listener.

So I decided to take my talents to Knoxville, home of the Cherokees. I knew absolutely nothing about the league or the team when I got there. I was expecting a bunch of felons on razor-sharp blades carrying weapons. The salaries in the East Coast Hockey League are not what you would call "lucrative"; I made $500 a week and the team paid for rent. But at the time I thought I was rich. And that's how I ended up in the farmhouse.

A CHRISTMAS STORY

When I arrived in Knoxville I knew almost no one. The good news was that most of the players on our team were fresh out of college or junior and didn't know anyone either. There were a couple of familiar faces, though. Doug Searle was at camp and I had met him a couple of years earlier when he was a teammate of my brother's in Peterborough. And because Knoxville was affiliated with Las Vegas, the coach, Barry Smith, had seen me play in training camp with the Thunder. Remember, I had played pretty well in the "mean nothing" games in Vegas, and Smith obviously witnessed them. I do recall a conversation in his office where he told me he didn't think I'd be with them that long; he thought another IHL or AHL team would sign me quickly. But in the meantime he was happy to have me.

As I've explained, most players, me included, don't aspire to play in the ECHL. The East Coast Hockey League is the minor league's minor league. It feeds into the American Hockey League (AHL) and, back when I was playing, the International Hockey League (IHL), which folded in 2001. If you're in the ECHL, something has gone wrong. (Unless it's a lockout year, and you're a millionaire looking to stay in shape.) However, after the initial shock of my situation subsided I started to settle in.

I got to know the guys on my team, and realized that although this wasn't anyone's dream it was our reality, so we might as well have fun with it. And that right there is the hook. It's why the ECHL is commonly referred to as "Easy Come, Hard Leave." The money isn't that great but it's enough to have a good time. You're usually in your early twenties, so how much cash do you really need? You're playing with guys that are between the ages of twenty-one and twenty-five. Most of them aren't married, and if they are they don't have kids. Add that up and it equals no responsibilities. So really, all you need to worry about is practising, playing, and knowing which bar has the best happy hour on which day. As with a majority of the minor leagues, in order to maximize attendance most of the games are played on Friday, Saturday, and Sunday. That left Sunday night and most weekdays to do some team bonding. Guys typically met up after practice, grabbed a little snack, and then tried to figure out the optimal number of beers to consume before dinner. Sure, we were professional athletes (sort of), but we were also young and wanted to have some fun. When you don't have wives or kids, your teammates are your family and support system. We were young men with many free nights. That adds up to more than the odd pint.

Life isn't too complicated. Then you find out you can stay there in the summer and do some part-time work and a couple hockey camps. Then life gets really easy. No responsibilities, playing hockey for a living, part-time job in the summer. Hit repeat on that a couple times and the next thing you know five years have gone by and you're a lifer in the Coast! The trick is to always remember in the back of your mind *why* you're there. It should be a stepping stone. I knew if I got too comfortable I wouldn't be making the next step. It would've been so easy to fall into the trap. I had high hopes for myself, and I was eager to prove I was better than the ECHL. I was excited for the season to start. I was on a mission.

I didn't know much about Knoxville before I arrived and in fact was unaware hockey lived in such parts of America. And, let's be honest, in Knoxville hockey was a ways down the depth chart when it came to most popular sports. The list started with college football and after that included high school football, Pop Warner football, and so on. If you didn't know (and I didn't, before I got there), Knoxville is where the University of Tennessee is located. Tennessee Volunteers football is like religion in that town. And if football was religion, Peyton Manning was the Pope. I couldn't believe the number of houseboats that would make their way down the river on Volunteer game days. And I really couldn't believe the number of newborns who were being named Peyton in honour of the Vols' QB. Those people in Knoxville were flat-out *crazy* about football. So at best, they were mildly psychotic about hockey. The fans appreciated hard work and physical play, and the crowds loved the odd scrap. The arena we played in was average to above average for the ECHL. It definitely had an old-school feel to it. Attendance was decent and beer sales were excellent. Knoxville Cherokees games were, if nothing else, a party.

Of course, parties often end in fights, and more than a few Cherokees games featured classic line brawls. They may be a thing of the past in the NHL, but back then, in that league, there was probably a brawl every ten games or so. I don't know if it's the atmosphere in those old barns full of beer-fuelled fans, or rosters made up of guys willing to fight their way up to the next league, or whether it's just lack of discipline. Maybe it's all those things. Maybe more. But my dominant memories of those days involve guys squared off around the ice, gloves and beer cups strewn everywhere, and fans up on the boards cheering on the mayhem.

The first game of my professional hockey career was one to remember. I had two goals and two assists and was named first star.

It was one of those games you don't want to end. Everything went right. If I had a cell phone back then I would have turned it on post-game and waited for the teams to start calling. Unfortunately I didn't, and apparently no GMs knew the number to the pay phone outside the dressing room.

It also could have been that everyone at the NHL level was dealing with the lockout. Gary Bettman, the owners, and the NHLPA executive committee were trying to hammer out the issues of cost certainty, revenue sharing, and the granddaddy of them all—the implementation of a salary cap. Some players took off to Europe to stay sharp, some sat tight, and some went to the AHL and IHL to specifically take away a job from me. Many of the stars (the guys who didn't have to worry about money) did some PR for the NHLPA. Remember the Four-on-Four Challenge? That three-day tourney in Hamilton raised a bunch of money for charity. Meantime, Wayne Gretzky and some select friends took off on a World Tour to play exhibition games to try to keep the players in a positive public light. And I just kept grinding away in the ECHL. (I can remember checking the Knoxville paper to get updates on the NHL lockout. Yeah right! As far as Knoxville was concerned the ECHL was the NHL, and if they never did work out a deal most of the people in Knoxville wouldn't give two shits. It was almost like being in hockey's version of solitary confinement with no communication with the outside world.)

As the season got going, I quickly realized that pro hockey was different from college. In college there's a lot of excitement and energy because you play only on the weekends and the season lasts only six months. The pro game was more businesslike. You didn't celebrate the wins for long or lament the losses for more than an hour. There was always another game coming up. It was a job. It was also a whole new routine for me. I'd usually get to the rink about an hour and a half before practice so I could sit and listen to some of the exploits from the night before. We'd practise for about an hour. After practice I'd hit the gym for forty-five minutes to an hour and that was the end of the workday for me. Sometimes I'd go home to relax, other times I'd go catch a movie. It took some time to stop feeling like I always had some place to go and something to do, but it was definitely a welcome change. In college, we had classes from 9 a.m. until 2 p.m. and then we'd go to practice. We'd practise for a couple hours and then lift weights for an hour. After that we'd eat dinner and go to another class or to study hall. Not a lot of downtime. Now, it was all about managing the downtime (which basically amounted to figuring out a way to stay out of the bar during daylight hours).

I'm not sure if it was an East Coast League thing or a Knoxville thing, but when we went on the road we travelled in style. We didn't use your standard hockey-issue Greyhound, we used a tour bus. That's right baby—we rolled in Bon Jovi's tour bus, or maybe it was some country music dude's ride. These buses usually had two card tables in the front, twelve bunk beds in the middle, and a huge wraparound couch in the back. We had so many rookies on the team I even got a bunk. Most of the time, however, I would hang out on the back couch and watch movies. My favourite bus rides were the ones on the way home after a successful road trip. When we won three games in three nights that bus really became a big-time rocker's tour bus (minus the hot chicks and drugs). The music was cranked and there were plenty of beers to go around.

In keeping with our rock star lifestyle, one night when a bunch of us went out to celebrate Halloween at least one of us may have had a little too much to drink. In fact, this particular player may have had more to drink than he could hold down as he sat in the back of another player's car on the way home that night.

In the morning, like the professionals we were supposed to be, we showed up for practice, perhaps a little worse for wear. After the usual drills, just when we were expecting to be dispatched to the showers, where our recovery would begin, the coach skated our balls off for forty-five minutes. At the end of our torment, he called us all in for a little talk. We were heaving and gasping, and he was leaning on his stick in the thoughtful pose made famous by Ken Dryden. He gave us a short lecture on being game-ready, but couldn't help breaking into a wry smile at the end.

"By the way, boys," he said in his best deadpan, "next time I'd advise you to clean the puke off the car before you come to practice." (A valuable lesson for all athletes.)

I didn't think about it at the time, but in Knoxville I was starting to become a pro. I was also having a good time doing it, even if I didn't want to admit it. I was playing well. Life was pretty good. And it was about to get better with an early present from Saint Nick.

In December of '94 I was lying on the couch admiring the way the lights were catching our newly decorated Christmas tree (Bud Light cans make for festive ornaments!) when I got a call from my agent, Pat Morris. I figured he was calling for his 3 percent of my $500, but he actually had some news. Pat informed me there was an NHL team that wanted to sign me when the lockout ended.

"Excuse me, Pat," I said, "but I thought you said *an NHL team.*"

"I did."

"Which team?"

"I can't tell you until the lockout is over."

"Screw you. Which team?"

"Honestly, I can't tell you. It's in your best interest if you don't know. But I can tell you that when the lockout ends you'll be signing your first NHL contract."

Any guesses as to my next question? Considering I had no heat or indoor plumbing in my luxurious farmhouse, I think it went a little something like this:

"WHEN THE FUCK IS THE LOCKOUT GOING TO BE OVER?"

I must say, Pat is a standup guy. If you ever need to rob a bank, Pat's your man. He will not talk. And he certainly wasn't about to let the cat out of the bag just yet. Once I realized that Pat wasn't giving anything up, there was a call I just had to make. To my parents? you ask. Nope. How about the girlfriend? Guess again.

"Hey Chris, how's it going? What have you been up to? How's the weather in Hartford? Staying out of jail? No? Oh well. One more thing … *when are you guys going to take the deal so I can get the hell out of here?*" About 95 percent of me understood why the lockout was happening and what the players were fighting for. But the other 5 percent wanted the guys in the NHL to come spend a week in the farmhouse and see what life was like on the other side of the ritzy hotel suites and chartered planes.

After I tried to guilt-trip my twenty-year-old brother into talking to the players' union on my behalf, I did make calls to my parents and the future Mrs. Journeyman to give them the update. Obviously, they were thrilled. My folks had been down a few weeks prior to Pat's phone call. Fortunately for them they stayed at a hotel and weren't subjected to crashing at the farmhouse. We had a room for them; shockingly, they just didn't want to use it. I can still see my mom's face as I took her on a tour of my home (farm) away from home. The look was one of shock, fear, pity, and amusement. Mrs. Journeyman, on the other hand, did have the pleasure of staying at the lovely chalet on the farm. Not one of our finer moments as a couple. Although, you can be sure it's true love when she comes for a visit and stays at your house with no heat and no cable and doesn't give you "the tap" afterwards.

Regardless, my situation wasn't what you would call ideal, so they all were relieved to hear there might be some light at the end of this tunnel. Again, looking back, I should have known that that light was an oncoming train.

Here was my predicament. I'm playing for the Knoxville Cherokees, and playing pretty well I might add. I have been chosen to play in the ECHL all-star game, which is good. I've been told I will sign with an NHL team when the lockout ends, which is *really* good.

But I want you to put yourself in my shoes for a second. You've been informed you're one step closer to your dream. How would you approach the games? Do you go 100 percent still? Are you the first one in the corner? Do you still want to go to the ice and block that shot? What if that "unknown" team that plans on signing you is watching?

As you can imagine, I was having trouble deciding whether I should go full out or play it cautious. I didn't want to get hurt and miss my window … again. But I also didn't want to let the team down.

The funny thing was that once the game started I didn't think about it. I just played. That was probably the only time my mind didn't play tricks on me. Off the ice, I was a little edgy. Picture me, if you will, waiting day after day by the phone, hoping for it to ring with news that the lockout was over and I'd be released from prison.

In January 1995, our beautiful Bud Light Christmas tree was still lit up in the corner of the farmhouse. Our plumbing was firing on all cylinders (finally). I was playing great (an ambitious way to describe my play, but I'm telling the story so grant some creative licence, please), and the mice were all dead.

Chris called and delivered the news: He was going back to work. As you can imagine, I couldn't call Pat fast enough to find out my new area code. And you know what he said to me?

"I don't want to tell you until I can work out the contract details."

Now, in his defence, his sense of urgency wasn't the same as mine. His previous three months hadn't played out as follows:

- Released by the Vancouver Canucks
- Head faked by the Detroit Red Wings
- Fed a nice "thanks for coming" burger by the Las Vegas Thunder

followed by

- Considering a move to England
- Settling in a state-of-the-art outhouse in Tennessee
- Being informed I'd be released from prison but they couldn't find the paperwork.

Needless to say, my take on the contract details was as follows: They make an offer, and we jump on it. Pat, again, didn't budge. And I had to play a home game the next day.

I made it through the game without incident and was working my way through a few Pabst Blue Ribbons when the phone rang. This time Pat had the answer.

"Ducks," was all he said.

"What?"

"You are now a member of the Anaheim Mighty Ducks!"

You may laugh, but that was one of the proudest days of my life. I couldn't have been more fired up to call my folks and my girl. And they couldn't have been happier for me.

My contract was unspectacular, but I didn't care. After all, I wasn't in a position of strength when it came to bargaining power. It was a three-year, two-way contract. My NHL salary would be $175K, and my minor league salary would be $35K. (This is actually a pretty common contract, so common the players call it the "John Lilley contract." It's the one you get when you have zero leverage.) True, I'd have to start paying rent. But, again, I thought I was rich.

I made plans to get out of Knoxville fast. Problem was, I couldn't get out fast enough. My flight was scheduled to leave a day after the Cherokees' next game.

What would you do?

Thank the boys and the coaching staff for the last couple of months, wish them the best, and sit out the game …

or,

Lace up the skates one more time with the boys and play (what you hope will be) your final ECHL game.

The morning of the game I went into Coach Smith's office to explain what was going on. He was disappointed to see one of his top players leave (shut up; I was one of his top nine forwards), but he was also happy for me. As for playing that night, he left it totally up to me, and added, "If I were you I probably wouldn't play."

Well, we were already short a couple of players (I think some Euros tore a heartilage), and I knew he needed me. The fact that he left it up to me meant a lot. Throw in the fact that Pat told me an injury couldn't undo the contract and I was in.

Before the game I told the boys it would be my last one as a Cherokee. They were genuinely happy for me. Sometimes in such a situation there can be jealousy and animosity toward the guy leaving, but I can honestly say I felt none of that.

I made it through the game unscathed. In fact, I did much more—I actually had one of my best games in Knoxville, scoring a goal and adding two assists in victory. I played on a line with Pat Murray and Dave Nielsen, and we had a heck of a game. Pat was happy for me, and I couldn't help feeling bad for him. He was such a great guy, and a great player. He had a real head for the game and a sweet pair of mitts. It would've been fun to play with him longer than a couple of games. Pat was in the NHL with the Philadelphia Flyers a couple of years before that season in Knoxville. As a rookie I thought playing in the Coast was a kick in the balls, so I could only imagine how Pat felt. If he was crushed to be playing two rungs below the best league on Earth, he never let it show.

Not to overanalyze things, but I have no doubt that my performance that night had something to do with the fact that the pressure was off. The deal was done and I knew I was going to be moving on, so I could concentrate solely on playing the game. It wasn't about work or impressing the coaches. It was about going full out for my teammates one more time. Not having to worry about "the job" allowed me to play more freely. You always hear players say they are at their best when they go out and have fun. And that's exactly what I got to do in that game.

After the game, the lads were loading up the bus for a quick six-hour trip to Birmingham, and I remember thinking to myself that I was abandoning them. You see, when you spend as much time together as hockey teams do you genuinely care about guys you play with. It's especially evident in the lower leagues because you're so far down the food chain you take on the mindset of "it's us versus the world." It's that mentality that brings teams closer together. When you watch a guy put his body on the line for the good of the team, it means something. When you watch someone stick up for one of his teammates, it means something. And it's that aspect of hockey that I love. So, when I was set to ride off into the sunset with my dream still moving in the right direction I couldn't help feeling a little guilty.

It was a lot harder to leave than I thought. I figured when the time came and I had the opportunity to sign an NHL contract I'd hit the road without a second thought. "See you boys, it's been real, it's been nice, it's been real nice. Don't call me I'll call you." I don't want to say it was unfair, but most of the guys worked just as hard as me and wanted it just as badly as me.

Still, I did leave.

I was scheduled to fly out at 7 a.m. the next morning, and I still hadn't packed up *my entire life*. Keep in mind that my entire life at the time fit neatly into a Jeep Cherokee. The plan was to load up my truck with all my belongings, pack a suitcase to last me a week or so, and meet my new team on the road in Phoenix. You know how when guys make it to the show they always thank their parents for all those countless hours driving them to the rink as kids? Well, my dad seriously one-upped those early morning rink trips. I needed to get my Jeep to San Diego (home of the Gulls, Anaheim's farm team and my new team). And having only played in the ECHL, I didn't know that clubs in the IHL took care of stuff like that if you asked them. And even if I did know, I might have been too scared to ask so as not to offend anyone.

So this is where Big Jim (also affectionately known as "Diamond Jim," because he too likes to partake in games of chance) enters the story. He was to be my vehicle re-locator. No biggie, right?

Well, Dad was in Dryden, Ontario, which is a two-hour drive

from International Falls, Minnesota, which is a one-and-one-half-hour flight from Minneapolis, which is a three-hour flight from Knoxville, which is a one-hour drive from the property formerly known as "the farmhouse," which is a 2,210-mile drive from San Diego.

To top it all off, Diamond Jim had to make the final leg of the trip without any music. I had decided that I couldn't be without my CDs on the road and packed them in my suitcase. Sorry 'bout that, Jimbo—and thanks, by the way.

Now some say karma's a bitch, but not my old man. After dropping off my truck and taking me to dinner, Diamond Jim decided to head back to Dryden via Las Vegas. After travelling for the better part of three days, Dad was due for some good luck, and he got it at the craps table. Diamond Jim walked away from the table with ten grand. Pretty good travel voucher if you ask me.

THE GULLS

Of course, when Pat said "Ducks" what he really meant was "Gulls," the Ducks' farm team down the highway in San Diego. But that was fine with me. I was part of an organization. I was on a depth chart.

Just where I ranked on that chart was about to become clear.

One of the skills you learn as a journeyman is the art of fitting in. Over the course of my career, I became a master of that art. Come to think of it, I should open a consulting business to educate new players on the finer points of blending in.

It wasn't always easy, mind you. Even for an experienced journeyman, the hardest thing to do is join a team in mid-season. The players have been together for half a year. Everyone knows everyone. Roles have been defined. Beers have been consumed. The family is set. And then, in walks the new guy.

In this case, the new guy was from the East Coast Hockey League. And a rookie to boot. Not exactly a leper, but close. I arrived at the hotel in Phoenix before the team, so I went to my room to grab a few winks before the team meal. I figured I'd just throw on some jeans and a T-shirt and head down to dinner. Not a good first impression for the new squad. I remember walking into the room and hearing, "I guess it must be a casual dress code in the Coast." At the time I wanted to crawl into my Canadian tuxedo and hide.

My first game didn't go much better. The coach dressed me as the tenth forward behind the usual minor league roster of up-and-comers like Steve Rucchin, Jason "Sheriff" Marshall, Denny Lambert, former Leafs pick David Sacco, and Darren "The Gimp" Van Impe. And grizzled pros like Hubie McDonough (legendary IHL scorer), Mark Beaufait (IHL and DEL top scorer), Ron "Dawg" Wilson (800+ NHL games). And who could forget goalie Allan Bester? A bunch of guys making a name for themselves, and a bunch more whose days of dreaming about playing in the NHL are behind them. They still love the game and could make a decent living at it.

There was a different feel between this team and my squad in Knoxville. It was more serious. Don't get me wrong—guys still liked to have a good time, but it was certainly a more businesslike atmosphere. I'm sure there were many reasons for that. First off, these guys were older. In the Coast our team comprised mostly young men. The Gulls were made up primarily of *men*. These guys had wives, families, and bills to pay. There was far more at stake. And since we were just one rung below our dream league, guys wanted to make sure they did everything to get that first chance, that next chance, or that last chance.

And then there was Sean Pronger. The tenth forward. Just hoping to get a shift.

The math is pretty grim. Three lines of three means that if you're the tenth guy, you're the odd man out. Most teams used the tenth forward spot to dress their hired assassin—the guy they don't actually want on the ice that often. But on that night, it was a slow-footed centreman who was not interested in showing off his pillow hands, and didn't get much of a chance to showcase any other skills. I got to play a little with every line, or every sixth or seventh shift. Nothing makes the new guy feel welcome like sitting on the bench watching everybody else jump over the boards.

The next month and a half was uneventful. I was in and out of the lineup. And when I was in the lineup, I wasn't really a part of it because I was playing only a handful of minutes a night. Even though I was one step closer to my goal of playing in the National Hockey League it certainly didn't feel like it. When I was in the Coast all I could think about was making it to this level, but in my dreams making it didn't mean sitting on the end of the bench trying to figure which line and what position I'll play next. I may have still been wet behind the ears, but I knew that no one gets called up to the show from the press box either! As bad as I wanted this to work, I wanted to play more. Throw in the fact that I was living in a Travel Lodge across the street from the rink, and at times Deliverance, Tennessee, didn't seem that bad.

Now, I wasn't alone at the lodge. There was a grizzled, crusty, veteran member of the Gulls that also lived there—with his wife and three young kids. One night Crusty called and asked me to come down to his room. En route I wondered if I was in store for some rookie hazing. Maybe have a bucket of water tossed in my face or something like that. But no, it was just Crusty and his three-month-old kid watching TV.

"Do me a favour?" he asked.

"Sure," I replied. I figured I was about to go on an errand for diapers or formula or a flat of PBRs.

"My wife just got a flat tire on the freeway and I have to go get her. Can you watch my kid?"

What the fudge? What do you say to that? Just OK, I guess. Now that I have kids I suspect the old bastard used me so he could go out for a couple beers. Veteran move if he did! Anyway, I felt like the boys in *The Hangover* when they found the baby. Thankfully, I handled things somehow and Carlos lived to poop his diaper another day. As the weeks went on, I got to know the other side of Crusty. The side that could crush six beers to my one. The side that came out of the gates quickly but wasn't much for stamina. Again, having kids of my own now, I realize he was just getting those beers in while he could. A life lesson I use to this day. Thank you for your wisdom, Larry DePalma.

So that's where I was on the depth chart: team babysitter.

From the outside it probably looked like I had it made. I was living in beautiful San Diego, California. Theoretically, I was just one step away from the NHL. All I had to do was roll out of bed, stumble across the street to the rink, and try not to get cut after practice. I would then hit the weights and maybe squeeze in a ride on the stationary bike. After that, it was back to my penthouse suite at the Travel Lodge to have a nap and get rested up before I went to explore San Diego's finest watering holes. Given the fact that my previous three months consisted of driving to a truck stop to use the facilities, you'd think I'd be a little more appreciative of my current situation. But I wasn't happy. I wanted to be a hockey player, and I knew if I kept this as my routine I would never get to where I wanted to go. So, I did what I never thought I'd ever do. I called my agent to *ask* to go back to the ECHL. Can you believe it?

I was in San Diego all of two months. In that span, I played eight games and put up zero goals and zero assists. No, I didn't exactly leave my mark on the IHL, and I'm not sure anyone except the bartender at Foggy's Notion noticed I left.

BACK TO THE COAST

At the time, I couldn't believe I was choosing to leave sunny San Diego to go back to the farmhouse. It was almost enough to make me fall to the floor and suck my thumb. Then Pat, my agent, called.

"Your flight to Greensboro leaves tomorrow at 8 a.m."

As I reviewed Knoxville's schedule I realized that Knoxville doesn't play Greensboro again during the season. "But Knoxville doesn't play Greensboro," I said to Pat. (So naive.)

"I know, you idiot. You're not going back to Knoxville. Anaheim has its own ECHL affiliate in Greensboro, and that's where you're headed." Of course. Since Anaheim's ECHL team is the Greensboro Monarchs, why wouldn't I be going there? I am an idiot. When I first decided I wanted to go back to the Coast I was thinking I'd just re-join the old squad in Knoxville. I knew them. They knew me. It would have been nice and simple. In all of my wisdom and preparation before placing my request I didn't even think to ask a) if Anaheim had an ECHL affiliate, b) where Anaheim's ECHL team was located, and c) if it would be possible to go back to Knoxville. Chalk that one up to another lesson learned: before you ask to go, find out where you're going.

Nothing like a cross-country flight to allow time for reflection and re-evaluation. I remember thinking that I was about to join my fourth team and I had only been a pro for six months. Talk about ominous foreshadowing. And I wasn't forced to go back, I actually asked for it!

My new team was the Greensboro Monarchs, coached by an angry sort by the name of Jeff Brubaker. For those of you who never had the pleasure of watching him play, you should know that his style was a tad physical in nature. Put it this way: he had twenty-five points to go with the 512 PIMs in his NHL career. And he coached the way he played. The Monarchs were a tough, physical team (employing Jeremy Stevenson, Howie Rosenblatt, and Davis Payne, who wasn't a softie by any measure), and I was supposed to bring a little offence to the squad.

There was just one problem. I was out of shape.

How, you ask? Why? Well, playing three minutes a night every five games in San Diego certainly didn't help. And to be honest, I got so discouraged during my time with the Gulls that I never felt like putting in the extra work I would have needed to be ready.

My first game wasn't too bad. I believe we won, and I might have chipped in with an apple. (See? *Offence.*) The next one was on the road in Raleigh, North Carolina, against Rod Langway and the IceCaps. Yeah, that's right, Rod Langway. The back-to-back Norris Trophy winner. The Rod Langway who played 1,000 games in the NHL. I grew up watching that guy. And for the life of me I couldn't figure out what he was doing playing in the ECHL. I never had a chance to ask.

We were on a five-on-three and I was standing in front of the net waiting for a teammate to shoot the puck. Well, he took the shot, and Langway re-directed it right into my face. I went down on impact and immediately knew something was wrong. Luckily, I was able to turn at the last second so the puck got me in the jaw as opposed to the teeth (and no, that's not what happened to my brother's pearlies). I thought my jaw was broken. And for some stupid reason, I also thought that when you broke your jaw it became unhinged, like a snake's, and just dropped. I bounced back to my feet holding my mouth shut. I was more worried about freaking out the fans in the front row than waiting for the trainer to get to me. When he ran out to see if I was all right, I skated past him and headed into the locker room. I raced to the nearest mirror and steadied myself for what was surely going to be a gruesome sight. As it turned out, there was just a lot of blood. And when I let go of my mouth, a funny thing happened: nothing. It didn't unhinge or anything. However, I could stick my tongue between my bottom teeth, which is something I definitely couldn't do before the game. I figured I had just lost a tooth. But when I took a closer look, none of my jibs seemed to be missing. Weird.

A doctor finally arrived to examine me. His expert opinion was that the puck had just bruised my face and the impact of it caused me to bite down on my gums. He told me that I was going to be fine. Now, I'm from a small town and I grew up believing whatever the doctor told me. So if this quack said I was going to be fine, then I was going to be fine.

I went back out and finished the third period, overtime, and the shootout. After the game I grabbed the doc and told him that something was *really* wrong with my face. He got serious this time, because he even pulled out one of those wooden thingies to poke around in my yap. Again, he told me I was fine and that I should just lay off the crunchy and chewy food for a bit.

Thanks, Tips. They teach that at vet school?

On the two-hour bus ride back to Greensboro I tried to wash down a slice of pizza with two pints of my blood and almost passed out from the pain. It was then I decided I needed a second opinion. The next morning I woke up at my new hotel home and my face did not feel any better. I got to the rink and told our own team medical guy that I needed to get my face checked out. And he told me that he would set up an appointment with Dr. So and So after practice.

I was thinking, "Practice? Are you kidding me?"

He wasn't. So, after enduring practice I went to the doctor's office and had an X-ray. He looked at the image and took less than a second to declare that my jaw was broken. Unbelievable. Apparently the force of the impact split my jawbone just above my chin, and that's why I could stick my tongue between my teeth. To top it all off I had surgery the next day to repair the damage and my mouth had to be wired shut. My season, perhaps mercifully, was done.

I had just arrived in Greensboro. I didn't have my vehicle. I didn't know anyone. And now I was living in a hotel with my mouth wired shut.

The night after my surgery was one of the worst of my life, because I didn't heed the doctor's advice to pick up painkillers before the procedure. Sure I felt fine after the operation, for a while, but then the drugs wore off. I'm not sure how to describe the pain I felt that first night, but let's just say it's the kind of pain you feel when a doctor wraps steel around each of your teeth to hold them all in place and then wires the whole thing shut for good measure. I swear I could feel my heart beating in my teeth. And there is no question I thought about busting into a pharmacy to steal some narcotics. I didn't, and I'm not sure why I'm telling you now that continual hot baths made me feel better, but they did.

When morning finally came, I grabbed a cab to the drug store and basically strangled the pharmacist for my painkillers. Then I went home and blissfully fell asleep.

After waking from my drug-induced nap, I remember going for a walk to the park so I could figure out what the hell I was going to do for the next six weeks of my life. I also wanted to contemplate whether this hockey life was for me.

To make this long story short, the answers to my life questions don't really matter except to say that I needed to see my girl, my friends, and my family. And, yes, despite everything I still needed hockey.

Finally, for your amusement, I also needed my car. The last time I saw the Cherokee, it was packed with all my worldly possessions in front of the Travel Lodge in San Diego. My Jeep was supposed to be picked up by a trucking company so they could haul it to Greensboro. Only problem was, when I called the trucking company they told me it had not been picked up. Because it wasn't there.

My next phone call was to the Travel Lodge, which really didn't help me in my investigation either. Once I finally got them to understand who I was (it shouldn't have been that hard; I lived there for two months) and what I was looking for (a late-model Jeep Cherokee with my number and initials on the licence plate— shut up, I was young), they told me how sorry they were but the vehicle was not there and they didn't recall the last time they saw it.

Who knew that Jeep Cherokees were the chosen vehicle of carjackers in California? Certainly not me, until I found out that my wheels had been stolen and driven to Mexico. I'm still a little miffed that a Mexican can somehow cross the border in a white Cherokee with Ontario vanity plates. Regardless, the Jeep was no longer driveable and I was no longer in possession of all my worldly possessions.

It was the perfect end to my rookie season.

4

—

THE LAME DUCK

If you made it through the previous couple of chapters without lobbing the book into the garbage bin, you're likely a sadist. And yes, since I continued with my career after a rookie year that included living in rural poverty south of the Mason-Dixon Line, playing with a broken jaw, and losing my Jeep and pleading with the Mexican authorities to get it back, then you'd be correct in calling me a masochist. Nowhere to go but up, right? Like Andy Dufresne in *The Shawshank Redemption,* I climbed through a mile of shit and came out clean on the other side.

Well, not exactly clean. And not exactly on the other side, either. However, after a long summer of training, soul searching, and getting the range of motion back in my jaw, I was no longer in Dixie. It was the fall of 1995. O. J. Simpson had just been found not guilty. The DVD had just been invented. The Dow Jones closed above 5,000 for the first time. The hockey team in Anaheim was still called the Mighty Ducks. And, in truly important news, Sean Pronger attended his first NHL camp.

I was eager to show everyone in the organization what kind of player I was and how lucky the Mighty Ducks were to be the highest (only) bidder. I had trained my ass off all summer long for this. I was ready to announce my presence with authority. It was a much different feeling from a year earlier when I had no idea where I was going, when I was going, or if I was going at all. It makes the early morning training sessions a little easier when you have a clear picture of your goal. You may have the impression that I am a guy who doesn't mind relaxing with a cool beverage from time to time, but I should be clear about what motivation can do. I was in the gym every morning at 7, going at it for two or three hours just about every day. That's not easy to do, day in and day out, especially when the people around you are on a strict regimen of beer-drinking and fishing. But all I had to do was think about training camp and my one goal—making the opening-night roster.

Upon my arrival in Anaheim, I couldn't help being impressed with how organized everything was at the NHL level. They had arranged a shuttle service at the airport to take us to the hotel! (OK, I was easily impressed at the time.) At the hotel, they had our keys laid out in the lobby. Pronger: Room 301.

It was a real thrill seeing my name there in black and white, written down by an NHL team. Well, part of my name, anyway. If the assistant's assistant who scribbled that list had included my given name, I might have been spared a little embarrassment the next day.

There I was in the morning, heading to the nurses' station for my physical, confident it would be proven I was among the Mightiest of the Ducks.

"Sean Pronger reporting for my physical," I announced to the waiting nurses as I swaggered up.

"I'm sorry, we don't show your name anywhere."

Are those alarm bells I'm starting to hear?

"Excuse me? Could you please check again?"

"Well, it says here I have a Chris Pronger, but no Sean Pronger."

As far as I knew the Blues hadn't traded Chris to Anaheim that morning. Fortunately, there were only about twenty players within earshot. I could hear them snickering like schoolchildren. Great; I'm sure this won't be brought up in the dressing room before each practice.

For the record, that wasn't the first time someone substituted Chris for Sean. And it surely wasn't the last. I've had referees, linesmen, coaches, teammates, opposing players, fans, media, doctors, trainers, strangers, and my parents call me Chris. Don't you think that one time payroll or accounting could have made that mistake? I guess I should consider myself lucky, at least, that my wife has never called me by my brother's name.

Having to endure "the physical" before training camp was never fun for me. You get poked and prodded like a head of cattle going up for auction. The medical team tests your knees and shoulders; there's a blood test, urine test, eye test, EKG, hernia check (cough, cough). You have to do chin-ups, vertical jumps, two-mile runs, wind sprints, max VO2 tests, and maybe a special torment called the wind gate (an exercise designed to reduce an elite athlete to a shuddering wreck in exactly thirty seconds). There's no shortage of motivation, though. You may have been training all summer, but so have the physical specimens around you. There are usually some absolute beasts in camp who can tear off thirty chin-ups without getting winded, though as often as not they can't play hockey. (Then there's someone like Steve Rucchin, who is built like a Greek statue but has never bothered hitting the gym.)

After the physical it's time for the welcome dinner. This is always an interesting event—when everyone is eying everyone up and pretending not to. The rookies are acting like they've been there before even though they haven't, the veterans pretend not to be threatened, and the journeymen just sit back and try to figure out how on Earth they could possibly make the team.

I have to admit, my first welcome dinner was a little intimidating. I knew a couple guys from the year prior in San Diego and Greensboro, but for the most part I was one of the new kids. And yes, I was trying to act like I'd been there before.

Now, it didn't take me many years to realize that this is an annual affair where management and coaches tell all the players that they want a competitive camp and no one's job is safe. Jobs will be earned. Play, not pay, will determine ice time. Everyone has a chance.

As a rookie, I ate up every word. But if I had looked around I would have noticed that guys like Don McSween and Oleg Mikulchik weren't paying attention. They'd heard it all before and knew the speech was road apples. McSween was one of the all-time great guys. I could relate to him. He played college hockey and seemed to have his shit together. He'd done a couple tours in the minors and was a guy whose war stories you'd love to listen to with a few pints.

As the dinner came to a close that day, Head Coach Ron Wilson stood up and said, "Check the list on the board in the lobby to see which ice session you're in tomorrow."

The list? What the heck is the list?

I remember sidling up to the list like it was no big deal, but those butterflies in my stomach felt more like elephants. I mean, there wasn't a list in Knoxville or at Bowling Green.

I glanced at the list and noticed it was composed of two teams. Questions swirled through my head. Is it better to be on Team A or Team B? Do they have me down as Chris or as Sean? Am I even on this list? It took me only a few moments to realize that I wasn't on Team A, and that I was listed halfway down on Team B. I didn't know much as a rookie, but I knew that probably wasn't a good sign. When I took a little longer to peruse the list, I figured out that these teams weren't random drawings out of a hat.

TEAM A	TEAM B
Paul Kariya	Dwayne Norris
Oleg Tverdovsky	Nikolai Tsulygin
Steve Rucchin	Jeremy Stevenson
Joe Sacco	David Sacco
Guy Hebert	Byron Penstock
Mike Sillinger	Sean Pronger

You won't find these lists in Ron Wilson's archives, but you get the idea. One side comprised veterans, established players, and a star. The other could have been named Sean Pronger and the Scrubeenees.

As a rookie, I thought it was no big deal. I was young and figured I'd be on Team A in no time. When it got to be training camp #3 and #4 I didn't even glance at Team A.

Since this was my first training camp I was excited to get started. Thankfully, I didn't know what to expect or I may have had a different attitude. Any thought of getting to hang out in an NHL locker room was quickly shot down when I was informed that only the veterans would be getting dressed in there. The scrubs would be suiting up in the dressing rooms reserved for the minor hockey association. (Although, I must say, the grey cinder block walls did have a soothing effect.)

Getting dressed and undressed with guys you're competing with is always a good time. Before practice there's a lot of small talk about who's played with whom from what team, or who played junior with whom. But really, all they're thinking is, "I hope you slip on a banana peel and blow out your knee." It's strange, though. Every guy in that room is ridiculously competitive, and has devoted his whole life to getting to this dressing room to beat the guy beside him. Still, there is almost no ill will. The thing is, the players in that room have more in common with each other than they do with pretty much anyone else in the world. As much as you want to succeed, the sense that you're all in it together is nearly as strong.

Of course, every once in a while a cocky kid will stroll in and make it clear he's moving on to better things. Most don't make that mistake twice, though, as there's always a battle-scarred veteran at hand to say something like, "Settle down, rook, and go get me my extra stick so I can tape it." And anyone who doesn't get the message in the dressing room will certainly get a little special attention on the ice.

For those of you who think that training camp is filled with golf outings and massage appointments, allow me to enlighten you on what really goes on: eat, practice, scrimmage, bag skate, weight training, eat. Kill time in the afternoon, eat. Kill time in the evening, sleep. *Hit repeat*. It's not as glamorous as you'd think. Oh yeah, and the whole time you're practising, scrimmaging, and getting bag skated, you have the entire organization watching and judging your every move. And all you hope for is that your hotel phone doesn't ring and that there's a jersey hanging in your stall the next day so you can run the gauntlet all over again. Whoever coined the phrase "one day at a time" must've been talking about a training camp.

My first training camp turned out to be fairly uneventful. I got into exactly one exhibition game and it was against the Rangers. I remember fighting for the puck in the corner with Adam Graves and I almost apologized to him. I couldn't believe that nine months earlier I was playing in the East Coast Hockey League and now I'm literally running into one of my favourite players from the Oiler days. Can you blame me for being excited? I was going up against a two-time Stanley Cup winner and former member of the Kid Line! In our brief battle for the puck I realized what many others already knew: this guy is as strong as an ox and impossible to move off the puck. He was a beast. It was so hard for me not to be star-struck—a problem I would deal with throughout my career.

My excitement was short lived, because the next day I got the tap to go see Coach Wilson.

"Sean, you've had a great camp ... go down to the minors and work hard ... you'll be back in no time."

At the time, I bought it hook, line, and sinker. As the years went by I learned how to spit out the hook. As much as it sucked to get sent to the minors, I was happy with my camp. I think I proved to the Ducks organization that I had the potential to be an NHL player. More importantly, I proved to myself that I could compete at the NHL level. Considering where I was just one year earlier, things were moving in the right direction

My arrival to Baltimore (Anaheim had moved its farm team from San Diego to Baltimore) was one to remember. This was the same day the not-guilty verdict was announced in the O. J. Simpson trial. We were staying at a Holiday Inn in downtown Baltimore and the city was going nuts. My first impression was fear and excitement. Almost the same as how I viewed the start to my first season in the AHL.

Unlike the year before, I knew some people on the team I was starting with. From the San Diego Gulls team I knew Darren Van Impe, Jason Marshall, Craig Reichert, and David Sacco. I also knew Jeremy Stevenson from my brief stint in Greensboro.

The locker room mentality was a lot different now than when

we were in the minors. In training camp we're all competing against each other. In Baltimore, we were a team with a common goal. Sure, we were all trying to get to the NHL, but it was more like we were working together. More than anywhere else, when you're in the minors you take on an "us against the world" mindset. After all, we're kind of helping each other get to the next level. And get to the next level I did.

The first time I got called up to the show reminded me of the scene in *Major League* when Jake Taylor (Tom Berenger's character) gets a call from the Cleveland Indians. Only I wasn't wearing a sombrero. I was playing for the Baltimore Bandits of the American Hockey League, and Walt Kyle was the coach.

It was my first year in the AHL, but not my first time under Walt. I had played for Walt briefly in San Diego the year prior. Seeing as I finished that year with zero goals and zero assists, I'm pretty sure I didn't leave much of an impression. I knew I needed to get off to a good start or else it was going to be a long year and a short career.

Well, I didn't exactly announce my presence with authority in Baltimore. I was a healthy scratch in only the second game in the regular season. Brilliant. A summer of hard training and mental preparation seemingly dusted by game two. I could already hear the banjos calling from Knoxville.

I learned very early there is only one way to climb your way out of the dog house: shut your mouth and work your ass off. After clearing that early-season hurdle I was able to develop some trust with the coach. I settled into a nice checking role along with Stevenson and Reichert. We didn't score a lot but we played the way the coach wanted us to and brought some energy to the team. I don't mean we fought all the time, but we did throw our bodies around and we could cycle the puck for forty seconds. We didn't get a lot of shots, but keeping the puck away from the other team is huge for momentum. It's not bad for defence, either. Things were going pretty well for the team and me. However, getting called up to the NHL was the farthest thing from my mind. After all, the parent club almost always brings up the player who has the hottest hand in the minors in hopes he can ride the streak right into the show. That's why it was such a surprise when I got a call from Walt.

"Sean, it's Walt. You're being called up to Anaheim."

"Very funny, who is this?"

"It's Walt, your coach."

"Seriously, quit messing around. Who is this and what do you want? I'm busy watching my soap opera."

If I had been scoring goals in bunches I would have been all over the call—I wouldn't have thought someone was trying to play a fast one on me. However, this wasn't one of those times. Sure I had been playing pretty well, but the Ducks weren't even on my radar. So I didn't think there was any way that I could be on theirs.

"Sean! Wake up, you moron—it's Walt Kyle, your coach!"

"Sorry, Walt. You know how guys are around here with all the practical jokes and stuff. What did you say?"

"You are being recalled by Anaheim."

I was so shocked, the only thing I could say was, "Why?"

"Valerie Karpov got hurt and they want you to come up for a game."

"It's just for one game? Is that it? What do I bring? Who are we playing? Who am I playing with? What time's my flight? Who's picking me up?"

"Sean, slow down. It's just one game for now, but who knows? Just go up there and play your ass off."

And then he hung up.

I sat there for a minute with a stupid smile on my face and thought about my previous year. Just eight months before I was sitting in a hotel room in Greensboro, North Carolina, with my jaw wired shut wondering where it all went wrong. And now here I was, needing to get my bag packed and get to the airport because I was going to play in the NHL. I didn't know Karpov and I didn't care he was hurt. Actually, I did care he was hurt. I was happy that his pain was my gain.

Since I was only going up for a game, I didn't put much thought into the packing process. I grabbed a few articles of clothing and jammed them in a bag in order to get to the airport as quickly as possible. I was so nervous about missing my flight (and my chance) that I took the first parking spot I could find at the airport; luckily for me, it was very close to the Departures entrance. It was much later that I figured out why I had been so lucky. I parked in one-hour parking. Quick, yes. Bright … no. To be honest, I was so fired up at the time I would have abandoned my car if I had to.

I knew it was the NHL the moment I landed. There was a guy with a "Sean Pronger" sign near baggage claim. They even spelled my name right. My driver chauffeured me to my hotel near the Pond in Anaheim. Needless to say, it was a pretty sleepless night.

The next day was a blur. I remember meeting with the coaches (Ron Wilson, Tim Army, and Al Sims) to go over systems and assignments but there is no way I could tell you now what they said. It struck me as funny that these were the same guys who made me walk the plank earlier in the season, and now they were trying to get me prepared to play in my first National Hockey League game. I barely remember the morning skate, or for that matter which team we were playing. I just wanted to get to puck drop. I wanted game time to arrive so I could finally say that I had realized my dream of playing in the NHL. And, as corny as it sounds, that's something no one can take away from you.

My usual routine of a pre-game nap was more like a pre-game sweat that day.

Luckily for me, I wasn't the only member of the Ducks staying at the all-inclusive Residence Inn. A fellow by the name of Alex Hicks had been called up a few weeks prior to me, so I had obviously played with him at the start of the season in Baltimore. Alex gave me a ride to the rink, offered up a few suggestions, and most importantly tried to keep me relaxed. He knew exactly what I was going through because he had just played his first NHL game too. And he delivered—none other than Barry Melrose of ESPN had picked him for first star of the night after a two-goal and one-assist effort. Interestingly, I don't think he scored two goals in a game when he was in Baltimore. It just goes to show there's a fine line between the NHL and AHL. You can be good enough to be a first star in the NHL, but not good enough to stick around. My goal wasn't to become first star in my first NHL game. My goal was to get the chance to play my second NHL game. Alex probably doesn't recall that ride to the rink, but it's forever etched in my memory. Our paths would cross again a couple years later when I was traded to the Penguins.

Warm-up took forever to arrive, and when it did I floated around trying to act like it was game number 800 for me. I was stretching along the boards when Robert Dirk approached.

"First game, kid?"

"Yep."

"First of many I'm sure. Have some fun out here." As a player who spent some time in the minors before establishing himself as a regular NHLer, I'm sure he could appreciate the road it had taken to get there and how exciting it was to play game number one. You could've blindfolded me and I would've known it was the NHL. The buzz of the fans, the smell of the popcorn, the sound of the passes going tape to tape, the echo of shots ringing off the glass. You could feel the intensity. Sure the routine was the same, but the rest was just ... different. It's tough to explain except to say that the difference is palpable. The energy is greater. The speed is faster. Everything is ramped up. I was definitely wired during the pre-game. I couldn't concentrate on my routine. I couldn't concentrate on my teammates. I couldn't concentrate on the crowd. Everything was a blur.

Ron Wilson, Anaheim's head coach, had a reputation for starting guys who were playing in their first NHL game, and sure enough I was on the ice for opening puck drop. Wilson could be a real hard-ass at times and there were moments when he left you scratching your head, but giving players the memory of a lifetime by starting them in their first NHL game is a really nice touch. And you know what? He still does it to this day.

So on November 29, 1995, Sean Pronger faced off against Dale Hunter, won the draw, and was credited with one game in the National Hockey League.

I wish I could tell you that I remember everything about that game, but I can't. My first NHL game is a wonderful memory but the details of it are fuzzy. My main recollection is that I had to work hard not to skate around the whole game with a smile on my face. I had to make it look like I belonged, or at least like I thought I belonged. Game face. Even though all I could think about was that my name would be in the NHL history books as having played one game. All the guys on the team were great. They seemed genuinely happy for me. Since it was an expansion team most of the players were "castoffs" from other organizations. They didn't take for granted where they were in their careers. Most had earned every inch the hard way. Randy Ladouceur, Joe Sacco, Mike Sillinger are a few who stand out from that day. Those guys told me to try to enjoy the moment. To try to savour it and remember it. They also made me feel like a welcome member to the club—the exclusive club that was the NHL.

As big as that moment was then, it is much larger now. At the time I didn't know that I was on my way to journeyman status as a hockey player. I still believed that game was just the first of many in what would be a long and storied career. Now, with hindsight being twenty-twenty and all, I realize it was one of the defining moments of my life in hockey. One of the peaks. Perspective allows you to redefine success. Since my career didn't include scoring titles, all-star selections, multiple championships, and awards ceremonies (except the ones I attended with Chris), then perhaps just playing in one NHL game was my Hart Trophy. Not exactly up to Scott Niedermayer standards, but who cares. I got to do what millions dream of but never get a chance at. I got to play hockey in the best league in the world. To this day that's something that makes me extremely proud.

I didn't dominate in that game by any means. In fact, if you were watching on TV there's a good chance you wouldn't have noticed me. But I can tell you that I didn't feel out of place, and I'm pretty sure I didn't look out of place. I kept up with the play, made the right reads, and generally fit in. Not a first star performance, but a performance to hold my chin up about.

So. Enough back patting. Let's get back to the reality of the situation.

Because I was just supposed to be playing one game with the team, I was waiting for the inevitable tap from one of the assistants when it finished. It never came. I wandered around the dressing room and hallways of the Pond hoping to make eye contact with someone of authority so they could give me the heads up one way or another. Chafing me further was the fact that the Mighty Ducks were leaving on a road trip the next day. When you're as green as I was then, you don't want to assume anything. Once again, a million questions were swirling through my brain.

What if I show up at the airport and I'm not supposed to be there?

Why isn't anyone telling me what's going on?

Why did I pack only enough clothes for one day?

Did I leave the stove on back in Baltimore?

When I finally got it figured out that I would accompany the club on its road trip, I looked at what cities the Ducks were going to be visiting. And if my day was already a sundae, the itinerary was the cherry on top. Detroit on Friday and then—brace yourself— Toronto on Saturday night! That's right—*Hockey Night in Canada*, baby! I had to make it to that game.

I'm sure most people look back upon some of the things they did when they were young and wish they could go back and throttle the young version of themselves. I'm no different. I'd love to give Young Sean multiple beatings.

There I was, on my first NHL road trip, striding up to the plane eager to prove that I belonged. As I looked around I saw Paul Kariya, Steve Rucchin, Mike Sillinger, Fredrik Olausson, and Joe Sacco. They were all looking very NHL in their custom-tailored suits. I suddenly became hyper-aware that I was decked out in a green blazer, khakis, and brown Doc Martens. Strong gear if you're going to a frat house keg party; however, not so appropriate for an NHL charter. First to greet me on the plane was Joe Sacco. After eyeballing me up and down, he shook his head.

"This is the NHL, kid. Go get yourself a suit, because that outfit is embarrassing."

(Author's note: Unless you win the Masters, there is no need to own a green blazer. Ever!)

After each veteran provided his critique of my ensemble I settled in for my first NHL charter flight. We flew from LAX to Detroit. I think the flight took a little over four hours, but it seemed like four minutes. When you've spent your life travelling on the "bone-rattler," a four-hour charter flight is heaven. And, by the way, charter flights are the *only* way to travel. First, our bus dropped us off right at the stairs to the plane. Second, we didn't have to go through security—we just marched right on board. Third, the food was fantastic. Fourth, I didn't have to sit next to some gigantic Western Leaguer; I had the whole row of seats to myself. When we landed I think the flight attendant had to forcibly remove me from the plane.

All I kept thinking before our game against Detroit was, "Don't give them a reason to take you out of the lineup." Don't get me wrong. I was excited to play the Red Wings. I grew up idolizing Steve Yzerman. Sure I wanted to be the hero in that game, but I thought it was important to set a realistic goal. Mine was nothing more than to make it to the next game. And the next game was against the Leafs in the historic Maple Leaf Gardens on *Hockey Night in Canada*. I ask you, does it get any better than that? I knew I had an entire town pulling for me. Everyone in Dryden was holding their breath to see if I could hang in there for a couple of games so they could watch one of their own on Saturday night. Sure, Chris had been on national television countless times, but everyone expected him to make it. Mine was more of a "rags to slightly better rags" story. I also had a bunch of friends in Toronto who were looking forward to seeing me play. But the topper was that the future Mrs. Journeyman was still working and living in Toronto at the time. I knew how much it would mean to her to see me play live in the NHL for the first time in Toronto. If I could somehow make it out of the Detroit game without disgusting Ron Wilson, there was a good chance she would.

I had a couple of things going for me. The Ducks were short-handed because of injuries, so they were travelling with no extra skaters. Even dressing a non-productive Sean Pronger was going to be more palatable for Wilson than playing a man short. The other factor in my favour was that we were going into back-to-back games. So any lineup changes would require a call-up from Baltimore. It wasn't outside the realm of possibility, but as far as I could tell there was no intention of doing so. However, I did know that if I played like ass they could try to find a way to get someone else in there. Then my "Toronto or bust" dream would have been just busted.

In the game against Detroit I learned a quick lesson from the officials. Rookies need to earn respect; it's not just given to them. Since I was a centreman I had to take some faceoffs. Back in those days they didn't have such strict rules as to where your skates needed to be when the puck was dropped. I remember taking a faceoff against the Godfather himself, Steve Yzerman. I was about to ask him to sign my jersey but remembered I had forgotten to tuck a Sharpie into my pants. It was a defensive zone draw for me, so I got to put my stick down last. As I was getting ready to put my stick down I noticed Stevie was practically turned sideways at the dot. In terms of faceoff technique, that is a huge advantage. And usually the linesman will sort out that kind of stuff before the puck is dropped. When I saw the linesman not doing anything, I had to say something:

"Can you square him up?"

"Shut up, rookie," he replied.

"But he's almost turned completely...."

Before I could finish my plea, the puck was dropped and I lost the defensive zone faceoff.

The officials weren't done with me yet. Later in the game I got a holding penalty—or, as I like to think of it, my name on the official game sheet as proof that I played—against Darren McCarty. We were in our defensive zone and McCarty was my guy. All I could think was, "If you want to play on *Hockey Night in Canada* tomorrow, DO NOT let him score." So I wrapped him up in a bear hug. Unless someone shot the puck off his ass there was no way "my guy" was scoring. I certainly wouldn't classify it as a "good" penalty, which are usually infractions that prevent a goal or a great scoring chance. This was more of a "desperation" penalty. One where a player (me) is so desperate to stay in the lineup he'll do anything. My bear hug couldn't be an easier call for a referee. When the ref blew the whistle I turned to question the call out of pure instinct. I didn't get a word out before the referee absolutely crushed me with a verbal assault the likes of which can't be printed on these pages. OK, it can be printed if I prune out about a dozen four-letter adjectives. Basically, he told me, "Shut the fuck up, rookie, and don't you ever question me again. Go take a seat." Afterward, I was so rattled I sought some input from one of the guys on our bench. "What is up with these refs?" His reply: "Play hard and keep your mouth shut." A lesson learned thanks to Bill McCreary.

We ended up losing to Detroit that night, but I thought I played pretty well. I had my guy, anyway. And then there I was, boarding the plane to Toronto with the rest of the squad.

On the plane I tried to play it cool, but anyone paying close attention would have noticed my focus on the coaching staff at the front of the plane. I wanted to see if they were huddled together making plans about something. Something like sending me and my green blazer back to the farm. As far as I could tell, Ron Wilson and company weren't scrambling to make any plans to change things up. I was fairly certain I would be in the lineup the following night. Even with the comfort of *thinking* no one was on their way up from Baltimore, it was another restless sleep. My body may have been tired, but my brain was running through every conceivable scenario that would keep me out of the lineup. I'm not sure I dismissed them all, but I did eventually drift off to sleep with thoughts of Don Cherry dancing in my head.

Since we played the night before, our pre-game skate was "optional." Maybe one day someone can explain to me what that word means. Optional?! This was Maple Leaf Gardens, for God's sake! They were going to have to drag me off the ice. I was skating around by myself before practice started just picturing the historic events of the building. I was remembering all the Saturday nights Chris and I spent in our basement watching the Toronto Maple Leafs play on TV. I grew up watching Rick Vaive skate down the right wing and hammer a slapshot past every hapless goalie in the league. Or Wendel Clark with his patented wrist shot. Or his patented fists. So much history and so many memories in this rink. I was going to get to cross PLAY AT MAPLE LEAF GARDENS off the bucket list. At least, I hoped I was going to get that chance.

I'll be honest, though. It wasn't *exactly* a dream come true. When you're a kid fantasizing about the NHL, you don't imagine yourself on the outside looking in on your own team. But I felt like a guest of the Anaheim Mighty Ducks, not a key player. There I was, in my green jacket, among the millionaires in their $2,000 suits, making sure I was laughing at the jokes but not so hard that I'd draw enough attention to myself and a veteran would bark, "What are you laughing at, rook?" Even at the pre-game meal on the road I had to be careful; the last thing I wanted to do was mess with another guy's ritual. Hockey players are absurdly superstitious. Some guys eat exactly the same food in exactly the same order every pre-game meal and they've been doing it for the last ten years. It's almost childish now that I think of it. What some might look at as superstition, others may call a routine. Who sits with whom may be totally meaningless, or it could be something a few guys have been doing since so-and-so scored a hat trick on opening night. I wasn't going to just scooch over beside the first Duck I felt like talking to, only to discover that I'd ruined his luck.

Then there was the matter of seniority. It's different these days—rookies now seem to assume they're entitled to the same privileges as everyone else. Not so back then. Everything from who got off the bus first to who ate where to who talked to whom was dictated by seniority. Pecking order was everything. I could be blasted with a withering "how many games do you have in the league?" for any mistake. And, as a call-up, I could have been carved by anyone on the team. I just shut up and tried to make sure I didn't end up in anyone's crosshairs. Of course, what I was forgetting was that the first sign you've been accepted is that guys start carving you. If they're letting you off the hook, it's because they can't be bothered with you. If they start giving it to you, you're one of them. Between ripping their teammates in the dressing room and chirping on the ice, hockey players get pretty intensive training in blistering one-liners. (Ron Wilson sidebar: I ran into Coach Wilson in Toronto about five years after he started me in my first NHL game. I was there for the 2000 NHL Awards ceremony because I had been nominated for the Hart Trophy and the Norris Trophy that year. Or was that the year Chris was up for those awards? Sometimes I get a little confused. But as they say, never let the facts get in the way of a good story. Most of the people attending the awards ceremony were staying at the Westin

Harbour Castle Hotel. Because I was such a committed athlete I wanted to get in a workout before happy hour. I was in the elevator coming down from my room on the way to the Fitness Centre, which was located one floor below the lobby. The doors opened at the lobby level and I saw Ron Wilson standing a short distance away from me. I called out to him, "Hey Ron." He casually looked at me, and then looked at the direction that elevator was going, and said "Hey Prongs, it looks like the elevator is headed in the same direction as your career." It was a solid line on such short notice it was one of the few times in my life I didn't have a barb to throw back at someone who had just cut me down.)

After the pre-game skate was over I still didn't know what was going on. I felt like an airport ticket agent who didn't know whether the flight was on time or cancelled. I still hadn't heard if I was in the lineup or out of it. I knew that I was probably in, but I didn't know for sure. I warned all my friends that were planning to come to the game that I wasn't 100 percent sure I was a go. When my phone didn't ring before the game I knew, at the very least, I would get to take warm-up. I think that was the only warm-up of my career I went without a helmet. And there may have been a little gel in the hair for good measure. Let's not forget, this was *Hockey Night in Canada*!

After warm-up I made myself scarce. I didn't stay in any one place too long. If they needed to tell me something—like, for example, "You're not going tonight"—then they would have to find me. When no one came looking I gave a quiet fist pump. I thought of my parents and everyone back home sitting around the TV.

I couldn't help thinking of Little Sean back in Dryden, Ontario, and what he would have thought had he known that if he kept working and dreaming he'd one day be on the same ice surface where he watched his favourite stars on all those Saturday nights.

Saturday night at Maple Leaf Gardens was electric. I can't quite put my finger on it, but there was just that something different. Maybe it's that it's all so familiar to hockey fans and so richly imagined that when you're there for the first time it's both brand-new and totally familiar at the same time. Maybe it's that when you first start watching the game, the players seem so huge, but then there you are, out there on that ice you've seen so many times before, only now you're one of the biggest ones. Then there are the guys you're playing against. I can't say I was a Maple Leafs fan growing up, but if you live in Ontario as a kid it's impossible to avoid the Leafs. They were and still are all-encompassing in that province. Every Saturday night at the Pronger household was spent watching *Hockey Night in Canada* on CBC. I felt like I knew the Leafs intimately. So you can imagine that facing off against Doug Gilmour felt a little surreal. It was as if I could hear Bob Cole and Harry Neale talking about me as I leaned into the faceoff dot. As I got ready for the draw I glanced up at "Killer." I could have counted the number of teeth in his mouth on one hand. I was also a good thirty pounds heavier than him and would have been able to eat a bowl of soup off the top of his head. Still, he was an intimidating man to be face-to-face with. It's something you don't often think of—how intensely personal a faceoff can be. Two guys, competing one-on-one, while both teams stand and watch. You can smell the guy who stares down from posters on kids' bedroom walls. It's a physical contest, but even more psychological—you're trying to get into the other guy's head, and he's trying to get into yours. (And if he's a future Hall of Famer, he's probably already succeeded.) It was at that moment I made a rule for myself. Never look a superstar in the face. Look only at the crest on his jersey. That way it would be easier to focus on the task at hand instead of the spectre of the player.

It was easier said than done, especially with 20,000 fans watching—one of whom I very much wanted to impress. God knows how many more were watching on television. Including my parents and friends and former teachers and probably everyone I ever played hockey with as a kid. All I had to do was beat one of the most intense competitors in the game.

I knew I shouldn't have been thinking about all that. I should have been focused on playing hockey. But on the other hand, some of the best advice I've gotten over the years has been to enjoy the moment. And for me, realizing that I'd accomplished something special just to be there to face off against Gilmour was a way to do that.

Winning the faceoff—well, that was even better.

NHL stardom did not happen for me that year. I dressed in four more games for a grand total of seven for the season. Not quite enough for the pension. It did, however, give me reason to believe I was on the right path.

5

REALITY CHECK AND THE SUMMER OF SEAN

I may have had appearances in only seven games during the 1995–96 campaign, but seven games is enough to know whether you have what it takes to play in the league. You're playing against the best in the world, and if you can hold your own shift after shift, then you must belong. Right? Seven games is a pretty good taste of life in the NHL. Enough to know I wanted more. More than enough to know what it takes. What it takes, I figured, was a summer of hard work in the gym, so I could show up in camp in the kind of shape I would need to be in to grab a spot on the starting lineup.

I guess I figured wrong.

The fall of 1996 did not start great for me. After training all summer with the intention of making the big club I had a disappointing training camp. I'm not sure whether I overtrained or didn't train properly; regardless, the train went off the tracks and I couldn't get it back on. I came into camp about five pounds heavier than I'd been the year before. It was five pounds of muscle, but I quickly learned that heavier isn't better. Especially if it makes you a half-step slower when you were already a half-step slow. Hockey players look huge in their gear, but most guys, even guys who play a very physical game, usually look pretty small when you see them in a T-shirt. All their power comes from their legs and glutes. Too much upper-body mass just slows you down, as I was figuring out the hard way. (If a guy has a huge upper body, chances are his job is punching people in the face, not skating.) I had busted my ass all summer, only to peak during the physicals.

The hard part of training camp when you haven't proven yourself is that you need to hit the ground running. There is *no* time to work out the kinks and get your legs under you. It wasn't so much that someone had a great camp and beat me out—it was more like I was so average they had no reason to keep me around. I'd trained all summer long with the goal of increasing my speed and finding my "fourth gear." Instead, I was red-lining in second gear the entire training camp. Every race for a loose puck was a losing proposition. I was mentally beating myself up after every ice session. I knew exactly what was wrong, but there wasn't a damn thing I could do about it. I'm pretty sure it would've been frowned upon to walk into the coaches' office and ask for a week or two off because I'd miscalculated my optimal playing weight. As a result, I found myself in a place I never thought I'd be again: sitting on a plane en route to Baltimore—with plenty of time to figure out what weight I should play at.

The demotion was a spark for me, though, and my play picked up as soon as I got there. Pucks were going in and points were piling up and I was having a blast. At one point, I was leading the league in goal scoring (I hope you were sitting down for that one). To be honest, I was never "untalented." It's just that sometimes you get off to a bad start, or the coaching staff has you slotted in a certain role, and next thing you know the season gets away from you. Just like when teams slump early in a season it's hard to dig out of the hole. The same goes with individuals. If you start poorly, it's tough to regroup.

I'm sure it's the same for every sport, but hockey is a game of split-second decisions that really amount to instinct. Ever notice how the puck just seems to bounce onto the stick of the truly gifted players? That's not luck, at least not every time. That's the confidence of a guy following his instincts. As soon as he starts thinking about it, he starts overskating that puck, or arriving a half-step too late. The guy who picks a corner with a one-timer has dozens of bits of information to factor in as he's winding up—the math is incredibly complex. But he's not doing math, or even thinking about it much. If he makes the shot, it's probably because he's not thinking about it at all. He's just playing hockey. If he *is* thinking about it, there's a good chance he fans on that puck, or it goes off the heel of his stick, or misses the net. The tiniest hesitation will make that happen. When something goes wrong you start thinking about it, and suddenly more things start going wrong.

And when things go right, more things start going right. The game starts to feel easy. Since good things started happening right from opening night, I was able to keep it rolling. To top it all off I was even selected to play in the AHL all-star game. It was the best start I could have hoped for that didn't include the NHL.

I think a big part of getting off to a great start was having Moe Mantha as coach. Somehow, we just clicked. Maybe it was due to the fact that I grew up watching him play for the Jets and I was trying to impress him. Or maybe I was just awestruck by the type of mustache he could grow. Whatever the reason, it was working and I wasn't about to overanalyze why. If I had to describe his coaching style I would say he was a player's coach. That's not to say he was soft or let the guys walk all over him. He just always had your back. And there was no B.S. with Moe: you knew where you stood with him because he was always upfront and honest. I loved playing for him. And I wasn't alone.

One of Moe's favourite pre-game speeches was to ask us how we wanted to be remembered as hockey players. He would get in my face and scream, "Prongs, what do you want on your tombstone?" As a young guy (which, when I played for Moe, most of my teammates were), that's not something I had thought of yet. Sure I wanted to win the Stanley Cup and be successful and make lots of money, but I hadn't really thought of how I would want my teammates to remember me. Thanks to Moe, I would ask myself that question before every game for the remainder of my career. It never failed to get me fired up.

Speaking of fired up, Moe was never shy to get emotional behind the bench. He could be very intense at times, because I'm sure he never lost that competitive edge he had as a player. But he could also be sympathetic when things went off the rails.

We, the Baltimore Bandits, were playing on the road against the Carolina Monarchs. It was one of those games where everything we did went wrong. And every mistake we made ended up in the back of our net. Mike Bales was our goalie at the time. With about six minutes left in the third the Monarchs scored to make it 12–5. That was pretty much all Bales could take. He went nuts and threw his goalie stick into the stands. Apparently, throwing your stick at the paying customers is frowned upon in the American Hockey League. Mercifully, Mike's night was over. Or so we thought. It's never fun to lose a game, but when you lose by a touchdown it can be miserable. As we were tiptoeing around the dressing room we found out we had five minutes to get on the bus and get out of Dodge. Instead of going directly to the freeway, our bus driver made a detour to the closest tavern. Moe grabbed Bales and the two of them marched into the bar. The rest of us were relegated to the bus. Almost on cue, as the two of them walked into the bar our assistant coach, Mike Gibbons, popped in the game tape for our viewing pleasure. I figured Moe had taken Bales in to buy him a beer and cheer him up after the shelling he took. They'll be back in ten minutes, I thought. Well, ten minutes turned into an hour. So, we sat in the bar parking lot, on our team bus, watching ourselves get our asses handed to us while the two of them sipped on a couple of Long Island Iced Teas. Just as the troops were starting to get restless, Moe and Mike walked out of the pub and climbed onto the bus. Not a word was spoken. The bus driver put it into gear and away we went. It was a six-hour ride back to Baltimore. In my head I kept replaying the scene from *Youngblood* when Coach Chadwick makes the boys put their gear back on after a drubbing. I would have been all right with it if Coach Moe made us do that or skate when we got back home, but what I didn't want to do was to have to watch any more of that fucking game that was still playing on the bus's entertainment system. I'm not sure if it was the second replay of the game or the third, but about four hours into our drive, as most of the players were sleeping, Moe made the driver pull the bus over on the side of the freeway. Since I couldn't sleep on buses I may have been the only one to witness Moe eject our game tape, open the bus door, and toss the tape into the ditch. Apparently he had seen enough too.

That blip aside, we weren't having a bad season as a team, and as I mentioned things were going swimmingly for me individually. So, sure enough, it didn't take long for the big club to come calling. That meant no AHL all-star game, and you know what? I didn't care at all, because the dream is not about being among the best in the minors. There was something extra special about this recall, because no injury had forced the team to come looking. Anaheim wanted a boost from the guy who had been leading their farm club.

Since I was providing offence with Baltimore I assumed that the Ducks wanted me to play an offensive role with them. I should have known better. Being the top dog down below doesn't mean jack squat when you move up the ladder. That's why it's really tough for some guys to perform with their NHL clubs upon recall. They are skill guys who are used to playing twenty minutes a game in all situations, and all of a sudden they are asked to chip in the puck, forecheck, and not get scored on. Luckily for me, my style of play didn't change too much from league to league. I was a grinder.

I went five games without a goal and was sure that when GM Jack Ferreira asked to see me after a game I was going to be handed my ticket back to Baltimore. Instead, I was told the words that all minor leaguers yearn to hear.

"Go find a place to live."

I was shocked. Sure, they're just six simple words, but they have the power to change everything for a minor leaguer. Why? Because they mean you're not a minor leaguer anymore! The team is saying "Hey, forget the hotel and find a place of your own." I couldn't wipe the smile off my face for the call to the future Mrs. Journeyman.

"Pack your bags, baby! You're headed to the show!"

Making that call to Mrs. Journeyman is one of my greatest memories. Obviously, letting someone know you've made it to the show is special. But if that someone happens to be your girlfriend, who quit her job and moved to a one-room flat on the outskirts of Baltimore, it's a little more than special. Mrs. Journeyman and I maintained our long-distance relationship during my first year (and what a year *that* was) and then my second year as a pro. She had a great job in Toronto with an advertising agency. She was on the fast track and everything was falling into place for her—with the exception of her boyfriend. He just couldn't give up on his dream. After my second year I realized that if this relationship was going to survive someone had to quit their job. I delicately suggested that she should come live with me. I told her to think of it as an adventure. It was probably her sense of adventure and not her scouting abilities that made her take a leap of faith. Because if she made that type of life-altering decision based on her expectation of me becoming an NHL superstar she most certainly would be regarded as one of the all-time worst scouts in history. But she took a chance, quit her job, and got to spend the first part of the 1996–97 season living in a 600-square-foot one-bedroom apartment in Columbia, Maryland. Don't get me wrong, we had a great time, but I couldn't help thinking that she gave up so much for this. She definitely deserved better. It was because of her taking that chance that we're still together (and because I'm an awesome husband and father). It's what made that phone call that much sweeter—because I felt like her sacrifice was paying off. Or hey, maybe she really is a sick judge of talent!

After I hung up, Steve Rucchin and Jason Marshall took me out for a celebratory beverage or four. It was one of the best days of my career.

It's funny what a vote of confidence can do for one's, well … confidence. Take a little pressure off yourself and things can really start to come together. The first game after getting notified to find a place I scored my first NHL goal (LA Kings, Byron Dafoe). Steve Rucchin had the puck on the half wall and fired a shot at Dafoe. I was standing right between the hash marks. The puck bounced off his pads right to me. I tried to go upstairs with it, fanned, and it slid along the ice just underneath Dafoe. It barely made it across the line but I didn't care. What a feeling! Actually, it was more relief than anything else. I put so much pressure on myself that I was glad to get the weight of the world off my shoulders. I do remember sitting in the locker room after the game, thinking "I just scored a goal in the National Hockey League." That's something no one can take away from me.

After I was done patting myself on the back it was off to the airport for our next game, which was a big one for me. We were headed to St. Louis—and yes, you-know-who was patrolling the blue line for those pesky Blues. I inaugurated the "Pronger Bowl" tradition with a highlight-reel goal (for me, anyway). It was one of those goals where I must have forgotten who I was for a minute because I had no business doing what I did. I was a left shot coming down the right side and cut in toward the net. As I got closer to the goal I slid the puck underneath the defenceman's stick (from my backhand to my forehand) and then tapped it through Grant Fuhr's legs. My celebration may have been a tad excessive; in fact, I've seen more restraint from players who scored overtime winners in the playoffs. But this put us up 4–1 on the road in a very important game in January. For all we knew, this may have been the difference for us in making the playoffs (at least that's how I tell the story to my kids). A certain gap-toothed defenceman was in the Blues lineup that night but unfortunately he wasn't on the ice. Can you imagine if he had been the blueliner I beat on that one-on-one? I know what I'd get him every Christmas: a brand new DVD of an unbelievable goal scored by his hero and older brother, me.

After I wiped the smile off my face, the Ducks returned home from the road trip and it was time for me to find a place to live. As someone who had lived in a farmhouse in Tennessee, a hotel in San Diego, a motel in Greensboro, and a one-bedroom apartment in the suburbs of Baltimore, trying to find a place in Newport Beach, California, was a welcome chore. And there's little doubt that my girlfriend was looking forward to it more than me. We were happy enough living in Baltimore, but checking out an oceanview apartment in Newport Beach certainly brightened things even more.

I remember signing our lease (month-to-month, of course) and feeling like we had made it. Here we were, both from a small town in northwestern Ontario, setting up shop in southern California. If it wasn't the top of the mountain it was pretty darn close.

What a great season that was for me and, more importantly, the team. We had two superstars, Paul Kariya and Teemu Selanne, leading the way. We had another player just coming into his own in Steve Rucchin. Throw a couple of savvy veterans, Jari Kurri and Brian Bellows, in with the rest of us hard-working role players and we made up a pretty good group. Good enough to put together a thirteen-game unbeaten streak during the months of February and March. For the first time in Anaheim Mighty Ducks franchise history, the team was in a good position to lock down a playoff berth. I'm not sure how much of a buzz there was around town, but there was a big-time buzz in our locker room. We were playing with confidence and it was a heck of a lot of fun going to the rink.

I even started dressing better. A few weeks after being told to find a place to live it was time to upgrade the wardrobe. Unfortunately, the green blazer and khaki pants look still hadn't caught on in the NHL and I was sick of taking abuse for looking like a minor leaguer. After all, I was in the show now. After consulting with some of the veterans on the team—and by consulting, I mean being told in no uncertain terms what to do—I made the call to one of their favourite tailors. I had to pinch myself. Was this small-town kid from Dryden capable of rocking a bespoke suit? You bet your Doc Martens he was. This particular tailor made house calls, so we invited him to our new apartment for the fitting. This guy brought his A game! He showed us fabrics, patterns, styles, cuts, colours, and combinations. He was going to set me up with a binder so I knew which pants go with which shirts and which shirts go with which jackets and what ties go with—what the hell? Are you kidding me?

This was like doing long division in Chinese. I just wanted a suit that wasn't green or khaki. How hard could that be? At the time I thought he must have thought I'd fallen off a turnip truck, but the league is full of small-town guys, so I probably wasn't the first or last hockey player he ever met who couldn't fold a pocket square. In the end, we kept it to a starter package of two blazers, three shirts, and two pairs of pants. All number-coded so even I couldn't screw up the combinations. I think he may have actually put in the binder, in bold letters, **Under no circumstances are you to incorporate the green blazer into the new look**. Whatever. I still think it looks sharp on the Masters Champion.

Early in April we had our first opportunity to clinch a playoff spot. The Mighty Ducks were home to the Dallas Stars. A victory meant a berth in the Stanley Cup playoffs. I had no doubt we would win that game. It's tough to explain, but there are times in hockey when the players in the room just know what the outcome will be. That was one of those times. The guys were loose, confident, and ready to celebrate a first for the franchise. And that's exactly what we did. Kariya and Selanne each scored a goal in a 3–2 victory. I'll never forget the sound of the crowd during the last minute of play. It may not be the same as the last minute before you're about to win a Stanley Cup, but it sure sounded that way to me. The atmosphere of that game was what I had waited my whole life for and it was better than I could have imagined.

In the first round we ended up playing the Phoenix Coyotes. The Coyotes had just arrived in Phoenix that year from Winnipeg. They were led by USA's dynamic duo, Keith Tkachuk and Jeremy Roenick. I have to be honest, I didn't think the city of Phoenix could bring it Playoff Style but I'll tell you what, they adopted the "sea of white" from Winnipeg seamlessly. In fact, the American Airlines Arena was an intimidating place to play that spring. The series was back and forth. We ended up winning the first two games in Anaheim and thought we were well on our way to the second round. However, as they say, it's not the first team to win two games, it's the first to win four. The Coyotes won the next two games in their rink and then walked into Anaheim and won a pivotal game five to go up three games to two and put our season on the brink. Game six was in Phoenix, and with our season on the line our best player stepped up huge. Who can forget Paul Kariya's wrist shot from the hash marks in overtime to force a game seven? Well, maybe you have, but it's a moment that is burned into my memory. A year of firsts was about to get another. Add my first game seven to my first season in the NHL, my first NHL goal, and my first NHL playoff game. Could it get any better? Yes, it could. The only thing better than playing a game seven is winning a game seven. And the only thing better than winning a game seven is setting up the winning goal in that game seven.

I wish I could say I carried the puck up the ice, beat one of the defencemen wide, and slid a goalmouth pass to a streaking Teemu Selanne. But it didn't happen quite like that. I tried to make a move on a defender, lost the puck off my stick, it went to Dmitri Mironov, and he passed it over to Dave Karpa who then pounded a slapper in the net. But you know what they say—there are no pictures on the score sheet!

The next round we had the pleasure (probably not the right word) of facing the mighty Red Wings. Not only did this team have Yzerman, but it was also the season Detroit rocked the five-man Russian unit. Sergei Fedorov, Slava Kozlov, Igor Larionov, Vladimir Konstantinov, and the Godfather of Russian hockey, Viacheslav Fetisov. Talk about intimidating.

The first two games of the series were in Detroit. That meant they had last change. So, whenever Sean Pronger's line was out there, Wings coach Scotty Bowman astutely sent out either Yzerman's line or the five-man Russian unit. He wasn't the best coach in league history for nothing, although I'm pretty sure the most dimwitted of beer league coaches could have figured out both of those two lines could chew me up and spit me out. How would you like to be a checking centre and to observe that the other team's coach is going out of his way to get his top lines out against you? I may have had only forty or so games in the league, and I was not exactly a Selke Trophy winner, but it is still an insult to be identified as a weak link by the game's most celebrated coach. And you know, I did take it a little personally. I took the faceoffs personally too. I'd square up to the dot (not that Yzerman ever had to) and think there is *no way* I am losing this draw. On the whole, I think I fared pretty well against the top two lines in the world that spring.

Asking which line I'd rather have faced is kind of like asking a death-row inmate what his preferred choice of execution is. With that in mind, I'd rather play against Stevie's line. He was like a bullet to the head—quick and painless. The Russians were like death by a thousand cuts. They could hang on to the puck forever and make you look like a fool. And that's before they start passing and regrouping all over the ice. I put all my energy into winning every faceoff against them. On TV—and even when you watch a game live—faceoffs appear to look like the centreman just takes nonchalant swipes at the puck in the hopes he can bat it to a teammate. I can tell you there is much more to it than that. Everything matters. It matters whom you're facing off against, what hand they are, which side of the ice you're on, and in which zone. If you're in the defensive zone it's much more important to not lose the faceoff than it is to win it. You don't want to give up any free shots. In the offensive zone you're trying to win it outright because it usually leads to a scoring chance. In the neutral zone sometimes it doesn't matter so much. I remember talking with Darryl Sittler (I played with his son Ryan in Baltimore) and he told me he sometimes lost the draw on purpose in the neutral zone so the opposing centreman would have a false sense of security and he could take advantage of that on an offensive zone draw. Unfortunately I wasn't a Hall of Famer (yet), so every draw for me was life or death. Especially when facing off against the Russian Five. If I lost the draw, my line wasn't going to touch the puck again.

It was a four-game sweep, but I can guarantee you it was one of the closest sweeps in NHL history. We lost in single, double, and triple overtime in that series. It was painful to lose in such a manner, but all in all the season was a success for everyone—the organization, the players, the fans, and even Sean Pronger, the mid-season call-up. We even got to say the eventual Cup champions knocked us out.

Making matters even better was the fact that I was up for a new contract that summer. The original deal I signed out of the East Coast League was up and I knew I was in for a raise. To be honest, though, I thought making 170 grand was awesome even if I was by far the lowest-paid guy on the team. My main goal in the summer was to secure a one-way contract. I didn't want the GM to have any extra incentive to send me down to the minors. Hey, if I played like ass and got sent down, then so be it. I just didn't want a cost-effective contract to get in the way of me having a fair shake to stay in the NHL. And I didn't think that was too unreasonable a request considering what had just transpired.

So I entered that summer with a swagger in my step. Not quite as much as Anthony Michael Hall's character in the movie *Johnny Be Good,* when he was strutting down Main Street in his nifty velour suit. But close. After all I'd been through, I felt like a legitimate NHL player. The way I figured it, the Ducks would offer me a contract, we'd accept it, and the whole ordeal would be over quickly. Unfortunately, the franchise didn't view things the way I did—and my agent, Pat Morris, knew it.

"Sean, this may not go as quickly as you'd like."

"Why, Pat? Why wouldn't they just get my contract out of the way?"

I failed to see the negotiation from their point of view. They had a few other players to worry about. And by that I mean they had a few (dozen) more important players to sign. Usually teams will take care of the big guys first and then spread around the scraps to the ham-n-eggers like me. Also, I think they wanted me to sit and think about it for the summer; some time without a deal would likely make it a little easier to grind me down.

Pat tried to calm my nerves.

"There's a process to it. I know you want to get this done so you can relax and enjoy your summer, but remember that you don't start getting paid until October. So it doesn't make a difference if a deal gets done today or in three months."

Foreshadowing.

"You're right, Pat, but if I have to sit on pins and needles for the whole summer waiting for this to get done I may have a breakdown."

More foreshadowing.

"Sean. Just train hard, try not to think about the contract, and let me worry about the details."

"Pat, I know you're experienced in these things. But please, if there's any way you can speed up the process you'll save me some hair."

"Try to relax and have some fun. You had a great season. Enjoy yourself a little."

Easy for him to say. My brother and a couple dozen other high-profile clients were paying his rent. I knew that it would be near impossible for me to relax if I was waiting for the phone to ring every thirty seconds for three straight months. That's a good recipe for insanity.

Regardless, I tried to take his advice to heart. That's why I decided it would be just fine for the future Mrs. Journeyman and me to join four other couples on a houseboat trip in Minnesota. Oh wait—three other couples and my brother, who decided to dump his girlfriend just days before the boat was to launch. It was a group full of folks who didn't mind blowing off a bunch of steam. Picture Fred Smoot and the Vikings on Lake Minnetonka without the peelers. However, since it was a long trip in the middle of training, Chris and I insisted on bringing workout gear on the boat. And by that I don't mean workout clothing. I'm talking about a complete set of dumbbells and a stationary bike. Yes, the top of the house-boat was turned into a little gym. Why wouldn't it be? It had a bike, weights, and a hot tub and waterslide. Those floating by us in the daytime must have done a double-take for sure, because they would have seen one guy riding a bike, one guy lifting weights, and seven others standing around them crushing beers. The co-author of this book tried to break me on many occasions while I was grinding out a forty-five-minute ride by offering me a shot every five minutes. I guess that was his version of intervals.

To go along with our mobile water gym we also had a satellite phone on board. Cell phones were just starting to make their mark in the world, and of course Chris owned one but it had no chance of working while we were floating on a lake in the middle of Nowhere, Minnesota. So, at a cost of five bucks per minute, I would call Pat daily for an update. And that update was always the same.

"There's nothing new to report yet Sean."

"All right, but if something comes up and you need to get in touch with me, call the lodge and they'll send out a boat to get me."

"Sean, I haven't forgotten your message from yesterday, or the day before. Just relax and enjoy your trip. Nothing's going to happen until you get back. Stop thinking about it."

"OK, but if you need to get in touch with me just call the lodge."

After the seven-day drinking and bike-riding binge ended it was time to figure out where I was going to skate before training camp began. I know a lot of guys don't like hitting the ice until September, but getting on skates as early as possible was a must for me as I was never the fleetest of foot. (Maybe I should have been a defenceman.)

As much as I loved going back to my hometown of Dryden, it caused a lot of problems when it was time to get back on the ice. Since Dryden is such a small town it doesn't keep the ice in the local rink all summer long. That meant I had to leave the comfy confines of my house on the lake every summer and take my pre-training camp on the road.

In 1997, St. Louis was the logical place to stay and train for the month of August. Since Chris was somewhat of a hockey player himself, it made sense to skate and work out with him. This was not a bad thing. Since he had a little more money at his disposal he was able to afford a personal trainer during the summer. Once a month he would fly to meet with his trainer, get evaluated, and receive a new training program. So, once a month, I would have a new training program. We got after it pretty hard in August. Chris and I would hit the gym five to six days a week as well as skate with a number of Blues and NHL players who lived in the St. Louis area. Throw in a couple of power skating sessions a week and I was feeling pretty darn good on the ice. After throwing in another puck past the shooter tutor during one of our scrimmages, I remember Al MacInnis yelling out,

"Will somebody give this guy a contract?"

Big Al was only half messing with me, but whatever, he didn't lead the month of August in scoring. It was my own special Art Ross Trophy!

I wish super-agent Pat had kept track of the number of inbound calls he received from me in the summer of '97. As August crept along I kept seeing other guys signing contracts all over the league. Obviously, that didn't sit well with me. I kept wondering, "When do I get to kick back and enjoy the summer?"

After each day of training I'd head back to Chris's place to see if Pat called. And each day there was nothing new to report. It wasn't like we were looking for a multi-million dollar contract with a no-trade clause. All we wanted was a one-year, one-way contract. They were handing those things out like candy to Europeans and Russians. Why couldn't a hard-working Canadian kid get a small piece of the pie? The Mighty Ducks obviously hadn't seen any tapes from the St. Louis Summer League.

As the calendar turned from August to September, I was mentally exhausted. Every morning from the first of July on I woke up hoping for some good news and every morning I was disappointed. I was like a kid running downstairs hoping to see presents on Christmas morning only to find there wasn't even a tree in the living room. Christmas Day sans presents had transformed into Groundhog Day. I'm not going to lie, I was getting more worried and anxious with each passing moment. I was weak and would have signed any contract the Ducks put in front of my face at that point. Thank goodness for agents.

When September rolled around, I still didn't have a contract and therefore I didn't know what the heck I was going to do for training camp. I couldn't stay in St. Louis and train with the Blues anymore. And I didn't know if going to Anaheim was the right move. I didn't want to make it look like I was desperate, even though I was, and I surely didn't want to risk an injury without a deal first. In four short months I had gone from a guy who was cocksure that a contract would land in my hands the minute the clock struck midnight on July 1 to a player who didn't know what the future held (again). There I was, feeling the best I had ever felt at that time of year thanks to a summer of hard work, and yet I didn't have a job to go to.

I called Pat to discuss our options. He said the Mighty Ducks were willing to fly me to Anaheim with the intention of working out a contract before the first day of the training camp. That worked for me. I was so desperate to get something on paper that I would have jogged from Dryden to SoCal. I landed in Anaheim two days before camp opened and checked into the Doubletree to wait for my next instructions.

David McNabb was the assistant GM of Anaheim at the time and was handling all the club's contract negotiations. That the Ducks flew me in less than forty-eight hours before camp was to commence gives you an idea of how long they felt negotiations would take with a guy who would be battling for their thirteenth forward spot. And it would have been easy *if* they had offered a one-way deal. Their first offer was a two-way contract with a good NHL salary component. Unfortunately, it had a minor league component to it as well. We countered with a one-way deal and McNabb immediately told us that there was absolutely no way that we would get a one-way contract from Anaheim. They didn't have to give us what we wanted and they knew it. If they caved and gave me a one-way it would open the door for any future player with similar numbers (unimpressive ones) to demand the same thing. It was a valid point and I knew it. Bottom line, we had zero leverage to make demands. Or at least

I thought so. What my agent told me to do next just about blew my mind.

"Sean, pack up your stuff and leave the hotel. We may have an offer sheet from another team."

"Excuse me, Pat? Who the heck would give us an offer sheet?"

For those of you unfamiliar with an offer sheet, it's when another team offers a group II (restricted) free agent a contract. Typically, offer sheets are for *huge* dollars to big-time players. Like the one Philadelphia offered to Chris Gratton (five years, $16.5 million in 1997), or that Carolina put in front of Sergei Fedorov (six years, $38 million in 1998). When a player signs an offer sheet the team that owns his rights can match that offer or let him walk and get compensation via draft picks. And when the dollar amount of the contract is big, then the package of draft picks is substantial.

I wish I could say my offer sheet was similar to the ones offered to Gratton and Fedorov. But based on a number of factors it was substantially less. Back in 1997, if a team signed a group II free agent to an offer sheet of $399,999 for one year and the other team chose to not match, there was no compensation in draft picks. That's how valuable guys in my pay range were deemed. We could be plucked for free! Anyway, Pat told me he had been talking with the Carolina Hurricanes about a possible offer sheet.

"How 'possible' is this?" I asked him.

"It's possible enough that I want you to check out of the hotel and go stay with one of your friends."

"OK, if you think this is our best move I'll check out."

"Good. I'll call you when I have more details."

"Thanks. Wait, does this mean I'm holding out?"

I had a hard time saying those words with a straight face. But it was true. After forty-six career NHL regular season games and a whopping nine playoff games, Sean Pronger was a training camp holdout. Just another one of those moments when I'd like to go back in time and punch myself in the face.

Since Anaheim was sure I was going to sign on the dotted line, the club had assigned me a roommate for training camp. Bob Wren was the lucky camper. He looked at me with amusement as I packed up my gear. I'd just met Bob and he seemed like a pretty quiet guy. However, I had seen his numbers in junior, he was an offensive dynamo. The one knock on him was his skating, and after meeting him I figured out why. He had the hands and vision of Gretzky but the body of a retired accountant. I'm sure he was thinking that "this Sean Pronger is a complete idiot but at least there's one less guy I have to compete with now." I know that's what I would have been thinking if I were in his shoes.

As advised, I checked out of the hotel and told no one where I was going. I went to stay with a good friend of mine, Steve Borcsok. He was originally from Toronto so he spoke the language but had moved to Newport Beach for work. In fact, he lived just a few steps from the ocean.

"Are you really holding out?" he asked.

"Yep," I replied with more than a hint of embarrassment.

"How much are we holding out for?"

"It's not so much about the salary as it is about the structure. We want a one-way contract."

"OK. How long do you think we'll be roommates?"

"I'm hoping I'll be gone by tomorrow."

"All right then, do you want to go grab a drink?"

Let's see. I had just spent the past two months getting in the best shape of my life. All of a sudden I was a training camp holdout with nowhere to skate and no idea how long I'd be off the ice. It was definitely one of those situations in life when you need to have some restraint and show a little discipline. It wasn't a vacation. On the other hand, it was 80 degrees out and I could not only smell the ocean, I could see it as well.

"OK, let's go. But just for one."

Before heading out for protein beers with Steve, I had to call Mrs. Journeyman to give her the update of what exactly had transpired. At that point she had no idea I was a holdout. I had a feeling she wasn't going to be too impressed with what had developed in the previous twelve hours. Adding fuel to the fire was that she was stuck in Dryden while I was just about to go rehydrate at a bar in Newport Beach.

"Hey babe, how's the weather up there?"

"Not bad. How's it down there?"

"Pretty good. Probably a little better than there," I said, as I watched the sun dance off the ocean in the distance.

"Have you talked to Pat? What's the scoop?"

Here we go.

"Pat has advised us to hold out. He told me to check out of the hotel and bunk with Steve until he can work out a few options."

Silence.

"Hello? Are you still there?"

"Yes. Are you telling me you will not be starting camp with everyone else?"

"Basically, yes. But there's a really good chance that it'll all get sorted out tomorrow."

"Sean, are you kidding me? We're in no position to be holding out. Pat better know what he's doing."

"Honey, this is what he does. Let's let him do his job. Besides, we don't start getting paid until October so it's not like we're losing any money."

It seemed like I was trying to convince myself as much as her.

From the way she said goodbye, I knew that I hadn't convinced either one of us.

Over drinks, Steve and I mapped out our new fitness program. He decided to take a couple days off work to be my training partner. At least that's what he said. I'm sure to him it was more about gaining a drinking partner for a few days instead.

The next morning we hit the gym. Then in the afternoon we went inline skating down the boardwalk, and then we followed that with a rigorous session of body surfing. Since I figured my holdout was only going to last about twenty-four hours or so, I enjoyed the day. I viewed it as a nice little mini vacation after an intense summer of training. It was exactly what the doctor ordered, I told myself.

My second day as a holdout felt much different. It was like I was playing hooky or doing something illegal. And then I made the biggest rookie holdout mistake ever. I went out and grabbed a newspaper. A word to all you potential holdouts out there: *do not* read the newspaper while you're on the lam. Don't watch television either, for that matter.

But, I figured, what was the harm in checking out what was going on at Ducks camp? As soon as I started reading the first article, I found out that I already knew what was going on at Ducks camp. I WASN'T THERE! McNabb was quoted as saying that it would be a shame if Sean Pronger didn't sign a contract soon because his NHL career could be over before it began. That stung. The first negotiating blow had landed and it pretty much knocked me to the ground. I called Pat immediately and left a message to call me back ASAP. We were but one day into our holdout and I was already wilting. So much for willpower. I could have handled losing my roster spot over poor play, but if I was bumped because of a holdout I would have been devastated.

Day two of the Newport Beach workout was not fun for my buddy Steve. I led him through a rage-induced weight workout that gassed the two of us. Anger fuelled the inline-skating portion of the program, and I went all out because it made me feel like I was staying somewhat in skating shape. In two short weeks I had gone from training with one of the best power skating coaches in Saint Louis to blading on the beach with a dude in jean shorts and a tank top. And if that's not sick enough for you, how about the fact that four short months before that metrosexual version of *Baywatch* I was going head-to-head with Steve Yzerman in the playoffs? I wish someone had some video of us inline skating near the beach that day. I was screaming along as if my life depended on keeping my speed at fifteen miles per hour or higher. I kept thinking my chances of playing in the NHL were slipping away. My blood was boiling. I was so hot that I completely forgot about my training partner, who was lagging fifty yards behind me. As he went into cardiac arrest, I just wanted to get to my phone.

The first couple days of my holdout I think I called my agent at least a dozen times. And I had to wait until I got back to Steve's place to call him. Can you imagine if I'd had a cell phone? I would run the bill up into the thousands. Between calling Pat, fielding calls from the future Mrs. Journeyman, and talking to my parents it felt like I was constantly on the phone. And no one was happy. Mrs. J. was stuck in Dryden just itching to book her flight to somewhere. Anywhere. My parents were hoping that the pride and excitement of having two boys in the NHL wasn't going to last just a few days. They knew that unlike Chris, my road to hockey's biggest stage had involved a number of roadblocks.

In super-agent Pat's defence, he was just trying to get the best deal he could. I really wanted that one-way contract, and he really wanted to get it for me. That's why day three of the holdout was such a tough one for the Pronger camp. Carolina called to say that an offer sheet wasn't coming. What little leverage we had went right out the window. The funny thing was that I wasn't that upset. Although I wanted a good deal, I certainly did not want to go to another club. I liked my teammates and I liked the organization. For those reasons I figured it was time to eat some crow and put the contract to bed.

Pat spoke to McNabb the day after Carolina informed us they were out of the Sean Sweepstakes. The Ducks offered us a two-year, two-way contract that would pay $350K in the NHL and $125K in the minors. That was a pretty good raise considering my last contract was $170K/$35K. Still, I had bigger plans. My AHL days were over as far as I was concerned, so I sure as hell wasn't going to commit to a two-year deal that included minor league pay. We countered with a compromise: a one-year deal for $375K/$150K with a clause that would drop the minor league pay if I played twenty-five games in the NHL. I thought that was fair. However, there was an underlying issue that was a sticking point. At that point in my career I had a total of forty-six NHL games under my belt. If I played fewer than thirty-four games that season I would have finished with less than eighty games' experience. In that edition of the Collective Bargaining Agreement, if you were twenty-five years of age or older and had fewer than eighty games in the NHL you were considered a group VI free agent. That meant I would have been an unrestricted free agent at the end of the season and free to sign with anyone. The Ducks weren't comfortable with our offer. They feared I would suffer a season-ending injury before the twenty-five-game mark and then they'd lose me at the end of the year to the highest bidder. Yes, it's comical when looking back at it now. But McNabb was just trying to cover his bases.

In the end, the two sides settled on a one-year, two-way contract for $375K/$150K with a clause that my minor league salary would be dropped after thirty-five games. Basically, if I played thirty-five games for the Ducks I would have the one-way deal I always wanted. It would also ensure the Ducks would retain my rights at the end of the season because it would put me over eighty games played and eliminate the possibility of becoming an unrestricted free agent.

When I look back, I still can't believe I held out. And if you do the math, I held out for an additional $25K. What's even more amazing is that the Ducks actually based some of their negotiations on the concern that they could lose me at the end of the season. But I guess it goes to show that the journeyman experiences just about everything the superstar does, including gut-wrenching contract negotiations played out in the media.

The Summer of Sean officially began on September 13, 1997. A good two and a half months after I'd expected it to. Regardless, I was ecstatic. I knew that I could finally join my teammates and play hockey, which was all it was about anyway.

I was a little concerned about my conditioning level since I had missed the first five days of camp. Sure, I had been in great shape when I arrived in Anaheim, but missing out on two-a-days for a week had no doubt set me back. Not good, considering the exhibition season started just one day after I signed my deal. I thought I would be allowed to ease my way back into things but I was horribly wrong.

I lasted two twirls into my first skate before Pierre Page, Anaheim's new head coach, approached me.

"Hey Sean, great to see you finally signed. Congratulations."

"Thanks Pierre."

"Make sure you get a good skate in today because you're playing against the Oilers tomorrow."

Was he kidding? Didn't he know my workout regime for the last week consisted of inline skating and body surfing?

"Fantastic! I can't wait to get in there," I lied.

Prior to the game I was nervous for a number of reasons. I was concerned about my fitness level and how my body was going to react to game situations. It doesn't matter how hard you train or practise, you can never match the speed or intensity of an actual game. I was also concerned my timing was going to be off since I hadn't played in a real game in close to five months. But mostly I was nervous that I was going to embarrass myself.

Somehow I made it through the first two periods without being cut from the team. With the game tied and about a minute to go Coach Page tapped my shoulder to signal my line was up. I almost turned around to make sure he knew that it was me he was sending out.

With time winding down I caught a pass up the middle and, with my new-found speed, split the defencemen. I'm still convinced time would have expired before I got a shot off, but Oiler defenceman Boris Mironov hauled me down just before the buzzer went. With one second left in the game Anaheim's training camp holdout was awarded a penalty shot? I was too winded, maybe too focused to think much about the situation. About how strange it was to be standing there, dead still, at centre ice, with 18,000 people watching and waiting in near silence. There's the puck just sitting there; there's the goalie ninety or so feet away. And here's the most neurotic inline skater to ever grace Newport Beach, thinking the most improbable beginning to the season just got a whole lot less probable.

I'm not sure how it happened, but Chris's brother converted on that penalty shot. I remember pumping my fist in the air and glancing over at the Edmonton bench after I potted the winner. The look I got back was, "Does this kid know it's just the pre-season?"

Ironically enough, that pre-season turned out to be the best of my career. Maybe I should've held out every year.

6

THE MINNOW OF
ALL TRADE BAIT

The NHL trade deadline is one of the most exciting dates on hockey's calendar. In Canada, deadline day is well on its way to becoming a national holiday. (Or national *hooky* day, I should say. How many guys come down with an upper-body injury—I mean a cold—on trade deadline day?) The three national sports networks provide wall-to-wall coverage from 8 a.m. EST on, trying to scoop each other on big news—like, say, Sven Butenschoen being picked up by the Blues for a conditional pick. Fans love it because they get to see how serious their teams are about making a run for the Cup. And hey, it's fun to talk about hockey, even if your team's not even in the race. Everyone wants to talk about which preening millionaire is going to be shipped out of town because he can't get along with his GM, or what veteran is going to finally get a shot at a Cup, or which guy is going to a contender as a "rental." Sure, it's gossip. Is that so wrong?

It's a huge day for general managers, because they get a chance to show how brilliant they are by picking up the final piece of a puzzle or perhaps instead by unloading what seemed like an untradeable contract. It's exciting for the coaches because they get to see if their wish lists have been fulfilled with that puck-moving defenceman or power-play specialist. And it's a monumental day for the media also. You could argue that deadline day for the sports media is bigger than any other single day of the year. Bigger even than draft day.

You know who else it's exciting for? The players. That's right, the pawns in the middle of all of the excitement. You think conversation is intense at the office water cooler on trade deadline day? Try an NHL dressing room. Of course, the players love to see who went where, which teams got better, which teams had a fire sale, what players went to a contender, and what players went to the Islanders. Which team just gave up on a guy they drafted? Did anyone you know get a free pass to the Conference finals? It never gets boring to see a GM absolutely lose his mind on deadline day, potentially crippling his franchise for years to come. Deadline day is a blast, without question.

Some players don't want to be traded. Those are the guys you see opt for season-ending surgery a week before the deadline. Not exactly elective surgery, but close to it. On the other hand, there are many guys who ask for a trade leading up to the deadline. Players who think the grass may be a bit greener on the other side. And, of course, there's always a number of pending unrestricted free agents who fully expect to be shipped elsewhere. Guys with some playoff pedigree who have zero chance of re-signing with their non-playoff-bound team. There are guys like Mark Recchi, who just seem to keep popping up on winning teams. And then there are the trades that happen for the sake of trades happening. Teams that pick up players hoping that a fresh start will do them good.

And with that, I must share my first experience of being traded in the NHL. It was March 1998, and my first full season in the league was coming to a close. Since I made it the whole year in the NHL it was a success for me, although I'm not sure you would call it a successful season. Nonetheless, it was eventful. I was a holdout in training camp (against my better judgment) and went on to have my best pre-season ever despite the fact that I only participated in one practice. I started the season on the second line, endured a thirty-three-game goalless drought, was a healthy scratch for the first time as an NHLer, worked my way back to the second line (with Teemu Selanne, although he didn't get seventy-six goals that season), and was playing the best hockey of my young career as the deadline approached. I felt as if I belonged.

My team that year, the Ducks, did not belong. Not in the playoffs at least, as we were *way* out of the race at that point. The magic Disney dust that was sprinkled on us the season prior had all but blown away. I'm not sure the exact reason for the huge fall-off from the year before. However—and I'm no genius—I'm fairly certain having Paul Kariya miss the first thirty-two games due to a holdout and then another chunk of games due to a concussion (thanks to a well-placed Gary Suter cross-check to the head) may have had something to do with it. That and the fact that we had only four players hit double digits in goals. But what the hell do I know, except that I wasn't one of those four players?

We had a few veterans and pending free agents who everyone figured would be moved for prospects or draft picks. I definitely did not fit on that list as I was just twenty-five years old and starting to hit my stride. Getting traded was the farthest thing from my mind (although every March that followed I was often found in the fetal position sucking my thumb on deadline day). It was a different story for my roommate at the time, Scott Young. Scott was going to be a UFA on July 1, so we just assumed he was as good as gone. Scott was a ten-year veteran, and more importantly a Stanley Cup winner with the Colorado Avalanche in 1996. In other words, the exact type of player teams hoping to make a lengthy run are interested in picking up. I remember hanging out in our hotel room in Chicago just waiting for the phone to ring. I felt horrible for Scott, as he had to sit there pretending to watch TV, when really he was nervously waiting for the hammer to fall. But it never did—2 p.m. CST came and went and our phone never rang once. Scott was relieved, because he had a wife and two kids back in Anaheim and if he had been traded he would've had to leave them behind for a couple of months.

That's the other thing about trade deadline day. Imagine you're an accountant or a garbageman or a teacher. You're doing a decent job, you think, but you start hearing rumours that your boss isn't quite satisfied. Then one day he calls you into his office and tells you that from now on you'll be crunching numbers (or collecting garbage, or teaching kids) in some other town—where your family doesn't live and you don't have a place to live and can't even find a good dry cleaner. Your plane leaves at eight. Deadline day can be fun for everyone talking about who's going where, but for the guys shipping out it's deeply inconvenient at best, heartbreaking at worst.

Once Scott was off the chopping block I decided that a workout would be the best way to relieve the built-up tension of the afternoon. I threw on the legwarmers and was just about to walk into the gym for jazzercise when there was an announcement over the PA.

Would Sean Pronger please report to the front desk?

Remember, this was a time before cell phones had taken over the globe. If someone wanted to get hold of you in the hotel and you weren't in the room, then to page via the PA was the only other option. Still, I was a little surprised to be paged because there wasn't anyone who should have been trying to get in touch with me. Perhaps I left my wallet at reception or something, I thought to myself. Not knowing the reason, I jogged over to the front desk.

"Hi there, I'm Sean Pronger. Someone just paged me. Did I forget something down here?"

"No sir, there is a message here for you to call your roommate."

Oh boy, Younger got traded after all! I grabbed the phone and called up to the room.

"Scotty, what happened? I thought you were in the clear."

"I am, Prongs. But Pierre called and he wants you to call him back ASAP."

Pierre? Pierre *Page*? Our coach? Why the heck does he need to talk to me? We don't play for another two days. Then it hit me. I was the one who was going to have to pack some bags. Holy shit. This isn't happening. With fingers trembling, I dialed the coach.

"Hey Pierre, it's Sean Pronger on the line. I got a message that I needed to call you?"

"Yes Sean. How are you? Have you spoken with Jack Ferreira [Ducks GM] yet?"

"No, I haven't heard from him."

"You better call him."

"Why?"

"Just give him a call, Sean."

I wanted to know right away. Hear it from the head coach that my services weren't wanted or needed in Anaheim anymore. But Pierre wouldn't give up the goods. He didn't have the courtesy to tell me that I had been traded. My next call was obviously to Jack.

"All right, where am I going?"

"Pittsburgh."

"For who?"

"Patrick Lalime."

A goalie? That's never good. You see, if you're a forward and you get traded for a forward that means there's one fewer forward on the team you're going to. An open spot that, presumably, will be filled by you. But if you're a forward and get traded for a defenceman or a goalie then there's no opening created by the departing player. So, either you're the odd man out on your new team or you get to take another guy's job. And you better hope he wasn't a favourite of the players already there, or it gets a little more difficult to fit in.

And just like that, my career with the Anaheim Mighty Ducks was over. In a haze, I shared a cab to the airport with Warren Rychel (one of the all-time characters of the game), who had just been dealt to Colorado. Here's a guy who once said to Richard Park, after Park played a great first game in Anaheim following being traded, "Parksy, great game kid. Keep playing like that and you'll have a great career here. Maybe you can open up a couple dry cleaners afterward." I know that's not politically correct, but hey—I didn't say it and Park loved the line.

During the drive we were both dumbfounded that I was one of the guys who had been traded. He kept shaking his head, telling me "I can't believe you got traded," not seeming too bothered by the fact that he was on his way to the airport too. The situation may not have been a shock to him, but it certainly was one for me. I was trying my best to convince myself that things happen for a reason. Pittsburgh must be where I belong. Yeah, right.

As a player, once you get over the initial shock that you've been traded it's kind of exciting to be heading to a new place. Your thinking quickly goes from the team that didn't want you to the one that did. Next thing you know you're in a new locker room with new teammates, playing the same old game. For me, the logistics of that first trade were easy. Grab a cab, head to the airport, and catch a flight to Pittsburgh. Pretty simple stuff, really. For the future Mrs. Journeyman, however, things weren't so easy.

An in-season trade in hockey can be an inconvenience to the player, but it's always a major monkey wrench as far as the family is concerned. It's not just a matter of Mr. Millionaire selling his mansion in that place and buying a new one in this place. OK, for some players it is. But for the journeymen of the world things work much differently. And most of the time it's up to Mrs. Journeyman to pick up the pieces left behind after a trade. These ladies have been through thick and thin if they've been with a fringe player from the get-go. Chances are they've followed their husbands through the ranks of the minor leagues. If so, then they've coordinated numerous moving trucks to pack up a half-dozen apartment/townhome/condos over the years. Not exactly the type of life that is conducive to carving out a career of their own, so most have put their lives on hold to support their husband's quest to play in the NHL.

It's nearly impossible for the journeyman family to establish roots in a community. It's such a transient lifestyle, almost like a fly-by-night business, touching down for a few days in one town before moving on to the next stop. That's not too difficult on the player because of the fact that his life revolves around the team. Even in a brand new city the player has built-in friends called team-mates, and a family of sorts in the team. Nearly 24/7 at home and literally 24/7 on the road players are around each other—in the dressing room, at practice, in games, on the bus, out for dinner, in the hotel. It's constant. The same can't be said for our significant others. Sure they can make friends with the other wives/girlfriends, but if you're new in town it's not that easy to integrate. For the guys hockey is the bonding point, the reason to be friends. For the wives/girlfriends there may not be a common point. Some are older with teenage kids, some are mothers with infants, and some are just young girls following their boyfriends around. Throw in the language barrier you get with the European players, and sometimes it's not easy to find a way to fit in.

Obviously, if you're able to stay in one place for a couple of years there is an opportunity to meet people outside of the game. That's a good thing for the player and a great thing for his significant other. Talk doesn't always revolve around hockey and it's possible to have a life away from the rink and the game.

My wife and I had that in Anaheim. We had friends within the hockey community, and outside of it as well. Mrs. Journeyman was especially happy because there was a group of girls on the team who were relatively the same age and in the same stage of life. And then, BOOM! It all got blown up.

"Honey, I've got some good news and some bad news."

"What happened?"

Someone like my wife who has heard it all wants to get right to the point and sees no point in playing games. In other words, don't try to sugarcoat things.

"We've been traded."

Pregnant pause.

"Where?"

"To a second-place team that's going to the playoffs!"

"Great. Where?"

"To the east coast."

"*Where,* Sean?"

"Pittsburgh."

Sigh. "OK, should I call the movers or will you?"

Like I said, this wasn't her first rodeo.

"Let's not worry about it right now. We'll keep our place in Newport Beach and get organized at the end of the season. The

Penguins are going to put us up in a hotel for the remainder of the year."

I arrived in Pittsburgh and was introduced to my twenty new friends. "What's up Jaromir? Hey Hatch. Hi Ronnie Francis, can you sign your rookie card for me? It's nice to meet you, Mr. Barrasso." A lot of my new friends on the team were players I grew up watching. I'm sure those guys thought I was some kind of stalker because I just kept staring at them like that kid stared at Santa Claus in *Bad Santa*. The hardest part for me was trying to act like I was one of them. I'm not sure what they thought of me, or if they thought of me. Pretty much everyone welcomed me to the team, and when they did I could almost see the wheels turning. I'm sure the guys were wondering, "How is this guy going to help us to win a championship?" It's always intimidating walking into a new dressing room, and this one was no exception. In Anaheim, I'd spent parts of three years with the organization so I knew everyone. Now, I had to go through the whole "get to know you" phase all over again. But like I said earlier, I had the easy job compared to the Mrs.

A week later she showed up late at night and cabbed it to the hotel. Since she was still on PST I decided to go about my business quietly in the morning and didn't wake her up before I took off to the rink. Upon my arrival back to the plush Residence Inn (yes, we even had a kitchenette), I found her standing over the sink staring out the window.

"Hey babe, I'm home!"

Silence.

"Honey, I said I'm home."

Silence.

"Hey, what's up?"

I walked over to her and turned her around. The floodgates

were open. Tears and mascara were streaming down her face as she was trying to not fully lose it.

"I'm fine, I'm fine. It's just going to take some getting used to our new place."

Since she arrived in the middle of the night she had no clue where our hotel was located. Pittsburgh is a fantastic city, but only if you're staying in Pittsburgh. Our hotel was about ten minutes out of town and in the middle of nowhere. The view from the kitchenette window was of a rusted-out tractor and some knee-high grass that surrounded the complex. In Newport Beach we lived exactly eighty-one paces from the beach, and let me tell you, that water is much nicer to gaze at than weeds.

That's why players always say "*we've* been traded," because they know they aren't the only ones involved in a deal.

My time in Pittsburgh was about as pretty as the view from the Residence Inn.

I played exactly five games during the regular season and then broke my foot. Oddly, it was in the same game that I scored my first and only goal as a Pittsburgh Penguin. Our coach, Kevin Constantine, was adamant about blocking shots and sacrificing our body. So, with time winding down in the third period and us up five to one, I made the ill-advised decision to lie down and block an Ives Racine slapshot. With the game in hand I just had to be an idiot. I broke the bone on the inside of my left foot right near the ball. Not a good place when you need to push off the ball of your foot to skate. There was only two and a half weeks left in the season and I was convinced I could make it back in time for the playoffs. I did not want to miss the first game of the first round. After all, it was against the Montreal Canadiens. How could I not be part of that? I was so desperate to be there for the playoffs that I basically forced the trainer to figure out a way for me to get my foot in my skate. He ended up devising some kind of tape job that he called a "moccasin." It felt OK, but I had no strength when I pushed off and it was difficult to stop quickly. Not a winning combination when my skating was already a question mark on a good day. I suited up for the first couple games of the playoffs against Montreal but was largely ineffective and eventually scratched for the remainder of the series—and, as it turns out, the remainder of the season, as we ended up losing that series in six games. There were a number of reasons why the Penguins fell to the Habs in the opening round, but the one that really stuck in my craw was that I felt our coach outcoached himself. I'm not sure why Constantine wanted to have our best line go up against their checking line, but he did. Alain Vigneault was the head coach of the Canadiens and he had moved Zarley Zalapski from defence to forward for the sole purpose of checking Jagr. To be Jaromir's shadow, so to speak. And Constantine played right into his hands. Hey, I can understand if you're on the road without last change and you don't get the matchup you want. But at home? Vigneault would send out his hybrid-checking unit and wait for Constantine to send out a line. And time and time again Constantine gave Vigneault the matchup he wanted. At least he could have made him work for it. Anyway, what started out as a new beginning and a shot at Lord Stanley quickly turned into a disastrous finish and a shot in the balls (foot).

Even with the bitter end to that season, I had a pretty great summer. There were two things I had wanted to do for a long time and I was over the moon to be able to cross them both off my list in short order. And I know I had the right agent, because he was involved in both. I have to say that for a player of my calibre I overachieved in the agent category. It may well be that having a decent hockey player for a brother *may* have helped me land a superstar agent. But my status didn't stop Pat Morris from going beyond the call of duty.

The first thing he accomplished on my behalf was to convince the Penguins that I was an essential part of their future. There was no need to hold out that year—long before I could develop another ulcer, the Pens put an offer in front of me. I had spent the entire season in the league for the first time in my career *and* I had arbitration rights, so perhaps they thought it would be best to lock me up for an entire year. And if that didn't floor you, perhaps this will.

The contract was a one-way deal. A first for Sean Pronger.

I closed another deal that summer, but one with a considerably longer term and no free-agency provisions. That's right—I finally made an honest woman of Mrs. Journeyman.

In order to avoid the paparazzi that would constantly hound us we decided to have the wedding in our hometown. The royal wedding was going to be held in Dryden, Ontario, Canada. The who's who of the NHL made the trek to the Great White North for the big ceremony: Chris Pronger, the best man (but not better man!), and yours truly, the handsome groom. What a star-studded affair! Also making the trip up to the mill town was none other than Ari Gold aka Jerry Maguire aka Pat Morris. In defence of everyone who didn't make the wedding, Dryden is not an easy place to get to. For most it requires a couple different planes and a rental car— or, in Pat's case, a Greyhound.

For Pat, the only people he knew in town were in the wedding. Obviously, he knew his star client, me, and his star client's brother, Chris. But he was also close with our friends and my parents. Unfortunately for him, we were all involved in the wedding and couldn't show him everything that Dryden had to offer.

About a half hour before the ceremony, the groomsmen and I were in a heated game of euchre in the church basement. My parents were busy entertaining our out-of-town family members. And my soon-to-be wife was at the Riverview Lodge (Hotel) with her bridesmaids and parents. Since Dryden is such a small town, there are really only two places worth staying at. One of them, the Holiday Inn Express, doesn't have a restaurant and so couldn't accommodate the reception even though it is a fantastic place to stay. (Shameless plug: Did I mention I'm also part owner?) So that leaves the beautiful Riverview Lodge.

When my wife-to-be came down to the lobby to meet her parents for the drive to the church, she noticed Pat floating around the lobby.

"Pat, is everything all right?"

"Yeah, I was just going to call a cab. How far is the church anyway?"

"Pat, it's fifteen minutes from starting, we only have one cab in this town and I doubt they'll be here in time."

"Oh. Is the church close enough to walk to?"

"Why don't you just hop in with us?"

"Really, you don't mind?"

"No, get in."

So, in the car over to the ceremony is my father-in-law, my mother-in-law, my wife-to-be, *and* … my agent. How fitting. On the drive over, Pat dramatically reached into his coat pocket and, without missing a beat, pulled out a folded piece of paper. "I guess this is as good a time as any to go over the prenup!"

Needless to say, everyone in the car burst out laughing.

If only more players were lucky enough to have an agent who would watch their back all the way to the altar!

Training camp, 1998. I thought I had solidified myself as a legitimate NHL regular. I showed up to training camp in great shape. I took it upon myself to go find a place to live. Presumptuous? Maybe. But I figured that's what you did when you hadn't spent a game in the minors the year before. I was a regular, so like any other full-time NHLer I was going to find a place to live in the NHL city that I was playing in. Maybe I wanted to give them the impression from day one that I intended to be there. Perhaps I thought it would be easier for them to send me down if I was staying at a hotel. It's also possible I didn't know what the hell I was doing.

As training camp began I could tell where they planned to use me—they wanted me to be the checking centre. Yep, the Penguins slotted me on the third line and my role was to play against the other team's top line and shut them down. This was A-OK by me. I just wanted to play. As camp progressed I *thought* I was doing the job. I'm not sure how, with all that had already happened in my short career, I allowed myself to feel comfortable. Because as you may have guessed, my job wasn't as safe as I thought it was.

By the end of camp I was moping around on the fourth line. My defined role was not so defined anymore. But I didn't panic. I tried to stay positive by telling myself it was OK. Just make the team and we can work our way back up the depth chart. Little did I know I was about to face a perfect storm of bad news.

There were a few players who I didn't think to include in my training camp formula when trying to figure out where I stood on the depth chart. In between stops in the Swiss League was Patrick Lebeau. He was invited to training camp and was looking good. Not only that, he was becoming a favourite with the coaching staff. Not good for any bubble player not named Lebeau. Not only that, after solid seasons in the minors it was looking like Jan Hrdina was ready for prime time. It also didn't hurt that he was from the Czech

Republic. He would fit right in with the seven other Czechs on the team. The storm would continue to worsen throughout camp.

On final cut-down day I wasn't nervous at all. That, more than anything, should have raised five alarm bells. How the hell was I not nervous on cut-down day? I arrived at the rink, saw my usual fourth-line jersey in my stall, and began my usual routine before practice. Hopeful after hopeful were called into the office to have their careers re-routed. Never once did I think they'd call my name. I remember talking to the boys afterward and saying, "Keep your chin up, you'll be back."

Who the hell did I think I was? A thousand-game vet? What an idiot I was to be talking to guys like that. I did not get cut that day. But I didn't make it to game one either. Two days before opening night, I arrived at practice to the news that Pittsburgh had picked up two players in the waiver draft. Both were forwards, and the kicker: we didn't lose anyone in the waiver draft. My heart stopped.

This can't be good. The math isn't adding up. Dan Kesa and Kip Miller were now members of the Pittsburgh Penguins. I had heard of both players. Kesa was a draft pick of Vancouver so I remembered his name from keeping track of the Canucks depth chart when I was at Bowling Green. From what I was told he was a solid two-way player. (Years later I had a chance to play with Kesa. He is a great guy and great teammate, but I confessed that when he got picked up by the Penguins I didn't like him very much.) I didn't know Kip Miller, but I had definitely heard of him and his family. He was a legend in college hockey who hadn't quite reached his potential as a pro. Pittsburgh was going to help him reach that potential.

As I was processing this news, Mike Eaves came up to me to say that our head coach, Kevin Constantine, wanted to see me. (Translation: He's not my head coach anymore.)

"Sean, we've made the decision to send you to Houston."

Here we go again. "Honey, pack up the new apartment ... we're getting another new apartment!" I wish I could say those were my only two residences that season. But I can't.

No one goes into a career knowing he's going to be a journeyman. But by the end, if you're a journeyman it's clear to the whole world. Somewhere in between, you realize you're not being sent down to get a little more seasoning before settling into a job as a full-time NHLer. Then it dawns on you: you're being sent down because it's part of your job to be sent down when it suits the big club. Just as it's your job to be ready to go back up when it suits the big club. *That's* the realization you're a journeyman.

So. That's what I was. A journeyman. Everybody in hockey knows what a journeyman is, but hardly anyone could define the role if they had to. I was going to try to come up with my own words to break down the definition of a journeyman until I decided to check out Dictionary.com (sorry, *Webster's,* it's 2012) and found that there was no way I could have articulated it nearly as well.

journeyman (n., *jur-nee-muhn*)

A person who has served an apprenticeship at a trade or handicraft and is certified to work at it assisting or under another person.

Any experienced, competent but routine worker or performer.

A person hired to do work for another, usually for a day at a time.

All three definitions of the noun can be perfectly applied to the hockey journeyman. An apprenticeship for NHL hockey is done in the East Coast Hockey League, American Hockey League, any other minor league, or overseas. As for being certified to work at it assisting or under another person? Doesn't that scream fourth-liner to you? After all, that's where the journeyman almost always ends up if he happens to make it to the NHL.

No further explanation needed. I mean, that sums it up just about perfectly.

In this definition I'd like to focus on the second part of the sentence, "usually for a day at a time." While it's true that some players are signed to ten-day or ten-game contracts, the vast majority of pro hockey players get deals with terms in years. That said, when a journeyman is called up to the NHL, his stay might be only a day or two depending on the situation. And a week or two if that particular player is lucky. No matter how long the stay, I can tell you that the journeyman is always thinking of his tenure as a day-to-day thing.

For me, season two with the flightless birds began with a flight to Houston and the IHL. After playing sixteen games with the Aeros I was re-called by the Pens and played a couple of games before assistant coach Mike Eaves gave me the tap.

"Coach wants to see you."

And you know what? I didn't care. I actually welcomed a trip back to the farm. We had a great team in Houston. There were plenty of solid, veteran guys who had been around and knew how to win. Coaching the Aeros those days were a couple of Daves, Tippett and Barr. Both were quality coaches and even better men. Throw in the fact that I had a very good start to the season and I was actually looking forward to going back. Another thing that didn't hurt was the one-way contract I was sporting that season. It didn't matter if I was playing for the Penguins or the Aeros, I was hauling in NHL dollars. That was the only one-way of my career, by the way. And because there was less income tax in Texas than in Pennsylvania, I actually made a little more money in the minors.

(Side story: Making more money in the minors is unusual, but it does happen. During the 2009–10 season, veteran defenceman Brad Lukowich was sent from Vancouver [NHL] to Texas [AHL]. Lukowich was on a one-way contract that paid him a million bucks. In the NHL Lukowich had to pay 14 percent escrow—a slush fund that players must contribute to in case the NHL doesn't generate enough hockey-related revenue to cover the players' salaries—as well as British Columbia's 44 percent income tax. In Texas he didn't have to worry about the NHL escrow, and since there's no income tax in the state of Texas he welcomed the demotion to the minors.)

For the first time in my career, getting called into the coach's office was a no-lose situation. Sent down = happy. Stay up = happy. Unfortunately, Kevin Constantine's message to me that day was neither.

"Sean, we've traded you to New York."

I was floored. That wasn't what I expected, to say the least. And for the obvious reasons I thought he meant the Islanders.

"You are part of a bigger trade. We sent Petr Nedved, Chris Tamer, and you for Alexei Kovalev, Harry York, and $15 million in cash."

Whoa! A blockbuster! And to the Rangers! Constantine was a little puzzled; I don't think he'd ever seen someone so happy moments after he'd informed them they'd been traded.

The way I figured it, the trade broke down something like this:

Nedved for Kovalev.

Tamer for York.

Pronger for $15 million.

Cut and dried. Simple.

I couldn't have been more pleased with the news. From Pittsburgh to Manhattan. From the Igloo to Madison Square Garden. And what a star-studded room the Rangers had. Mike Richter, Brian Leetch, Ulf Samuelsson, Kevin Stevens, Adam Graves, John MacLean, Wayne Gretzky … and to top it all off, Sean Pronger. So many of those guys I watched on TV as a kid. Whether it was Officer MacLean scoring the goal to get the Devils into the playoffs, or Adam Graves and the Kid Line winning a Cup in Edmonton, or Ulf versus Neely or Stevens patrolling Mario's wing on back-to-back Cup champions—I couldn't glance around the room without conjuring up a memory. And oh yeah, did I mention Gretzky?

And it was New York. Mrs. Journeyman was delighted to be in the Big Apple. You know the saying—happy wife, happy life. It's a cliché for a reason. And the icing on the cake was that my best friend from childhood also lived in New York City. (Also, did I mention Gretzky?)

7

MY 99 LINE

To say I was a Wayne Gretzky fan as a child would be like saying that my brother has a small gap in his teeth. The Oilers were my team and Wayne was my idol. When Chris and I played hockey in the basement, I was always Gretzky and he was always Mike Bossy. Two of the most creative offensive forwards of all time were our idols, and Chris turned into a Norris Trophy–winning defenceman and I—well, that's what this book is about.

We grew up in Dryden, a small mill town in northwestern Ontario, 400 kilometres east of Winnipeg. At that time, the Jets were still in Winnipeg and they were in the classic Smythe Division. That meant the Edmonton Oilers came to town often to torture the Jets and their fans. One year we made the journey to the 'Peg and by chance, or perhaps by stalking, the Prongers were staying in the same hotel as the Oilers. I can still remember sitting in the lobby with Chris watching the Oilers walk through on their way to breakfast. Kevin Lowe walked by and Chris casually said, "Hey Kev" as if they were old buddies. Who knew years later they would *be* buddies? That is, until Chris wanted out of Edmonton after year one of a five-year deal. But how about we leave that story for Chris's book, huh?

I didn't see Gretzky go through the lobby, so I went over to the restaurant to have a look. And wouldn't you know it—my idol was in fact there. I can still remember Wayne was eating eggs benny that day. As I was spying on him, an old man came up to me and said, "Hey kid, can you go get Wayne's autograph for my son?"

Now, understand I didn't want to ask because the Great One was eating. On the other hand, the autograph was for the man's kid. What was a well-raised, crazed Gretzky fan to do? I think you know the answer to that. Of course I asked! (If I'd had any brains in my head I would've got one for myself as well. No one ever said I was a genius.) Years later I came to the realization that the guy was just an autograph hound, using star-struck kids to do his dirty work so he could sell sports memorabilia. Yes, I am far more jaded now.

(Soapbox note: If you want an autograph from someone, do not bother, annoy, or interrupt that person while they are eating or sitting in a restaurant. Let them at least finish their meal and then try to catch them when they are leaving. That way they're not trapped at the table when everyone else in the restaurant figures out who is sitting there and then decides to get their napkin signed.)

Fast-forward about twenty years, and wouldn't you know it—I got traded to a New York Rangers team that included none other than the Great One. What a weird feeling that was. And I'm not talking about being traded. Somehow the first few trades of my career somewhat numbed me to being dealt. I'm talking about Wayne going from idol to teammate. I felt like I was a fantasy camper. Looking back, I see that may be one of the reasons my career never took off the way I thought it would. I never felt like I belonged because I was always looking through Young Sean's eyes at my great teammates.

From November 1998 to February 1999 I was a Ranger and a teammate of Wayne Gretzky. Any chance I got to hang out with him I did—although most of the time he had no idea we were hanging out. If we were getting off the bus to go to a restaurant, I would hang back and wait until Gretz (that's what his buddies call him, I think) walked by and I'd file in behind him.

How? Well, the seating plan on a team bus usually goes like this:

Front: Coaches, management, and trainers.
Middle: Rookies, bubble boys, and scratches.
Back: Veterans, cool guys, and good players.

As you can imagine, I was usually as close to the front as you could get without sitting on the equipment manager's lap. More often than not, because I was right on Wayne's heels, I would end up at his table for dinner. "Isn't it funny how we always end up sitting right beside each other, Gretz?"

I'm pretty sure he'd have had a solid case for filing a restraining order against me if he wanted to. I wasn't exactly Glenn Close from *Fatal Attraction,* but then again, Wayne didn't travel with a bunny rabbit.

As it turned out, the 1998–99 season was Gretzky's last in the NHL. Luckily for Wayne, he did not retire without having played with me. That's right, on my line.

Allow me to set this up, please. I was traded in November from the Penguins to the Rangers. I flew directly to Buffalo to meet the team for a game that night. I should have known things weren't going to be much different with the Blueshirts. When I arrived for the game, I saw that I was a healthy scratch. Craig MacTavish, an assistant coach at the time, came up to me and said, "Prongs, you're not going tonight. We're sitting you out."

Again, if I had a dollar for every time I heard those words over the course of my career, they might have added up to one of Chris's game cheques. Even when I was the lucky "Black Ace" (an extra player the team carries who gets inserted into the lineup from time to time) that our head coach John Muckler pulled out of the deck, it only added up to three to five minutes a game. I had teammates in New York who took longer shifts.

Joining me on the bubble that season in NY were Manny Malhotra and Darren Langdon. We were in and out of the revolving door that was the extra spot on the fourth line. One night (because of a perfect storm, you might say) Malhotra, Langdon, and I actually made up a line.

Mucks ran a short bench that game, because Manny and I finished with zero minutes of playing time each. Malhotra remembers another game in which he had four shifts for thirty-three seconds. How is that even possible? As for Langdon, whenever he was in the lineup, he would always make sure to take one twirl on the ice. When he was done, he'd come back to the bench and say, "There's another game towards the pension, boys."

As I write this book, Langdon is running his bar in Newfoundland and Malhotra is in the midst of a three-year, $7.5-million contract with the Canucks. I guess Muckler went two-for-three in regards to his decision making back then. Goes to show there are many gems buried on the fourth line.

I figured it was time to man up and speak with the coach to remind him I was still on the team. I loved New York and I wanted to stay. If I were going to remain a Ranger I needed to figure out a way to get in the lineup and stay in the lineup. After two months of building up the courage to talk to the coach, I finally decided to do it. On my way to John Muckler's office I stopped to talk to his assistant Craig MacTavish to gauge whether talking to Mucks would do me any good. He seemed to think it was a good idea and told me to let him know how it went after I talked to him. I was more than a little nervous. Remember, I grew up an Oilers fan. I still thought of Mucks as the big dog that took Wayne and company to the promised land in the eighties.

I summoned up the courage and banged on his door.

"Come in."

"Hey Mucks, do you have a couple minutes?"

"Sure, what's on your mind?"

"First off, I love playing here. Second, I want to play a bigger role on this team. Can you give me a little direction as to what I need to do in order to get in the lineup and stay in the lineup?"

I blurted it out so quickly I'm not even sure he heard or understood what I said. He stared at me from behind his desk for a time that seemed like an eternity but in reality was probably about five seconds. He looked intimidating. He also wouldn't have looked out of place with a whiskey in one hand and a cigar in the other.

The words that came out of his mouth have me confused to this day. He went on for about fifteen minutes about how players of my day and age didn't know how to give-and-go anymore. He talked about his Oilers teams and how they knew how to use open space properly. He kept going on about the Oilers and their dynasty. At one point I thought he may have lost his mind and thought he was still in the eighties.

As I walked out of his office with my head spinning I ran into Mac T.

"So, how did it go?" he asked.

"Honestly Mac, I have no idea. What I can tell you is that you guys certainly made an impression on him back in the day."

I joked about it, but the fact is, sitting out sucks. Most people don't understand just how much. They think, "Take that silver spoon out of your mouth and get a real job. You're in the NHL making big bucks. How hard can it be?"

And you know what? In the big scheme of things those people are right. Even when a journeyman like me pulls in an NHL paycheque, he makes a lot more money than the average dude who lugs his lunchbox to work every day. I get that. But I'm not complaining about the money. Just the opposite—I'd rather *work* for my paycheque. Getting paid to sit in the press box and watch your teammates go about their jobs is the opposite of what a hockey player wants to do.

Guys make it to the league because of their drive and determination just as much as their skill. They are competitors. They want to play. Even guys like me who are on the fringe of the league want to prove themselves every day. In fact, guys like me have *more* to prove each day. Yes, it's great to be a part of an NHL team—but when you're not playing, you don't feel like you are a part of that team. Remember how bad everyone felt for Phil Kessel when he was picked last for the all-star game? Poor Phil Kessel, the last of the millionaire superstars? Well, at least he got to play in the game. Every night, in every NHL rink, there are guys who have devoted their lives to the game, but find themselves in street clothes, eating popcorn, feeling a lot worse than Phil Kessel. Because their coach didn't want them on the ice *at all*, basically saying, "We have a better chance of winning tonight if you don't play." Fantastic. Fans may think these guys are getting paid to watch hockey, but really what they're doing is worrying themselves sick.

Is this the beginning of the end?

What did I do wrong?

Maybe I don't have what it takes.

It's the closest thing to a demotion without actually getting sent down. And once you're a healthy scratch, the only way to get back into a lineup is if:

1. Someone gets hurt.
2. The team plays awful.
3. Another player in your position is struggling or just plain sucks.

Now, no one wants one of his teammates to get hurt. (Well, usually.) And you don't want the team to struggle because that increases the odds that management will do something drastic like trade someone or send someone (you) down to the minors. Is there such a thing as a triple-edged sword? Anyway, that pretty much leaves door number three. One of your mates needs to play just poorly enough that the coach thinks the best thing for the team is to remove him from the lineup and re-insert you. And when that happens, let me say that you better play with some fire in your belly because coach and GM will surely be paying attention to see how you react.

I have to admit, it is easy to sulk when you sit out one game. And then you sit out another. And then you're benched once again. You start to feel hard done by, thinking you haven't gotten a fair shake. You're a marionette puppet and some evil coach or GM is pulling the strings, not allowing you to control your own destiny. You try to remember where you came from (farmhouse) and all the different obstacles you overcame to get to where you are. You tell yourself that you wouldn't be there if you didn't deserve to be.

Ah, but the mind is a powerful tool. Day by day, more and more doubt creeps into your head. Maybe I don't belong here, you think. And when it gets to that point, you're screwed.

You see, as a journeyman, a tonne of people don't believe in you. So if you don't believe in yourself, well, it's time to fill out the Walmart greeter application because your hockey career will be a short one. Everyone is watching how you react. If you're lucky, a coach will take you aside and tell you to pull it together. If you're not, they'll just get rid of you. Bottom line: sulking is not an option. Ever wonder how goalies who get pulled manage to talk about how great the guy who replaced him has been playing, or how a healthy scratch can go in front of the camera and talk about how happy he is the team is doing well and that he'll be ready to go when the time comes? They do it because they have to.

I can't explain how hard it is to go from being in the lineup, to out of the lineup, to in the lineup, to out of the lineup once again. When you're playing all the time, there is a rhythm to the games. It's about reading and reacting and making the proper play without hesitation. Even if you do make a mistake, you know you'll get a chance to make it right, honestly believing you can. And that attitude reflects in your play. But when you're a fourth-liner, playing five minutes every three games, it's difficult to get into a flow. You overthink things and second-guess yourself and that leads to mistakes. And those mistakes lead to Popcorn Row.

It would be like playing a heads-up golf match against someone who was allowed to practise after every hole, while you had to sit and watch until he was ready to move on to the next one. He gets to hit balls, stay in rhythm and work out the kinks, while you lose any momentum you may have had. I can't imagine it would be easy to have confidence in your swing if you were taking only a few lashes every half hour or so.

But enough of my sports analogy; let's deal in some facts. As in the logistics of being a "healthy scratch." The things the average fan simply doesn't think of when he hears a player won't be playing.

Believe me, for that player it's not as simple as just showing up to watch the game. There's *much* more to it, friends.

During the morning skate, one of the assistant coaches usually gives you the tap (I think we all know what that means by now). The thing is, a guy knows when he isn't going that night. It's pretty easy to figure out during the morning skate if you're anchoring the "helicopter line" (no wings) or the "doughnut line" (no centre). What's even more of a giveaway is when you're a forward paired with the defenceman who is two weeks into a three-week rehab for a knee sprain.

"What? I'm not dressing? I thought we were throwing off the other team? You mean you guys don't want to use me as a rover this evening?"

Shocker.

This exchange is followed by what is supposed to be a half-hour bag skate, which usually ends up being closer to an hour. Once that's finished you can either hit the weights, get on the bike, or head home. You see, if you're a healthy scratch then you have to get in another workout on game day because it's not really a game day for you. I usually went right home. That way I could at least kill some of the time at the game with the mandatory workout. In other words, take out my frustrations on the stationary bike. I would punish myself while watching the game in the gym. Yes, I was spinning my wheels, going nowhere.

Being scratched only gets harder as you go from being a prospect to a veteran. Imagine what it's like to come home, give your kids a hug, and announce "Daddy's not playing tonight." Another brilliant situation for the healthy scratch is when Mom and Dad pay a visit from out of town. They fly halfway around the continent (no direct flights from Dryden to anywhere, by the way) to watch their boy play in the show. "Sorry, not tonight folks."

Remember how my old man drove my Jeep from Deliverance, Tennessee, to San Diego? Well it wasn't the only time he spent long hours behind the wheel for me. About a month after that cross-country drive, Big Jim, along with a friend of mine, Ollie, decided they would travel to Minneapolis to see the Gulls take on the Minnesota Moose. No problem, just a leisurely sixteen-hour round trip to catch what would no doubt be an exciting game from the IHL. I remember thinking, "What if I don't play tonight?" Up to that point I had been in and out of the lineup, and when I was in, it was as the team's tenth forward. As you can imagine, the extra forward was not the centrepiece of the offence back then. This being pro hockey, I couldn't exactly go ask the coach to let me play because Daddy was coming! So before Big Jim started the trek, I warned him there was a chance I might not be in the lineup. I probably should have told him to save the gas money, because the odds were much better that he'd hit a moose on the drive than see me play against the Moose that night. Sure enough, Dad and Ollie drove eight-plus hours in a snowstorm to enjoy the game alongside me in the nosebleed section. I'm sure it was worth it.

By the end of my career my parents had it figured out. Fool me once, shame on you. Fool me twice, shame on me. Fool me 437 times and I'm not paying for another flight to whatever damn city you are living in this month.

Sometimes, even though you're a healthy scratch, you'll be asked to take the pre-game warm-up. Why? Well, it could be for a number of reasons. The coach wants to make you feel included. The coach wants to make sure your head is still in it. The coach somehow thinks the other team will spend warm-up on pins and needles wondering if it will be Sean Pronger or some other plug playing five minutes on the fourth line that night. Whatever the reason, I never minded taking warm-up even though I knew it was the only ice time I'd see all night.

Ninety-nine percent of the time a healthy scratch does not take part in the pre-game warm-up. If I wasn't asked to skate (neither a good nor bad sign), I would try to time my arrival at the rink for when the players were still on the ice. That way I could change into my workout gear and get into the gym before the guys came back into the room. Heaven forbid a scratch was still milling around when the players were done their skate. You don't want to bug the regulars, after all. It's all about not being seen and staying out of the way.

As grim as that sounds, it's a lot easier to manage being scratched at home than while on the road. The road is a different beast for the healthy scratch. There is a lot more planning involved. Consider this typical team itinerary for a game day on the road in Colorado:

10:15 a.m. Bus to Pepsi Center
11:30 a.m. Game-day skate
12:30 p.m. Pre-game meal
1:00 to 3:00 p.m. Pre-game nap
3:30 p.m. Pre-game snack
4:05 p.m. Early bus to game
4:45 p.m. Second bus to game
5:30 p.m. Team meeting
7:00 p.m. Game @ Colorado Avalanche

The only thing the team doesn't schedule for you is the pre-game nap that takes place between the pre-game meal and the pre-game snack. So I threw it in there for good measure. Guys in the lineup follow that itinerary to a T. However, it's a whole different ball of wax for the players who are sitting out that night. Let's have a little peek at how it differs.

GAME-DAY SKATE

In the lineup: Skate for twenty to thirty minutes doing various drills. Never give it much more than 75 percent effort; just get the legs going and work up a bit of a sweat. When finished, deal with the media, take a shower, and hop on the bus to head back to the hotel.

Scratched: Participate in the usual pre-game skate while watching the coaching staff like a hawk. Play mind games with yourself by asking questions like: Are the coaches looking at me? Why are the coaches looking at me? Why aren't the coaches looking at me? Why am I playing defence? Why am I being summoned over to the sideboards to have a one-on-one with the assistant coach?

Then comes the tap, of course. Once you know for sure you're not in you just wait for the rest of the team to leave the ice. Then the group known as the "Black Aces" goes to work. The Black Aces is the team within a team that consists of the healthy scratches, players close to returning from injury, the backup goalie, and one assistant coach. This lucky select few go through some more drills on their own before the inevitable bag skate. I'm not sure when this skate was officially named "bag," but the definition is obvious because you skate your bag off.

Either way, it's no fun. Bottom line, you don't get to play BUT you get to skate until you nearly puke. Once the rinsing is done, you shower and then may talk to the one beat reporter who hung around to see if you'd take a shot at the coach for not playing you. Then it's time to hop on the bus to go to the hotel. But wait—there is no bus, because it left forty-five minutes ago to take the real players back.

Memo to all you future journeymen out there: get the trainers to call you a cab as soon as you leave the ice so it's there and ready to go once you shower and get dressed. Otherwise, tack another thirty minutes on to your already awesome day.

PRE-GAME MEAL

In the lineup: Peruse a wonderful smorgasbord of dining delights. Take your pick of fruits, salads, chicken, steak, and fish. Replenish what you lost after the morning skate and fuel up for the rest of the day. Pretty much anything you'd like to eat is at your fingertips. (There's a reason some people call the NHL the Never Hungry League.)

Scratched: Pick through the scraps that were left by your ravenous teammates. Soggy lettuce, half-eaten chicken breasts, and honeydew just waiting to be consumed. I once returned to the hotel so late that the entire room had already been cleaned out. On that day, two of my favourite things were taken away: playing time, and food. Devastating.

PRE-GAME NAP

In the lineup: Shut down the mill for one to two hours. Sure it's a little childish, but it's one of the most important components of the pre-game ritual. Naps are awesome. If your boss let you shut it down for ninety minutes a day, wouldn't you do it? Of course you would. It's kind of like preschool all over again. Once a nap is incorporated in the daily routine, it is very tough to break the habit of enjoying one.

Scratched: The best-case scenario is if your roommate is a Black Ace as well. That way you can catch a nap if you want to. However, if that's *not* the case, you can pretty much kiss the mini sleep goodbye. Since you are late getting back to the hotel, your roomie is probably crawling into the wrapper at the same time you're eating a wonderful mix of cold salmon, warm yogurt, and loose grapes. Remember, it's never a good idea to bother the regulars—so you can either rush up and pretend to sleep for ninety minutes, or try to kill the afternoon in the city you're in. If that city happens to be Chicago or New York, then it's no big deal. But if you're in, say, Buffalo or Detroit, then good luck. Now before you people from those two wonderful cities start composing hate mail to me, let me say that I know there are beautiful suburbs in both Buffalo and Detroit. However, Joe Louis Arena is not in Auburn Hills. And downtown Buffalo doesn't have much to offer in the daytime unless you're looking for a high-interest loan.

GAME TIME

In the lineup: Take the team bus to the arena. Go over some scouting reports, review power play (so I'm told), and review penalty kill. Get dressed and play.

Scratched: First of all, you need to figure out if you're going to take the bus over with the team three hours before the game or grab a cab closer to puck drop. If you choose the latter, it usually involves trying to talk your way into the arena. "Honestly, sir, I am a player. I know I'm not playing tonight but if you just let me by the security gate, I might be able to wrangle up my jersey from the locker room in order to prove it to you."

Either choice bites, by the way. If you hop on the bus and arrive early, you have to find a way to occupy your time for about two and a half hours. Most coaches don't want the Black Aces floating around the locker room when the REGULARS are getting ready. We might make eye contact with them and throw them off. Or worse yet, bump into them and give them the "hands of stone" disease. On the road there is no change room or weight room to hide in. Basically, the choices are press box or stands. Great! In the press box, you'll have management and scouts eyeballing you with a look of disdain. They know you're not being held out for a possible trade. On the other hand, if you choose the stands you might as well have HEALTHY SCRATCH tattooed on your forehead. Put it this way: not many guys in the upper bowl of NHL rinks are wearing suits. For example, while I was playing (loose term) for the Rangers, we had a road game in Colorado. Esa Tikkanen and I were given the night off. We opted to sit in the stands to watch the game. This turned out to be a bad move. As we were walking up to our seats, in our suits, an entire section of Avalanche fans began chanting "Health-y Scratch! Health-y Scratch!" Man, I hated playing in Denver.

It wasn't until late in my career that I found the best place to watch a game on the road was the team bus. Most were equipped with satellite TV. So I could sit and enjoy the game with my new BFF, Mr. Bus Driver.

Here's another tale from my life when I was a healthy scratch with the Rangers. We had just come back from our two-day Christmas break, and the team was struggling. The captains called a team meeting before the guys hit the ice for the morning skate. The message was simple: Start winning games or management would start trading players. Believe me when I say that no one wants to get traded from New York. Not Long Island or New Jersey, but New York. That said, all the guys were suddenly viewing that night's game as the most important of the season. The morning skate was business as usual for me as I was anchoring a fifth line with Darren Langdon as my only winger. At the end of our morning twirl, assistant coach Craig MacTavish gave me the option of opting out of the bag skate because Todd Harvey had a bad hand and his status for the game was questionable. Mac T was almost positive that Harvey would be able to go, but I could take the rest of the morning off just on the slim chance he couldn't. In the two months I'd been a Ranger, I had averaged maybe four minutes a game in the few for which I had dressed. So to show the coach I was committed, I said I would tough it out and do my laps and lines. Besides, I didn't want to leave any soldiers behind because an extra body on the ice helps everyone. So we completed about an hour of pure skating drills and headed back to the hotel for some food.

My Normal Pre-Game Meal: Soup, salad, pasta, chicken, steak, vegetables, and maybe a scoop of ice cream. Have I mentioned how much I miss life in the NHL? Nobody eats better.

That Day's Meal: Two bowls of chocolate ice cream followed by a warm brownie. SOOO good.

My Normal Pre-Game Nap: Two hours.

That Day's Nap: No winks at all. My roommate at the time—Chris Tamer, a fellow member of the Black Aces—and I decided to watch a couple of movies instead of napping.

My Normal Pre-Game Routine: Tape sticks, read scouting report, check skates, ten-minute bike ride, stretch, and maybe a ten-minute massage.

That Day's Routine: Four cups of coffee, hang out with equipment guys, watch TV, no taping of sticks, no stretching, no bike warm-up, no massage, and no scouting report. (Harvey was going to play, after all.)

My Normal Pre-Game Warm-Up: Standard NHL warm-up with a couple hard laps and a couple starts-and-stops to get the legs going.

That Day's Warm-Up: Float around, stay out of the way of everyone, and get off the ice as soon as possible.

Now, keep in mind that the entire day I was preparing to be a healthy scratch. But when I came off the ice, Mac T pulled me aside and said "You're in."

I'm not sure if I even knew what those words meant. Anyway, I figured it wouldn't be such a big deal because I knew I could handle four minutes of ice time with even the crappiest of preparation. But the coach had different plans for me.

"You're going to play a lot tonight. You're on a line with Adam Graves and Marc Savard."

From that point there was a lot of nodding, sweating, and panicking. I remember thinking, What have I done? Why didn't I just leave the ice this morning when I had the chance? Why did I have to gorge myself on two tubs of ice cream? Why didn't I nap? Why am I such an idiot?

As it turned out, my fears weren't realized. The team played great and I was solid with a couple of assists in a 6–1 win. I had it all figured out. I had been trying too hard my entire career! I finally learned that less is more. Or maybe I *was* just an idiot, because I was a healthy scratch for the next five consecutive games. So much for the theory that you are never supposed to mess with a winning lineup. Thanks a lot, Muckler.

Now, it wasn't always the Rangers messing with me. I sometimes had a little fun to mix things up. More often than not, it was Mac T who told me I was going to be enjoying the game from up top. So sometimes when I saw him coming my way at the end of the morning skate, I would pretend that I didn't see him, then take a shot on the backup goalie, sprint to the red line, and coast to the other end. While at the other end I would continue to keep a furry eyeball on him because I knew eventually he'd have to come back my way. As he got closer, I would take another shot, sprint to the red line, and then coast to the far goal line once again. I figured that I would make them work to give me the news that I never wanted to get. Juvenile, I know, but I had fun doing it.

Anyhow, you get the idea of what it was like for me with the Rangers. In the lineup one day, then out for a week. One step forward, four steps back. However, in light of my situation, I did everything I could back then to try to get in the lineup. I arrived early for practice and lifted weights. I stayed on the ice after practice and worked on my skills (diminishing as they were and not in abundance to begin with). I had the strength coach design a special bike program for me to complete after practice. I put in as much time on the bike as I did on the ice. You could say I was the NHL's version of Lance Armstrong, but without the success or the allegations. I was putting in a tonne of work but I wasn't reaping any benefits. I couldn't get in the lineup and stay there. After weeks of being a human yo-yo, I was fed up. The frustration of watching game after game from the press row ate at me. I was having a tough time being a cheerleader night after night.

Pretending that everything is fine when it's not is a tough thing to do. But as a fringe player, you have to grin and bear it. You have to keep a positive attitude. No one wants to see a fifth-liner complain about ice time. If Mucks had seen me in sulk mode back then, I would have been on the first Greyhound to Hartford. So, one night, I decided to go blow off a little steam. See what the Big Apple had to offer. After all, I wasn't stupid. I knew that my days in

New York were likely numbered. Why not go out and see what the city was like while I was still there?

As most of you likely know, New York does not lack for things to do. Translation: there is an Irish pub on every corner. Couple that with the fact that my best friend since childhood, Chris "Herbie" Hancock, was living in New York at the time and you had a recipe for fun—and disaster! When I got traded to New York, Herbie and I decided we needed to pick our spots in terms of what nights to go out. I was a professional athlete with a career to worry about, after all. Before New York, our simple rule was to only go out on days that end in "y," so we figured we needed to set boundaries.

Anyhow, on this particular night we threw the boundaries out the window. The fact that a practice was scheduled for the next day did not weigh into our decision making one bit. Herbie, my wife, and I found a nice little tavern for a bite and a few carbonated wheat sodas. One led to another, which of course led to another four, and the next thing we knew my wife and I were strolling home at 4:30 a.m. New York is a little like Las Vegas with its hours of operation. Nothing ever closes! I think I got to bed around 5 a.m., which was great because I had to get up at 7 a.m. to drive to the practice rink. I got a solid two hours' sleep before the buzzer woke me from my coma. To be honest, I wasn't too worried because I had been practising on defence the day before. Not a great sign for a forward. I was literally a practice fill-in. (Good thing a goalie never went down during my tenure as a Ranger.) I somehow managed to get my car to the practice facility in Rye, NY. I arrived in plenty of time for my usual routine, which consisted of changing out of my street clothes, drinking an extra-large coffee, and choking down a jumbo chocolate-chip muffin. Everything was going according to plan. With chocolate all over my lips I strolled into the dressing room to make my way to the couch to watch a few hockey highlights from the night before. But as I walked through the room, I got the sense that something wasn't right. Something was definitely off, but I couldn't figure it out.

"Did we get a new player?" I wondered aloud.

After scanning the nameplates over the stalls, I concluded that we hadn't picked up anyone else. But I still had a feeling that something was up. You know when you come home and your wife/sister/mom has made a slight change to the furniture or moved a picture? You know something is off but you can't put your finger on it. That's the same feeling I had. I walked over to my stall.

"Wait a second, that's the wrong colour sweater hanging in my stall."

I looked around, wondering if my gear had been moved over a couple of stalls. But no.

I returned to my normal locker, looked past the red jersey, and sure enough my equipment was hanging exactly where it should be. The only question: *Why is there a red jersey here?*

You see, in NY I was a yellow jersey (Lance Armstrong, again). It was my colour. Typically, it was Darren Langdon and me anchoring the Yellow Line. We were special. Red, on the other hand, was for Gretzky, Adam Graves, and Kevin Stevens. I do not look good in red. I decided someone must be messing with me. I scanned the room to see who was trying to have some fun. Not a person in the room. No one running to hide. Then I came to the conclusion that the trainer must have put the wrong one in by accident. I grabbed the red jersey and headed into equipment manager Mike Fogilin's office.

"Fogs, you gave me the wrong jersey."

"No I didn't," he barked back.

"Yeah you did, you gave me a red jersey."

"No I didn't, Sean. You're wearing red today, my friend. Kevin has the flu."

Mouth agape, I ran back into the locker room to confirm what I had just been told. Sure enough, there was no practice jersey in Stevens's stall.

I'M PLAYING ON GRETZKY'S LINE TODAY. Are you kidding me? I just got to bed three hours ago and now I have the (practice) opportunity of a lifetime? A million thoughts and questions rushed through my head.

What have I done?

Why did I stay out so late?

Why don't they close the bars earlier?

Where is my camera?

How hard would Young Sean punch me in the face right now?

And he'd be right to do so. My first chance to play with the Great One and I had a bad case of the brown-bottle flu.

OK, calm down. Breathe deeply. You can do this.

I jumped in the shower and drenched myself in freezing cold water. Time to wake up and get ready to go.

Now, I know what you're thinking. Slow down, Chris's brother! It's not like you're playing the Islanders tonight. This is practice, after all.

I know! But you have to understand that for us fifth-liners, practice *is* the game. And when you're playing with Gretzky, it's the all-star game.

As the skate loomed closer, I wondered if I should have a talk with Gretz. Just a little chat between first-liners to let him know what transpired a few hours earlier. Or maybe I should just suck up to him and lie about my state.

"Hey, Wayne. I'm like, really looking forward to practising with you. Um, I've been a big fan of yours since I was a kid. Boy, it's too bad that I seem to have come down with a bug today. Must be the same one Kevin got, huh?"

Instead, I opted to come clean.

"Gretz, I'm hungover. Maybe even a little drunk still. Can you keep the puck away from me today?"

I could not believe I was saying this even as the words were coming out of my mouth. Was I really telling the greatest player in the history of the game—not to mention the finest passer ever—to keep the puck away from me?

I was. And the Great One was great about it.

"No problem, Prongs, I've been there myself."

Wait. Did he just call me Prongs? He knows my name? Somehow, that one line from Wayne put my mind at ease. Wayne knew my situation and he had my back. What a guy. I was calm as I got dressed. I knew that unless Kevin Stevens was on his deathbed, this would be the first and last time I was on the same line as the Great One. Romantically, though, I couldn't help but dream that Wayne and I would have some undeniable chemistry together which would force Muckler to do the right thing and keep me on the top unit. We'd become as tight as two coats of paint.

Right.

I could barely contain my grin as we began to wheel around the ice before drills started. There was a strut in my step, and not the "Guinness legs" I'd expected to be carting around.

"That's right, boys, the coaches hand-picked me for the first line today!"

I completely shut out the fact that the coaches likely didn't want to mess up the other lines by moving someone up to play on the Red Line. The conversation that set up this dream day of mine probably went something like,

MacTavish: "Hey, John, Kevin's not here today. What do you want to do?"

Muckler: "Throw one of the yellow scrubs in there to take his place."

However it all came about, the rest of the practice was a nightmare. My thought that I could just skate around and bang in the odd rebound to make an impression was delusional. And the idea that Wayne was on board with my "situation" turned out to be false. The Great One had no intention of playing pitch and catch with Graves all day so I could have my walk in the park.

Every single pass Gretz made was to yours truly. And I'm not talking about those beautiful saucer passes you see in his video *Hockey My Way*. I'm talking about wobbly hand grenades that would blow up as soon as they hit my stick. And by the way, I was playing the off wing. That's right, I had to try to catch those bouncing Betties on my backhand.

The practice that started as a chance of a lifetime turned quickly into a series of drills that I furiously tried to execute so I wouldn't be cut.

I remember a three-on-two drill that started with sweat pouring off my face. I was busting down the right side fully aware a puck was heading my way. Sure enough, Gretz lobbed another wounded duck my way and the puck landed somewhere near my blade. Then the whistle blew and Muckler was starting the drill over again.

"Where did the puck go?" Graves asked.

"In the stands!" someone replied.

Apparently, when Wayne passed the puck over I did such a good job of receiving it that it hit my stick, blew up, and flew over the glass. It was like someone had a joystick and hit the jackass button *every time* the puck came to me.

Thinking the whole episode was my fault, I formulated an apology as I headed back to the line.

"Sorry, Wayne," was all I could come up with.

He said, "Prongs, don't worry about it. I'll try to give you better passes from now on!"

And he delivered the line with a wink.

Turns out Wayne thought it would be fun to mess with me from the get-go. How awesome is that? The greatest player ever to lace them up went out of his way to thoroughly embarrass a hungover grinder. And you know what? That made me feel more included than if he had played it straight.

I often hear of people meeting their boyhood idols and being disappointed to find out they are complete assholes. Not so in my case. I've also had the opportunity to play with some unbelievably talented players who turn out to be less than ideal teammates. (What's up, Jaromir?) Again, not true in this case. Gretzky was awesome. He was a regular guy. If you walked into the locker room and knew nothing about hockey or anything about Wayne you would have no idea that he was one of the greatest players who ever played the game. There was no arrogance about him. And he had passion for the game and for winning.

For instance, one night I was, again, not in the lineup. (I still think they were resting me for the playoffs. At least that's what my shrink told me to think!) Anyway, I was hiding in the "healthy scratch" room—the place you go after the team loses and you're not playing, because you don't want to give the coach another target when he comes in to berate the boys—after another loss and figured enough time had gone by for me to reappear. If Muckler hadn't come in to breathe fire by now, he wasn't going to come at all. With the coast clear I was about to open the locker room door but stopped when I heard someone behind it launch into an absolute tirade. Being the coward that I am, I decided to stay on the safe side of the door and just listen. Someone in there was peeling the paint off the walls. F-bomb after F-bomb with a few other four-letter words thrown in for effect. I'd never heard such a tongue-lashing. I couldn't make out the voice at first, but soon realized it was the Great One who was delivering this chew-out to end all chew-outs.

It's not a secret that screaming happens in locker rooms. But most of the time it's just one of the guys going nuts for fifteen seconds to get something off his chest. Wayne went at the lads for about five minutes that night and the point of his fire and brimstone sermon was that mediocrity was not to be accepted. I wanted to feel bad for the guys, but to be honest I loved every minute of it. I loved the fire. I loved the passion. Wayne was fed up. He didn't want to allow his team or himself to be average.

I've heard people say they didn't enjoy watching Wayne in his later years because they felt it somehow diminished their memories of his glory days. They lump him into that group of athletes who were at some point great but end up looking ordinary because they held on to their careers too long. And while I agree that sometimes athletes look foolish when they don't realize their best-before date, I would not put Wayne Gretzky in that category. In my mind the true greats can't tarnish their legacy by looking "human" near the end. Put it this way—will you remember Jerry Rice as a Seahawk or a 49er? Will you remember Pete Rose as an Expo or a Red? Jordan as a Wizard or a Bull? It's not even close to a debate. Ten years from now the only real memory folks will have of Wayne as a Ranger will be of him skating around the rink waving goodbye in his final game. The rest will be all Oilers and Kings highlights. And don't even talk to me about the Blues.

Sure, Wayne had lost a step or two by the time he played his third year for the Rangers. And yes, 62 points is a long way from 215. But sixty points in a season still gets you $4.5 million per year in this day and age. So he wasn't that bad. You have to remember that Gretzky at 70 percent was still better than most of that Rangers team at 100 percent. You could still see the vision. Some of the things I got to witness him do were incredible. One particular play comes to mind. It was your typical three-on-two drill and Gretzky had the puck going wide down the left side. He was just below the bottom of the circle and it looked like his only play was to go behind the net, into his "office," and look to pass to someone from there. As he was skating toward the back of the net his winger, Kevin Stevens, set up camp in the left faceoff circle between the hash mark and the dot. Instead of going behind the net, the Great One waited until he had just the right angle and banked the puck off the side of the net right to a waiting and wide open Kevin Stevens, who hammered it home.

I'm sure that it was frustrating for Wayne that his body couldn't always do what his brain told it to do. But I believe that he felt he owed it to the game to keep playing those final years. He wanted to mentor some of the younger players on the team and in the league. He wanted to share his leadership skills with the veterans. Plain and simple, he wanted to leave a legacy. And he did. I think players of today could learn a lot from Wayne, especially the way he acted and carried himself publicly. He was always willing to do what was best for his team, and what was best for the league. If you think about it, without Wayne, the league wouldn't be able to spell San Jose, Phoenix, or Anaheim.

Unfortunately, what I could barely spell was "ice time." I was a healthy scratch against the Carolina Hurricanes. Not a great sign since this was well before their rise to respectability. I spent the entire first period on the stationary bike desperately trying to stay in some sort of game shape. After showering I was greeted by the

143

Rangers PR guy, who told me that our GM Neil Smith wanted a word with me. That was the first (but not the last) time I got the tap from a PR person. So as you can imagine, I was a little rattled.

"Don't worry, it's not what you think," he said to me. Which was interesting, because I didn't even know what I was thinking at that point.

We were nearing the GM's box when the PR guy decided to chime in again. I think he wanted to make me feel better about the walk and impending message, because he blurted out, "Don't worry, you're not getting sent down."

"Thanks, dude, I appreciate the info. Do you have anything else you want to tell me?"

"No, I'll let Neil tell you the rest."

I'll never forget walking into Smith's box at MSG, because right when I entered the Hurricanes scored to make it 1–0 for the visitors. Smith, slumped over in his chair, was mumbling to himself. I held back so as not to bother him, but it wasn't long before he motioned me over.

"Sean, what do you think is wrong with us?"

Excuse me? The architect of the '94 Cup-winning Rangers team was asking a guy who couldn't crack his lineup why his collection of star players was faltering. Luckily for me, a skirmish broke out on the ice before I was forced to answer the question. And when everything settled down at ice level, Smith said his piece.

"Sean, we've traded you to the Los Angeles Kings for Eric Lacroix."

It was a relief to know that at least I got traded for another forward. I certainly wasn't an expert on Lacroix's game, and couldn't even tell you which team won the trade at that point. But the impression I got was that while the Rangers wanted a guy they thought would actually fit into their lineup in a way that I never did, they also wanted to find a good spot for me as well. I figured it was going to work out for both parties.

How about a moment to reflect on all that transpired that season. Training camp in Pittsburgh (I signed there as a free agent in August), re-assigned to Houston at the end of September, called back up in mid-November, and promptly traded to New York only to be shipped to Los Angeles a few months later. Is it even possible to get mail after all that? No wonder my credit score was in the low 600s; by the time any bill caught up to me it was a late payment notice. (On a funnier note, there was a point that season when the Rangers were paying my rent in Pittsburgh, and the Kings were paying my rent in New York.)

As for my tearful goodbye with the Great One—well, it was brief but it left a lasting impression on me. After the game during which I got traded, I said my goodbyes to teammates and friends outside the green room at Madison Square Garden. Wayne walked by and pulled me into the room.

"Prongs, make sure you talk to Pete Miller when you get to LA. Tell him I said to take care of you. He's a good man. Good luck." No, he didn't say much, but it was more than enough. Getting traded pretty much always sucks and he was trying to provide a guy like me a soft landing on the other side. If only I had asked for the keys to his place at Sherwood.

You want to know the best part about that season? I can tell my kids that the one year I played with Wayne Gretzky he scored just nine goals more than I did, and I only played in fourteen games. Of course, I'll leave out the fact that Wayne scored just nine goals.

It's no fun being traded out of New York, but I can't say LA was without its appeal. When you grow up in the north of Ontario where winters are harsh, sun and surf from October through March is pretty damn appealing. Plus, having played in Anaheim previously, my wife and I knew a number of people in the area. This made the move somewhat easier. It may sound uncomplicated to be traded to sunny California, but it's not as easy as you'd think. If all you know is a Canadian market or east coast lifestyle then it's a culture shock to get dealt to the southern hockey city. The obvious difference is the weather. It may sound a little weird, but I actually found it easier to get into hockey mode in a typical hockey climate. Snow storms, ice storms, or below freezing winds just felt like hockey to me. Flip-flops and shades felt like beer. Playing in Anaheim or Los Angeles could feel dangerously like a vacation, and for someone in my situation that's not a good thing. Luckily I had already experienced driving to the rink in shorts, so this time around I wouldn't be fazed or distracted by it.

Since I was traded for another forward I felt pretty secure in thinking that I'd be walking into a spot in the lineup. When you're traded it's also important to get into the mindset that a team wanted you more than another guy, instead of that your old team wanted the other guy instead of you. I successfully did that after the trade, so I was convinced my ice time and productivity were sure to improve with the Kings. Sometimes it's also uncomfortable if you're traded for a player who was really popular in the room. Usually there's no animosity, because guys know you didn't trade yourself. I had no problem walking into the room, so I felt good about that. And by no means is that a shot at Lacroix. Funny enough, Eric and I had a conversation on the phone after the trade when he was trying to figure out places to live in New York. I think I may have recommended a few pubs as well. I was happy with the trade and was eager to prove the Kings' management made the right decision.

Another reason I was happy to be heading to LA: Rob Blake, the Kings' captain, was not only a Bowling Green alumnus, but also actually the guy who took me out to dinner on my recruiting trip. Blake is a truly formidable hockey player (in fact, no one has ever hit me harder than Blake did one game when I was in Anaheim— he caught me with one of his patented ass-checks right in the chest as I was reaching for a bad pass), and an even better guy. And one of the assistant captains was Garry Galley, the guy who drove halfway across the continent to kick in the door at the annual reunion. There probably wasn't a team I'd rather play for.

Plus, the hockey gods were smiling on me in a way I hadn't even known about when I was en route to the Kings. It turned out the coach couldn't scratch me from the lineup even if he'd wanted to.

The legendary Larry Robinson was our coach and we were fighting for our playoff lives. Every win was an amazing high and every loss seemed like doom. After a couple of contests in which we finished on the wrong side of the ledger the leaders of our group decided it was time for some team meetings.

Now, team meetings can come in a three different forms:

Coach-initiated: This is the most common and it can happen on the ice or in the dressing room. The head coach will usually give his opinion as to what is wrong with the team and what has to happen to turn things around. This can be anything from a pep talk to an all-out scream show. These types of meetings are called after a really ugly loss or a short losing streak, or before an important game. The coach usually just wants to make sure his players are focusing on the right things.

Captain(s)-initiated: This type of team meeting is a little more serious and can include the coaches. Anyone is invited to speak their mind in this setting, although usually the talking is reserved for the leadership group of the club and the head coach. Things have started to slide quite badly for a meeting like this to be called, so it doesn't happen all that often in a season.

Players only: No coaches are allowed during these closed-door meetings in the dressing room. Many times these can be initiated because the players don't like something the head coach is doing, so they pass on the information to the captain to take up the ladder. There also may be a problem within the room that needs to be addressed. Things have gone almost completely off the rails for a players-only meeting to be called.

In LA that spring, the team had already graduated to #3. Veterans went around the room to offer their observations on how the team's problems could be remedied. Once that phase failed it was on to the next step, one that could bring a team together or tear it apart: laying personal blame. We were told that everyone would have to come up with something for the meeting so we were to be prepared.

Imagine how great that was for me. I had just arrived from New York. Now I was going to start pointing fingers? I figured since I was a new guy I could get out of the exercise, so I approached our Blake (who I knew on a personal level prior to my arrival in LA) and voiced my objection. Thank goodness for me the hockey world is a small one.

"Blakey, do I really need to stand up and give my opinion as to why the team is playing like shit? I mean, I just got here and it may not go over too well."

"Don't worry about it," was his reply. "It's totally anonymous. Write down your thoughts on a piece of paper and give it to me or one of the assistant captains. We'll read through them together."

What a relief that was. I honestly didn't know enough about the situation or the makeup of the team to offer an honest or insightful opinion, so I just jotted down that the team needed to stick together and some other kumbaya garbage. Well, little did I know that when Blake said "we'll read through them together," he meant the entire team. Yes, Blake and our two assistant captains, Garry Galley and Luc Robitaille, stood at the front of the trainers' room and read each one aloud. Talk about uncomfortable. Our entire team was crammed in the trainers' room and we had to discuss each note that basically tore our team to shreds, piece by piece. Not exactly what you would call a warm and fuzzy exercise, believe me. The best part was that it was supposed to be anonymous, but somewhere in the proceedings Blake took one of the notes and saw that the author had attached his name to it. He read it anyways.

"Steve Duchesne is what's wrong with this team. Signed Ray Ferraro."

Apparently Ray didn't want to sugarcoat things. And since Duchesne was sitting only about five feet away at the time of his declaration, things were a little awkward. Everybody just went silent. Steve kind of laughed at first. I think he thought Ray was messing with him, but this was no time for jokes. Making matters worse for Duchesne was that Ferraro wasn't the only one who mentioned his name (shockingly, Duchesne was dealt to Philly at the deadline that year). Another popular target was the coaching staff. Many of the players thought that the coaches played with the lineup and shuffled the lines too much. The feeling was that it was tough to get any rhythm or flow with guys constantly moving in and out of the lineup.

Once we finished our group hara-kiri, Blake took the feedback and delivered it to the coaches. A future Hall of Famer going nose-to-nose with a guy who was already there. But Larry

Robinson didn't dig in his heels. He got it. So he called another team meeting to say that he appreciated the comments and was willing to make some alterations to his philosophy. He told us that if we won, there would be no changes to the lineup unless it was due to injury.

We played hard the next few games and strung together a little winning streak. Luckily for me I happened to be in the lineup for those games, so as per the new rules I got to stay in the lineup. However, during the morning skate after one of those wins I got that old scratch feeling once again. I'd developed a sixth sense for that type of thing over the years. Sure enough, when the skate started I was on the fourth line. Normally that wasn't such a big deal, although that day there were four of us on the fourth line. That's a little disheartening.

In the dressing room, Larry had written the lines on the board. Normally, the fourth line looked like this:

PRONGER   FERRARO   COURTNALL

However, there had been a little twist to it:

PRONGER/JOHNSON   FERRARO   COURTNALL

Obviously, the call between Matt Johnson and me would be a game-time decision. Because I was always trying to read stuff into things, I figured that since my name was on the outside I would be on the outside looking in once the game started. While I was convincing myself that I was going to be a scratch, the coach came over and confirmed it to my face. See, I'm not crazy.

Luckily, Blake saw the exchange between Larry and myself and followed the coach into his office after it was done. Not two minutes later Larry came out of his office, walked right up to me, and said, "Prongs, you're going tonight."

Music to the ears of a guy like me. Thanks, Captain.

I'd like to say I took that opportunity and helped the Kings on a successful stretch drive and playoff run—however, I blew out my MCL a few games later and my season was done. In a strange twist of fate I was upended by my old teammate Travis Green against my old team, the Ducks. Luckily my injury happened before the trade deadline, otherwise I may have been forced to pen another chapter in this book. The Kings weren't much better off. Steve Duchesne may have been a problem, but getting rid of him didn't solve the problem. Los Angeles missed the playoffs. Any way you dice it, the 1998–99 season was a lesson in frustration, air miles, and moving trucks.

And that was it. It's funny. For so long I'd been thinking a one-way contract would solve all my problems. But until they come up with a contract that includes not only a no-trade but also a no-scratch/no-injury clause, there will still be problems that lawyers and agents can't solve.

8

SOMETHING UGLY IS BRUIN

A hockey season usually doesn't end with the fans' applause or a lap around the ice with the Stanley Cup. If you're fortunate it does, but I'm sure you've figured out by now that nobody's ever had a reason to call me "Lucky" Pronger. Only one team per league wins the final game of the season. The rest wait one day after their final loss and then it's the annual ritual of locker clean-out day. There's not much to it, really. It's the day the members of the media get their final crack at the players. It's also the time pigeons like me hound the stars of the team to sign sticks and other bits of memorabilia.

"Hey Blakey, can I trouble you for an autograph or ten?"

Mostly it's for keepsakes, but for me it was more like proof that I was actually on the team! Locker clean-out day is also the time when envelopes of cash find their way to the team's equipment and medical guys. Most of the time the captain of the team (or a veteran) will set the minimum amount of tip that's acceptable. And I never had a problem with it. Equipment and medical trainers work their tails off all season long to try to make life better for the players and the coaches, and they usually do it for mediocre pay. The cash was like a year-end bonus and the amount was probably never enough. (Disclaimer: If anyone from the IRS is reading this book, I know for a fact that every cent of said bonus is claimed as income. Honest.)

The locker room clean-out is also the time that guys will try to "borrow" as many sticks as possible to take back home so they can barter a few at their local summer tavern, give them to buddies, use them for summer hockey, or build an addition on their cottage. Before leaving for cottage country you also have to do an exit physical to identify any problems that need to be addressed during the summer. If everything looks fine then the team gives you a clean bill of health so if they decide to trade you the other squad can't claim you're damaged goods. When you're all done coughing for the doctors it's time for the year-end meeting. If you've had a good season you welcome this sit-down with the GM and head coach. Everyone likes to hear that he's done a good job, may get an expanded role the next season, or will get a contract in the summer. However, if you've been sent to the minors once, traded twice, and finished the season on the IR the meeting will be a little less than special.

Since the Kings were lucky enough to have me last they had the duty of cutting the cord. My year-end meeting with GM Dave Taylor went something like this:

"Sean, we've decided to go in another direction."

"Which direction is that?"

"The one that you're not going in."

At least he was honest. It's not like it was a tough decision for the Kings, considering I totalled zero goals and four assists in twenty-nine games with the Kings, Rangers, and Penguins that season. I'm not sure what's more impressive, the fact that I had no points or that I played twenty-nine games *combined* for three NHL franchises in one season. The Kings chose to save a couple hundred thousand bucks by not re-signing me.

That left me as an unrestricted free agent as soon as July 1 hit. I couldn't wait. Now I know what you're thinking, "This plug just got bounced from three different teams during one season and he thinks the offers are going to start piling up once the clock strikes midnight?"

Hell yeah! I mean we're talking about a veteran of 142 NHL games at this point. I figured there were lots of teams that would be interested in a good character guy with great bloodlines (and yes, I do believe that bloodlines flow upward from a younger brother to his older sibling).

I couldn't wait. I had my fax machine ready to go. Rod Tidwell had nothing on me. I woke up the morning of July 1 like a kid wakes up on Christmas.

"Did Santa come last night?" I asked my wife.

"Not even Santa would offer you a contract on day one" was the reply. I would never have married her if she didn't have the required talent for one-liners.

As it turned out, Santa didn't come to the Sean Pronger household until August. It stung a bit, I'm not going to lie. I was just coming off the first one-way contract of my career and the Bruins had the gall to offer me a two-year, two-way deal? But after getting traded four times in a calendar year, one should feel lucky to receive any offer outside of the California Penal League.

Beantown, here I come!

A tenth time to make a first impression. Of course I checked out the roster before camp started, and I thought there just might have been a spot for a big ole lumbering centreman with no hands. It also helped that I knew a few guys on the roster and a former teammate of mine was one of the assistant coaches. That's right, the legendary Ken Baumgartner was one of Pat Burns's assistants that year. Kenny was another guy that I grew up watching. He was a scary man to watch on TV—and let me tell you, he was even scarier when he was on the other team. He was a menacing presence on the ice. I remember playing (as a member of the Mighty Ducks) against him in Maple Leaf Gardens and thinking to myself that he wasn't "all there." He just had a look to him that made you feel like he would kill you at any given moment for no particular reason. On this night I overheard him say to Denny Lambert (one of our tough guys) "I'm giving you an invitation, kid." The puck dropped and away they went. It didn't go very well for Denny but at least he took him up on the offer and showed up. I remember hoping—or, more precisely, praying—I wouldn't get the invite. Thank God the invite never came. I'm not sure what I would've done but I am sure I would have embarrassed myself.

Thankfully, I played more games with Ken than against him. I had the privilege of playing with him in Anaheim a few years prior and he's one of those guys you'd want on your team any day. Most people think of Bomber as a fighter, but what most people don't know is that he was a decent player and could play both forward and defence. Mind you, he did get a lot of room to operate.

As comfortable as I felt around Baumgartner, I felt the exact opposite around the late Mr. Burns. Don't get me wrong; Pat Burns was a great man. He was straightforward, which as a player is the most you can ask for from your coach. On the flip side he could be really, really tough. Not a huge shock when you consider he was a former cop with a mullet, mustache, and quick temper. Put it this way: Pat Burns did not exude rainbows and teddy bears. Players certainly did not get the warm and fuzzies around that guy.

Speaking of NHL legends, suiting up at the Bruins training camp meant skating alongside Ray Bourque. That is, skating behind Ray Bourque. During one of our early skating sessions I witnessed the ultimate show of respect. It was near the end of practice and we were doing a lengthy drill without pucks—aka the dreaded bag skate. It was ten minutes of continuous skating. The drill started with four groups of skaters. Each group started on the blue line (where it meets the boards). We were to skate in a counter-clockwise direction around the nets. The coach wanted to see if one group (or individual) could catch the next. I happened to be in the group behind Bourque. The whistle blew and off we went. After about five minutes of skating our group had caught up to Bourque's group. Bourque was leading his group, so there's about twelve guys piled up behind him. After another couple minutes the group that started behind us had caught up, so all of a sudden eighteen guys are skating directly behind Ray. At about the nine-minute mark the last group had caught up. We now had twenty-four skaters directly behind the living legend. For the entire skating drill no one dared to pass Ray Bourque. He set the pace and we followed it without even considering showing how much gas we may have had left in the tank.

As it turned out, I had a decent training camp. I played in almost all of the exhibition games, which I took to be a good sign. Of course, it had nothing to do with my play. I found out later I had enough NHL experience to be officially considered a veteran. And in the pre-season each team must dress at least ten veterans to ensure fans see something that could pose as a real NHL team with some semblance of skill. What a rip-off for the Bruins faithful in the fall of 1999. Believe me when I say the folks weren't jumping over the turnstiles to see "the other Pronger" trip over the blue line.

Fans pay full rent for their tickets in the pre-season, yet they're often treated to a roster not anywhere near full of NHL players. So obviously the crowd's give-a-crap meter is at about 60 percent

This is where it all began. Big Jim and I at the 1991 entry draft in Buffalo. Had I known then what I know now I would've snuck around and got my picture taken in front of ALL of the team banners. You know, just in case!

The glory days! (Cue Bruce Springsteen.) This was quite possibly the best line ever to play in Dryden minor hockey. At least that year ... on that team. (Left to right: Chris Hancock, Sean Pronger, Brian Armit)

All I kept thinking was, "Isn't this the guy who took a twenty-five-game suspension on Pierre Turgeon back in the day? I'll be sure to keep an eye on him if I score."

This was the year I started to become a pro hockey player.

This is a collector's item. Without this shot there may not be a record of me playing for the Rangers … at least not in a game!

I really wish things had worked out with the Kings. And I really wish they'd worked out for another thirteen years, because then I'd be a Stanley Cup champion.

This was the last time the Great One and I were ever going to play in Maple Leaf Gardens. The team wanted to make sure we captured a photo. Wayne and I agreed they should have a memento of us.

Some of the best hockey of my career was played in Syracuse. It was also where I earned the most Air Miles. Called up to and sent down from Columbus seven times in one season!

Below: Some of the worst hockey of my career was played in Providence. This would be one of my "do-over" years if I could.

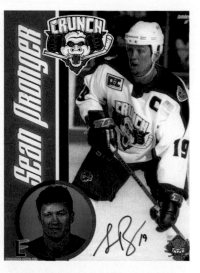

I refuse to acknowledge this period in my hockey career.

At my wedding to Mrs. Journeyman. Better than winning the Hart Trophy, I won a real heart. This is my all-time favourite picture (not including pics of my wife and kids—had to get that on the record). (Left to right: Chris, Big Jim, Sean)

What a great year for the Pronger family. Chris with his Norris Trophy and me with the Hart Trophy. Or was this the year that Chris won both? So confusing.

This is where Murph and I originally hatched the idea of the *Journeyman* book. Herbie, our former book agent, wanted too much in agent fees, we didn't know how to spell or write, and Mrs. Journeyman just thought we were morons. So we shelved the idea. I guess we'll have to wait to see who was right. (Left to right: Murph, Herbie Hancock, Mrs. Journeyman, Sean)

Ladies and gentlemen, I give you the wolf pack! (Chris Pronger's wedding, 2001)

Here's the wolf pack about to go on a fishing trip to a remote location on a lake in northwestern Ontario. We were told we could pack only what was absolutely necessary. I can assure you none of those cases made the return flight. (Left to right: Chris "Herbie" Hancock, Sean, John "Hummer" Cummings, Steve "Rock" Roll, Chris "Weasel" Pronger, Darcy "Mit" Mitani)

This was the only year Chris had the privilege of playing with his older and wiser big brother. I think he did a good job of learning what it takes to be a successful peewee player. I'm at the back in the middle, Chris is in the front, second from the left.

This was a surprise retirement party orchestrated by Mrs. Journeyman. I was completely stunned to walk into the restaurant and see fifty or so friends and family in attendance. She also reached out to former teammates and had them write a sentence or two about their experiences playing with a living legend. After listening to all the kind words it became overwhelmingly clear that I was an AWESOME teammate (and extremely modest). Seriously, it was a night I'll never forget. Thanks, babe!

watching exhibition hockey. It's a bit of a shame, really. Games that mean so much to a handful of players (guys on the bubble) mean very little to the people watching them. You're grinding your balls off trying to make the right impression, and if you do come up with a big play most of the fans missed it because they are too busy scanning the program trying to figure out who the hell #46 is.

After the final game of training camp, which was in Montreal, we boarded a plane for Boston. There were about five guys left for one or two spots—depending how many bodies the Bruins wanted to carry. We got into our usual card game on the flight, and I will say that's something I really miss about my playing days. Dealing some hands and having a few brews with the guys on the plane is about the best form of team bonding you can have. As the plane levelled out, I noticed Kenny Baumgartner walking from the front of the plane toward the back. Nothing unusual about that, as Kenny was not that far removed from his playing days. So it wouldn't be a shock for him to leave the front of the plane to shoot the shit with the fellas in the back. As he was making his way back he stopped and whispered something to one of the Euros. The Euro stood up and started walking to the front of the plane.

"Hmmm, that's interesting," I thought at the time. "Why is that dude going to the front of the plane? What did Kenny whisper, and what is the real reason he looked like a dead man walking to the back of the plane?"

Then it dawned on me. They were shooting guys on the flight home! I mean, I figured they'd at least wait until we got to the practice rink the next day. I couldn't help but feel for Kenny, as he was sent to play the role of the Grim Reaper. It wasn't long ago that he was one of the guys sitting at the back, and now he was being forced to make guys walk the plank. You could tell it was a chore he didn't enjoy. I continued to play cards while keeping a furry eyeball on Kenny. Usually I would have been counting cards, but this time I was counting the number of guys who had to make the lonely walk up to take a seat beside the head coach. As Kenny approached our game I buried my face in my cards, hoping he'd pass us by. My heart was racing as I knew there were only a couple of us left that Kenny would potentially call on.

"Please don't let it be me, please don't let it be me, please don't let it be me," I repeated in my head as if a mantra would have any impact on the situation. I was slow playing in the hope of delaying the inevitable. If I'd had a cell phone, I would have pulled it out right then to make a pretend call to someone, anyone.

Well, Ken was gracious enough to let us finish the hand. But as soon as the cards went face down I felt the cool blade of the sickle touch my shoulder.

"Hey Prongs, Burnsy wants to see you."

"I don't really want to see him, Kenny."

"I know you don't, but I don't think you want him coming back here, do you?"

"Good point. He's not going to give me a parachute is he?"

I turned to the boys to add some levity to what was a very quiet time on the bird.

"Well fellas, it's time to face the firing squad. Deal me in; I'll be right back."

I'd like to tell you Pat's speech was different from all the rest, but I can't. So go back and read Ron Wilson's words to me when he dropped the axe on my neck in Anaheim and there you go.

The Bruins paid for sending me down by promptly dropping their first five games of the season. Desperation must have set in, because I was re-called. We played one game at home (a loss) and then headed out west for a two-week road trip. After a couple more losses on the road, the club was a healthy 0–8. Perhaps I wasn't the solution the club was looking for. No one was happy, especially not Pat Burns. On a good day, the ex-cop was an intimidating man. As you can imagine, Burns was as approachable as a hungry grizzly at this point. We had a couple days off in between games while we were staying at a resort in Phoenix. Under normal circumstances, that would have been a great thing, but considering the calendar was nearly November and the team was oh-for on the season, it was a nightmare. Days off during times like that are easily turned into two-hour practices without even a hint of a possibility of having a good time. At one of those practices, we were doing a neutral zone regroup drill. The puck was to go from D-man to D-man up to a winger and then turn into a three-on-two. Mattias Timander was the first D-man. I can picture it now.

The whistle blows to start the drill. Timander tries to take a pass from the coach and can't handle the puck. Burns stops the drill with a whistle.

DO IT AGAIN!

Mattie takes the pass cleanly and fires it up to his D-partner but the puck rattles off his shin pad.

TWEET. "DO IT AGAIN," Burns yells.

Mattie, shaking now, sends a pass behind his intended target.

TWEET. "AGAIN!"

You can feel the tension. Things are getting uncomfortable. Everyone is hoping Mattie can hit his partner on the tape soon, because every messed-up drill is a step closer to the dreaded team bag skate.

"C'mon Mattie, you can do it," someone urges. It sounds more like a prayer than encouragement.

Mattie's next pass blows up off his partner's stick.

TWEET. "Do it again," Burns says, seething. This time, though, he is quiet. Not a good sign at all.

The pressure is too much for poor Mattie. His last attempt is a foot too high and the drill is blown dead once again.

"MATTIE! GET THE FUCK OFF THE ICE!"

Timander, dejected, was forced to head to the locker room a good thirty minutes before the rest of us finished up. Heading into the room after practice, I saw him showered and dressed, still sitting in his stall. I threw an arm around him to try to cheer him up.

"Don't worry about it, buddy," I said.

When he lifted his head, he stared at me and I could see embarrassment, frustration, and anger in his face.

"Don't worry about it? Prongs, I was just a healthy scratch from practice."

Better him than me, I guess.

I played a grand total of eleven games for the big club. I played OK, not great, and it surely didn't help that I felt like I was *persona non grata*. Sometimes the threat of being sent down can light a fire under a player. Other times it just makes him tentative and awkward on the ice. The worse the signals are from the coach, the worse you play.

Still, even though I worried incessantly about being sent down, I was still caught off guard when the axe finally fell. We had suffered a tough loss in Buffalo one night and had to get right back home for a game in Boston the next night. I can't say that I played poorly, but after a thumping from a division rival I should've known that something had to give. Looking back at a game like that, I realize now that I needed to do something to show the Bruins I wanted to stay. Run somebody over or get in a dust-up. Something. Anything. As I learned throughout my career, just enough is never enough.

Since it was a back-to-back situation there was no morning skate for the home game. When I walked into the dressing room around 4:30 p.m. to start to prepare for the game there was another player in my stall. I nonchalantly strolled around the room to make sure I hadn't just been moved to another spot, but couldn't find my nameplate anywhere. I knew what that meant. I mean, it's not like I was Joe Thornton. Wasn't that nice of them to give me a heads up? I found the equipment manager and he just shrugged his shoulders and told me to talk to Coach. I tried to find a place where I could hang out and be seen by the coaches but not by the players. Finally, Burns came into the room to let me know that sure enough I had been put on waivers and if I cleared that I would be sent down to Providence. Thanks for keeping me in the loop, fellas. I'm pretty sure this could have been done over the phone and without the embarrassing trip to the rink. I hope it was just a case of one hand not knowing what the other was doing with the Bruins.

I found my gear neatly packed in the equipment room. For the life of me I don't know why I didn't grab a couple dozen Ray Bourque sticks. Perhaps theft would have made me feel better, but instead I was forced to hang out in the equipment room until the guys went out on the ice for warm-up. If it seems like I spent a lot of time at the rink hiding from my teammates so there wouldn't be an awkward goodbye, that's because I did. Once they cleared the room I had to lug my gear out of the building and load it up in my car in the parking lot. It's a weird feeling when your team is warming up and you're standing in the parking lot trying to cram a hockey bag in the trunk of a car hoping not to get recognized. OK, maybe "recognized" is the wrong word there, so let's say hoping not to get noticed. Fortunately and unfortunately, it's a relatively short drive to Providence from Boston. There's not much time to beat oneself up about getting sent down AGAIN. There's also no chance to claim the airlines fucked you over so you could miss a day of practice.

This demotion by the Bruins felt different from the one that happened at the end of training camp. The first time I was sent down I played pretty well for the Baby Bruins because I truly believed the big club was going to come calling for me. And it did. Now I didn't have any faith that the Bruins would come knocking for "the other Pronger" anytime soon, if at all. And so began a real dark period in my career.

I had just spent the previous six-plus months filling out change of address cards only to find myself in the minors once again. I was pretty sure I was on the back nine of my NHL career and I was having a tough time coming to terms with it.

The Bruins had won the Calder Cup the previous year and there were lofty expectations that the club would repeat. Making matters worse was the fact that head coach Peter Laviolette nominated me to be captain of the team. I could certainly see the argument for naming me captain. I had a decent résumé in the NHL and a solid one in the minors. I had always relished getting a letter on my jersey, and anytime it was the "C" I threw myself into the role. But the timing wasn't right that year; I was still reeling from the previous season and I was devastated to be starting things off in the minors once again. What would normally come naturally to me as captain suddenly seemed forced and insincere. I felt like a fraud. I didn't have a lot of self-confidence, and that's not a good trait for any leader. I knew I wasn't the guy who could lead them to another title. And unfortunately I was right.

Both the big and little Bruins had injury problems for most of the year, which is a nightmare for any organization. When players in the NHL club go down, the AHL is raided of its best players to fill the holes. And then if some injuries occur at the minor league level, things go sideways in a heartbeat. That's what our season was like from start to finish. I was never on a team that had as much turnover as the Providence Bruins did that year. It's never a good sign when in one season five different players wear #21 *and* #30, four wear #23, and three wear #71. Couple the injuries with the high expectations and no one in Baby Bruin land was in a good mood. And I surely wasn't helping things by playing the worst hockey of my career, and, worse yet, not caring that I was doing so. Even though the American Hockey League is a step below the NHL it isn't one where you can just throw on your gear and everything falls into place. Just about everyone there is good enough to play in the NHL. Take a shift off and you're going to be just as embarrassed as you would be in the big league. To try to get by with a half-hearted, half-assed effort was a waste of everyone's time.

I think my season in Providence can be summed up by two games. We played the Springfield Falcons in a home-and-home series at the end of December. The first game was in Providence. We lost the game 8–4 on home ice. Not good. It was one of those games where everything that could go wrong, did. We had a rookie defenceman by the name of Nick Boynton. Yes, future NHL all-star Nick Boynton. In the first period he gathered the puck behind our net and rung it around the boards to a winger that wasn't there. One of Springfield's D-men corralled the puck and fired it right back at our net. Nick found his way to the front of the net just in time for a perfect deflection by our stunned goaltender. Not only did Nick score the own-goal, he also assisted on it. I had never seen it before and I can assure you that Boynton hasn't done it since. The next morning I walked into Coach Laviolette's office, because as captain I felt like I had to show my face to see if there was anything he wanted me to pass along to the team. Surprisingly, Laviolette and assistant coach Bill Armstrong were in a relatively good and calm mood. They took it upon themselves to show me the Nick Boynton goal and assist. I can assure you, the play was a little funnier the day after. When you lose a game in such ugly fashion all you want to do is play your next game. You don't want to have too many days in between games after a big loss. Luckily, we played the same team the very next day. In the room I tried to fire up the troops. Gave them the old "they embarrassed us on home ice and now they're laughing at us" speech. Told the fellas we could return the favour and forget about the night before. Apparently, I am not General Patton. We got blown out that night 14–2. Oh man, 8–4 would have felt good. If I could've dug a hole from the bench to the Dryden Mill I would've. In my career I've never been a part of anything like that. And the cherry on top was that I was captain of the Providence Titanic! I had no idea what to say after the game. When all eyes were on me to offer something, I just sat there in stunned silence. Normally, I would've gone bat-shit crazy. Probably smashed something and called out a few guys, but I didn't. I just sat there. At that moment I realized my heart wasn't in it. However, I would like the record to show that I was even for that game with an assist. Jesus, I sound like a European.

If I could have one "do over" in my career it would be that season. I was in a bad place mentally and couldn't find my way out of the darkness. To be a leader when your heart isn't in it is not good for anyone, and for the Providence Bruins that season, it was just another ingredient in the recipe of disaster. Safe to say, I was not surprised when the phone rang that spring.

"Sean, it's Lavy. We traded you to the Manitoba Moose. You have a flight tomorrow morning. Good luck." His phone call was the culmination of a year of frustration, high expectations, and infrequent results. I wish I could say there was one decisive incident that sealed my fate, but there wasn't. It was a slow burn that was always just below the surface. I did not play well. He knew it and I knew it. We both would have been better off if he'd pulled me into his office and read me the riot act. That may have been the wake-up call I needed to pull my head out of my ass. Instead, it was just mediocrity and I was gradually excluded from conversations about the direction of the team. That's usually a bad sign when you're the captain. What added to the frustration was that I knew I was playing badly and tried to regroup, to be a leader and play better. The problem was I couldn't. The well was dry. A sure sign it was time to move on.

I put up a front about how disappointed I was to be leaving, but deep down I knew the trade was not only best for the Bruins, but also best for me.

9

OUTWARD BOUND

Winnipeg, Manitoba—or, as it's more affectionately known, Winter-peg, Man-it's-cold-out-here! An outpost, as far as many are concerned, but I was thrilled. Winnipeg was a homecoming of sorts for me. I grew up a short three-and-a-half-hour drive east of the 'Peg, and many times in my childhood the Pronger family hopped into our wood-panelled minivan to make the trek to the big city. To get traded there was exciting. And Manitoba was in the IHL, which was my preferred minor league (it's sad to have a preferred minor league, I know). Randy Carlyle was the general manager and head coach, and Scott Arniel was his assistant. Talk about a walk down memory lane. Chris and I had watched both of them as members of the Jets. Back then Randy chose to wear a mullet instead of a helmet. Nevertheless, he was a crafty defenceman who played with an edge; kind of like the way he coaches. Arniel was a smooth-skating winger with good hands. They both had a wealth of hockey knowledge and the respect of the players because of their résumés. The assistant GM at the time was Craig Heisinger (aka Zinger), and I would get to know Zinger very well over the following year and a half.

It's funny to look back now and see how things could have been different. I truly believe if I didn't get traded to Manitoba my hockey career would've been shortened by about four years. Winnipeg reignited my passion for the game. That was my first time playing for a Canadian team, and even though it was in the minors I couldn't help but feel the energy the city had for the game. Yes, there are some great minor league cities in the States. There are proud franchises with enthusiastic fan bases that support their team. But there is just something different when you play in Canada. No doubt I'm biased, and I do consider myself an unabashed over-the-top patriot. Still, playing in Winnipeg meant playing where people knew who you were. The Moose (although not the Jets) were Manitoba's hockey team at the time and fans cared about the guys who played for the club. The Moose were not second fiddle, and as a player I could feel that.

When I arrived at the Winnipeg airport it felt different from the million other times I had landed there. Instead of it being a brief stopover on the way home, it *was* home. The air was crisp. It was hockey weather. Heisinger picked me up at the airport and I didn't know what to make of him. He showed up dressed like he'd just got back from ice fishing (which he very well might have). He casually grabbed my stuff and started walking to the car. This is a guy who worked himself from trainer in the Western Hockey League up to assistant general manager in the National Hockey League. Little did I know that the future assistant GM of the Winnipeg Jets was carrying my hockey bag.

Prior to arriving in Winnipeg I had checked out the roster to see if there were any friendlies on the team. I discovered I had played against a few of them, but that was it. The only guy I knew was the guy I got traded with, Keith McCambridge. Yet another time in my career I had to try to fit in on the fly.

It was so cool to walk into the Winnipeg Arena for the first time. I had been there often as a kid, but always as a wide-eyed fan. The arena was an NHL facility and the Moose ran the team like an NHL team. Just what the doctor ordered, as far as I was concerned. During morning skates I would look up to the seats where we used to sit as fans and try to appreciate how far I'd come from childhood. It was the minors, sure, but how could I not be excited to play in that city? When I came out for my first pre-game warm-up I was hooked. It was not what a minor league game is supposed to feel like. The buzz was NHL-like and you could seriously feel the energy from the crowd. It was the middle of March and the playoffs were looming. The intensity level was ramping up. The Moose were in a fight for a playoff spot. Or, more specifically, a fight to avoid a best-of-three play-in to see which team would get the right to play in the playoffs.

There were only fourteen games remaining in the regular season when I arrived. I played well. If I hadn't been so fired up, I probably would have had around ten or twelve goals. But I was so excited my hands couldn't catch up to my feet, and that was a feeling I'd never experienced before (or since). I felt like a kid again. I was playing in an NHL rink without the NHL pressure. I played on a line with Bill Bowler. Here's Bill in a nutshell for those of you who may not know him: he's not much of a skater, but he's a world-class passer. He set me up more times than I can count, but I just couldn't finish.

We ended up having to play the "mini-playoff" against the Long Beach Ice Dogs. This wasn't your typical best of three series. Game one was to be held in Winnipeg, and games two and three were in Long Beach. Luckily, it was just a quick six-hour flight away. We lost game one at home and then it was off to Long Beach to try to win the next one or our season was done. I wish I could say we found a way to win game two and then completed the comeback with a win in game three, but alas—it was not to be. We lost game two in overtime. It was an unspectacular ending to what was an overall disappointing year, with one catch: for the first time in a long time, I was excited to see what the future held.

I couldn't wait for the next season to begin, except for one thing: training camp would be in Boston once again. That's right—the Moose owned my minor league rights, but I was still a member of the Bruins as far as my NHL rights were concerned. Talk about awkward. I would get to see the coaches and management who thought so highly of me they didn't even want me on their minor league team. Fantastic! Even with those less than ideal circumstances I somehow still believed that if I had a great training camp, I had a shot at making the team. Man, was I an idealistic idiot.

In camp I must not have made much of an impression, because I spent most of it skating as the fifth-line centre on the "C" squad. Still, I refused to put two and two together and told myself things weren't going that badly. As training camp was winding down, we were scheduled to have our intra-squad game. At least, some of us were. The staff had posted the lineup for both teams in the main locker room at the practice rink. I didn't rush over to see who I was playing with because I knew it was going to be the usual assortment of prospects and plugs. Once the crowd cleared, I scanned Team White and didn't see my name on the list. Then I scanned Team Black only to find that my name wasn't there, either.

"OK, if I'm not on Team White and I'm not on Team Black, then I must be...."

Oh yes, I was a healthy scratch from the intra-squad game. Not exactly the confidence boost I was looking for. I remember having to sit in the stands with my fellow scratch Keith McCambridge while the Bruins radio guy, Bob Beers, told us not to worry.

"They know how you guys play," he said.

And he was right, because two days later we were both on our way out of Boston.

After I got over the mental beating I took at the hands of the Bruins organization I was excited at the thought of playing for the Moose. For once it wasn't going to be a bus ride, three connections, and a rented U-Haul for Mrs. Journeyman to join me. Since we spend the off-season in Dryden, it was only a three-and-a-half-hour drive straight west.

We had a strong team that year. Some of the notables: Brett Hauer, Philippe Boucher (who, after leaving the Moose, would go on to play another 500+ games in the show), Scott Thomas (who was part of the LA Kings team that upset the Red Wings and then took the eventual Stanley Cup champion Colorado Avalanche to seven games), Dan Kesa (a veteran of almost 140 NHL games, who I finally got to confront about stealing my spot on the roster in Pittsburgh), Johan Hedberg (this was where his nickname "Moose" came from), Kenny Wregget (who was an absolute classic), and, rounding out the dream team, none other than John MacLean.

John MacLean was a flat-out beast on the ice. As old-school as you can get. Tough, great character, and team first all the way. Mac didn't light the International Hockey League on fire when he arrived. It's a bit of a culture shock for someone who's never stepped foot in an IHL rink. The game is a little more disorganized on the ice than the NHL so it takes some getting used to. He was one of our go-to guys late in the game when we were up or down by a goal. He was also one of our shoot-out guys. One time I think he forgot where he was after he scored and started jumping around like he did when he scored that big goal in '88 to get the Devils into the playoffs. I loved seeing the old guy get excited. It was no secret

John was getting a little long in the tooth. After all, he had been in the NHL for the better part of two decades. But I'll tell you what: He played his ass off in Winnipeg. It would've been so easy for him to just mail it in, fake a groin injury, and collect his $2.5M from the sidelines. But he never let up. I did have to chuckle a couple times when we were on a long bus ride and I noticed him looking around. I don't know if he woke out of a dead sleep or what, but I felt obligated to remind him there were no stewardesses on these flights! He couldn't help but laugh. I was fortunate to play with John a couple of times in my career, and he just might take home the award for the "Sean Pronger greatest trade story of all time."

While in Winnipeg the club decided to do some "team building." What this basically means is picking an activity that everyone can do, and then adding some brews to the mix. It can be bowling, pool, darts, or curling, basically anything to give the guys a mental break from the game. On this particular day our activity was ice fishing. How awesome is that? I can honestly say it was the only time I ever did that for a team building exercise and I'm sure our city of residence had a lot to do with that selection of activity. The team set us up with everything we needed (and believe me, I'm well versed in the necessities of ice fishing)—fishing rods, bait, ice auger, and so on. All we had to do was bring something warm to wear and something cold to drink.

John MacLean was with the Moose at the time because the New York Rangers had loaned him to us. His nickname, or at least what I called him, was Officer MacLean. Yes, an obvious reference to Bruce Willis's character from the *Die Hard* series. (Hey, as a hockey player I had the right to not give anyone a good nickname.) He and I did a little time together in my brief stop with the Rangers, and I can tell you he is one of the all-time great guys. To set the stage, picture a grizzled fifteen-year NHL vet with a Stanley Cup on his résumé sitting in the middle of nowhere in an ice shack having the time of his life. I grew up watching John play, and here I was crushing beers on the Red River with him, listening to his war stories. That right there sums up why I miss playing. As we were discussing how our careers had derailed to the point of ice fishing together in Northern Manitoba, his phone rang with none other than Rangers GM Glen Sather on the line. Slats informed John that he had just been dealt to the Dallas Stars (where he would become an integral part of the Grumpy Old Men line). I can still picture it now: Mac with one of those Russian fur hats on his head, sitting in a freezing ice shack in the middle of Nowhere, Manitoba, fishing rod in one hand and cell phone in the other, learning that his career had just taken another abrupt U-turn. I'm not sure whether we caught any fish on John MacLean's last day as a member of the Moose, but I can guarantee we caught a buzz.

If I had to choose a single word to describe my 2000–01 season, it would be "liberating." I was still owned by the Boston Bruins, but it would've taken an act of God for them to call me up to the Big Club. So unless something drastic happened, I was going to be in Winnipeg for the year. Did you hear that? It was going to be one city, one team, and one address for the entire season. I grabbed all of my change of address cards and threw them in the fireplace. I can't tell you the peace of mind I felt knowing I wasn't going to be jerked around.

Even though I wasn't playing for an NHL team, that time with the Moose might have been the most fun I've had on a team in my career. At the time the Moose were still an independent team, so we had castoffs from all over the NHL. We were all in the same situation, and basically in the same place in our careers. We'd all played in organizations that treated us "poorly" and now we were in a great hockey city with a group of guys who liked to have a good time on and off the ice.

I loved to have friends from Dryden reach out to say they were coming up and wanted to know if I could get them tickets. It was as if I'd come full circle. It was so refreshing to no longer be nervous about people coming to watch in case I ended up sitting beside them. I was more concerned I couldn't get them the seats they wanted.

Despite the blast I was having, though, the 2000–01 season did have its share of ups and downs. I got to experience a ten-game winning streak *and* a ten-game losing streak. Just the type of consistency all franchises strive for. And speaking of consistency, what would a season be for me without that quintessential humiliating moment?

As I mentioned, my NHL rights were still owned by the Boston Bruins, so my paycheque had the Bruins logo on it. The Moose, being an independent team, weren't anyone's minor league affiliate. After a couple of months I opened my multi-hundred dollar paycheque only to find it had an Islanders logo on it. Hmmm, must have picked up the wrong stub. Double-check. Nope, Sean J. Pronger was the name, and the dollar figure certainly looked correct. Weird. I made a quick call to my agent, Pat Morris, to try to solve the mystery.

"Pat, why does my paycheque have an Islanders logo on it?"

"Let me look into that for you, Sean. I'll call you right back."

A couple minutes passed before the phone rang.

"It turns out the Bruins had too many players under NHL contracts. A team is allowed to have a total of fifty players. They can be playing on different teams in different leagues, but they can't go over fifty. They must have negotiated a deal with the Islanders to take over your contract."

"Obviously, they have big plans for me since they were keeping it a secret from everyone, including me."

"I'm not sure what they want to do."

"Do you know whom, or better yet what, I got traded for?"

"I don't, but if I had to guess, probably not much."

"Thanks Pat, you're the best!"

Are you kidding me? How does someone get traded and not even know it? If I'd had direct deposit I would never even have heard about that blockbuster. And I remember vividly where I was when I had that conversation with Pat: standing in the cereal aisle at Safeway. Pencil that one down as another low point. I spent an entire season with one organization but still managed to get traded. Wasn't I playing with Gretzky just a year ago?

Despite the unknown trade to the Islanders, that season was still a very positive one in my career. After the time I had in Boston almost any situation would have felt like a step in the right direction, but I'm telling you the city of Winnipeg and the Moose organization really re-energized me. That season also provided me with one of the more memorable (in a good way) moments of my career.

It was the first round of the playoffs and the Moose were down three games to one versus the Houston Aeros. Since the cities were so far apart in the IHL, the format of a playoff series was 2-3-2 (and it was all commercial travel). We were the lower-seeded team, and after a tough home ice overtime loss in game four we were facing elimination. But I had played on a lot of teams, and there was something about this particular group that led me to believe this loss would not be the defining moment of the series. Our leader and captain, Brian Chapman, had made a costly turnover that led to the overtime winner. But Chappy, a grizzly veteran, didn't hide after the game; he faced the music like a man. You could just see the other guys watch as Chapman answered all the tough questions. Guys take notice when they see their leader go through what he did and how he handled it afterward.

Game five was the next day in Winnipeg, and it went to overtime as well. Not wanting to let down our captain, we battled hard. We outplayed the Aeros badly. But, as in all playoff games, who had more shots or more scoring chances or who took the play to whom is irrelevant. All that matters is who wins the game. I would argue that having the opportunity to play hockey in a situation where, literally, the next goal ends your season is the closest thing to being a kid again—but with much higher stakes. You remember those street hockey games: when it's time to go home, the next goal wins. Well, the next goal *would* win, and depending on which team scored it would determine how many teams got on that plane to Houston. The hero that night was Sioux Lookout's (pseudo local boy) very own Jimmy "The Chin" Roy—meaning the Moose was alive for at least one more game.

After a day used primarily for travel, the Moose and Aeros once again would need overtime to decide game six. Sometimes when you're so caught up in the moment you don't take the time to truly appreciate what's happening. Three consecutive overtimes is pretty rare in a series, and I had lived it. Overtime is the place where you lose yourself, and find yourself. This is where the world stops and every ounce of energy and focus is on the next shift. You don't even think about the next period. All you can think of is your next shift and whether you can muster the energy to beat the guy across from you. Because that's usually how it ends. Somebody loses his focus for a split second and then boom—it's over. And you do *not* want to be that guy! This time, in game six Steve Brule stepped up big for Manitoba and suddenly Houston, for the first time in the series, found itself in an elimination game on home ice.

After coming back from being down three to one in the series and winning games five and six in overtime, I can tell you the players in our room felt there was no way we were losing game seven. We could feel the wind go out of Houston's sails and blow right into ours. Momentum doesn't always factor into playoff series, but sometimes if the series goes long enough it does. What's great about the playoffs is that the work and energy you put into the first part of the series can sometimes only be realized when you get to the seventh game. All the bodychecks you throw at their defence in games one through six finally add up to a turnover in game seven. Even though we were in their building for game seven, given what had transpired in the last two games we felt confident we'd broken their spirit and would take this series. To have the chance to play in a game seven, no matter what league, is an incredible experience. I played in a few in my career and could probably give the play-by-play for each of them to this day. And from that game seven, this would be the play I'd have the easiest time calling.

The score was 1–1, and their defenceman skated with the puck around their net. I was giving chase. When he came around the net and was nearing the bottom of the circle, I sensed he had to move his stick back toward me to make an outlet pass. I quickly lifted his stick, stole the puck, turned—and fired the puck over the glove of their goalie, Frederic Chabot, before he (or I) knew what was going on. It was a big goal in a big game that we would eventually win 3–1. I didn't think much about who had maybe seen the goal since the game was played in Houston, Texas, and this was long before highlights were immediately available on the Internet. I mean, how many people pay attention to the IHL playoffs? Well, apparently they do when there's a Canadian team involved. Especially when that team rallies back from a three-to-one series deficit. I remember a friend of mine telling me they showed my goal on *Hockey Night in Canada.* That just goes to show you that hockey fans love a good comeback. Go figure—my only highlight on CBC is when I'm in the minors!

After we made that magical comeback—and yes, I believe it was magical—we had no time to sit back and enjoy it. We went straight from game seven in Houston to game one in Chicago just two days later. It was a series against our archenemies, the Chicago Wolves. We played our guts out but lost in six games. I think that after our seven-game series that included three overtimes we simply ran out of gas.

After the season ended, I had a sit-down with GM Craig Heisinger to see what their plans were for Sean Pronger for the next year. The IHL was shutting down, and the Moose had agreed to an affiliation with the Vancouver Canucks and would be playing in the AHL from then on. I was never really a fan of end-of-season interviews (for obvious reasons), but my conversation with Zinger couldn't have gone better. He said he was going to speak with the Canucks about their willingness to sign me to a two-way contract. At worst, he told me, "If they don't sign you, we'll sign you to a minor league contract here. We want you back."

Yes! Someone wanted me. I can't tell you how refreshing it was to hear that. I told Zinger I loved playing in Winnipeg and I wanted to come back. He told me to give him a few days to get it all ironed out.

While I waited for Zinger to close out some sort of deal, there were more urgent matters to take care of—namely, the Manitoba Moose year-end golf blowout. My group consisted of Moose captain Brian Chapman, assistant coach Scott Arniel, and team owner Mark Chipman. I got to know Chipper pretty well during my time in Winnipeg, and he was/is one of the best owners and all around hockey management types I've ever met. It just seemed like he really cared about his players. Conversations with Chipman weren't just in passing. He always asked about the wife and the family. He was really committed to and invested in his franchise. That's why I wasn't surprised he was one of the main guys to bring the NHL back to Winnipeg in 2011. I can't think of a more deserving owner or fan base.

At that time, however, I was thinking more about how he could help me. I don't think it ever hurts to play golf with the owner of the team you're trying to land a deal with. Hey, I had just gotten my career back on track, and I wanted to make sure it stayed on the rails. I was not above sucking up to the brass to make that happen.

After a half-dozen cigars and twice that many beers, our round was nearly done. Arniel and I were tied on the eighteenth green and I needed to sink a twenty-five-foot putt to take him down. I'm not sure how I managed to stay balanced enough to drain it, but I did—and then I proceeded to run around the green and scream like an idiot about how clutch I was. It was during my victory lap that teammate Jimmy Roy drove up to our group in his cart.

"Prongs, where is your phone?"

"Battery's dead, Jimmy."

"Your wife's looking for you; she's called me three or four times already."

Oh, shit. "What happened?" (And, more importantly, how does she have your number?)

"How the hell should I know, I'm not your secretary."

I borrowed Chipman's phone and called the Mrs.

"Hey babe, what's up?"

"Have you talked to Pat today?"

"No, I've been drinking, smoking cigars, and playing golf all day. In that order."

"Well, superstar, try to keep your phone on next time. You just got picked off waivers by the Columbus Blue Jackets."

"What! How is that even possible?"

"I don't know, call Pat."

Pat filled me in on his negotiations with the Islanders. Since the Islanders had no intention of signing me, he'd asked the club for my outright release. It was only May at the time, so a release would give us a head start in the free-agent market because most of the other players were signed until July 1. The Islanders agreed and released me, so all I had to do was clear waivers to be home free. Didn't happen. Somehow, I was still available when Columbus had a crack to pluck me off the wire—and they did.

While I was upset that I wouldn't be going back to Winnipeg, I was also pretty excited to get another shot at the NHL.

It's funny sometimes how the game and life work out. It seems the man who insisted that Columbus pick me up after the Islanders dumped me was one of their higher-ups in scouting, a man by the name of Bob Strumm. The same Bob Strumm who, as the general manager of the Las Vegas Thunder in 1994, had put a bullet in me at the end of training camp. From executioner to saviour. Karma, baby.

I guess I hadn't played all that poorly back in Vegas after all.

10

SLAVA BLACKSOCKS AND THE YO-YO YEAR

So. It turned out I *did* still have an NHL career.

I must admit, there were times when I thought my charter-plane days were over, and I was almost OK with that. Almost. You spend your whole life trying to get to the next level, trying to get a little bit better. But that can't go on forever. Everyone has to plateau at some point. I look at guys who've signed multi-year, multi-million dollar contracts, and a lot of them seem to lose their appetite for going into the corners, or for blocking shots, or whatever. People say those guys are lazy. And I'm sure that's part of it. But only part. I think a bigger part is that they worked for years to get as far as they could, and once they figure they've gone as far as they can, once it stops being a challenge to see how far they can go, it starts being a job.

My point is that money is only part of the reason why guys want to play professional hockey. The challenge is a huge part of it. Once you think you've reached the highest point you will ever reach, you begin to approach hockey differently. Obviously, you think about what you *could* have differently from what you *won't* have. I was beginning to think that I'd had my run in the NHL.

So to get another shot at the big time was a welcome surprise. Just when I thought it was over, I packed my bags for Columbus. For those of you keeping score at home, the Blue Jackets was NHL organization number six.

I remember walking into the Blue Jackets locker room a few days before camp. Surprisingly, I didn't know that many guys. When you play for as many teams as I did the over/under is around five former teammates. I knew two. Mike Sillinger, whom I'd played with in Anaheim, and Tyler Wright from my Pittsburgh days. Sillinger was a thirty-year-old man who looked like he was forty and acted like he was twenty. (I'm quoting him, by the way.) He was one of those guys you couldn't help but like because he was always such an affable dude. Columbus was organization number eight for Silly and it would be far from his last stop. And he was not afraid to make light of the fact that he was so well-travelled. He was a great guy, a great teammate, and someone I looked up to. He had made a tour of the Western and Eastern Conference teams and still kept his sense of humour. Move over, Gretzky, I had a new idol!

When I played with Tyler Wright in Pittsburgh, Coach Kevin Constantine had him anchoring the fourth line on a team that only played three. He played sixty-one games that season and finished with zero goals, zero assists while averaging about two minutes of ice time per game. The following season, with Constantine still the coach, he started in the minors. And as soon as Constantine was fired, the Big Pens recalled Tyler; he went on to have a breakout year. In the summer the Columbus Blue Jackets took him in the expansion draft. In his first season he was an instant hit and quickly became a fan favourite. His story gave guys like me reason to believe and keep the faith that a break would eventually come. Journeymen always need to know there's still a chance and that we just need to be in the right place at the right time.

When you're the new guy it's always nice to have a few familiar faces around to settle the nerves. The only problem was that neither had arrived at training camp yet. As I was standing at the front of the locker room trying to figure out where to put my gear without pissing off any real veterans (looking and acting like a rookie, I might add), Lyle Odelein walked up to introduce himself. Lyle was the captain of the Blue Jackets.

"Prongs, welcome aboard. Put your equipment wherever you want, most of the guys won't be here for a couple days. Let me know if you need anything."

It was always an unsettling feeling walking into a locker room for the first time. And it can be even more unsettling when you're a player who spent the past two years in the minors. I was a bit intimidated being back in an NHL room and maybe a little embarrassed that I hadn't been in one for quite some time. So, as you can imagine, Lyle's words were definitely comforting. The fact that he knew who I was and took the time to walk over and introduce himself meant a lot.

There's no question that I knew who he was. Anyone who's watched the game has seen the heavy hitters on his dance card. He was typical of many tough guys in hockey in that he was really nice and approachable. Nothing like the animal he could turn into on the ice.

Before we were to begin the on-ice portion of training camp, we had the off-ice tests to get out of the way. Off-ice tests were never one of my strong suits. It's not that I didn't train hard or spend a lot of time in the gym in the summer. I put in the work and then some. It's just that I was never the fastest or the strongest guy on my team. I tested OK, but was never at the top of the list with the genetically gifted freaks. Good thing they never picked teams from the weight room.

For some teams, off-ice testing is not a big deal. However, it's been my experience that the worse a team finishes during the previous season the more off-ice testing there will be. The fact that Columbus had been in the league only a couple years made me think we might not see the ice for a while.

At my first training camp in Columbus we had to complete a timed two-mile run for one of our off-ice fitness tests. I remember stretching with the rest of the team when an SUV rolled up and dropped off another player. A Russian. You know how I could tell this dude was Russian without knowing his name or hearing him speak? Well, he was pimping black dress socks with white jogging shoes and the old-school running shorts. He might as well have had the Russian flag draped around his shoulders. He had literally just landed from the motherland and taken a ride to the track.

When the whistle blew, our new Russian friend bolted out of the blocks and proceeded to crush everyone in attendance. It wasn't even close.

I found out from a reliable source that Columbus management discovered this guy in Russia and they thought he would take the league by storm.

The only thing that held me back from suckering the guy was that Slava Blacksocks was a defenceman. The one thing I didn't need was more competition at forward. It's tough enough to win a job at camp. It's even tougher when management has its heart (and sometimes reputation) set on a guy.

Slava's story was that he played in the Russian League for a couple of years, although looking at him, it could have been a couple of decades. I always found it tough gauging the age of some of my Russian teammates. They could look forty but only be twenty-five. Or they could look twenty-two and actually be thirty-five with a doctored passport that said they were twenty-eight.

Turns out the Blue Jackets' brain trust decided it would be a good idea to shell out a hundred grand just to lure Mr. Blacksocks to training camp. I mean, are you kidding me? One hundred thousand dollars just to attend camp? Did they have to lure him away from his ten-million-dollar deal in the Hawaiian Co-ed Nude League? He was playing in Russia, for goodness sakes. And this was way before the KHL started handing out its ridiculous contracts, so there was no way he was making much jack back home. I would have thought a plane ticket, a hotel room, a few meals, and a chance to play in the NHL would have been enough. Nope. I was back to wanting to sucker the guy.

The cherry on the sundae is that at the end of one of the on-ice training sessions that camp I overheard one of the scouts tell Tyler Wright that our secret Russian had a drop shot. Yes, you read that correctly. A drop shot. Who did they think this guy was, Nikolay Davydenko? I almost crashed into the boards when I heard that. I even clarified the scout's statement with a laughing Tyler Wright.

Blacksocks should have had it made. Management had a vested interest, not to mention a financial interest, in him. He should have been a shoo-in for at least the seventh defenceman spot. When you think about it, he didn't have to do anything good at camp; he just had to avoid doing anything bad. But he couldn't. He played in every pre-season game and was awful in all of them. CBJ was forced to cut him and ship him to Siberia (literally) with his running shorts crammed full of dollars.

In hockey, like all sports, the cream rises to the top. If you're good enough and stick with it you'll get to the NHL. If you're a pretender, you may fool folks for a bit, but you'll end up getting exposed. Believe me, I know. I played for sixteen teams, after all. And I'm guessing you'd like to know Slava's real name. It is

SLAVA BLACKSOCKS AND THE YO-YO YEAR

Alexander Guskov, and he continues to put up pretty impressive numbers in the KHL to this day.

I was not unlike Slava that season. The Blue Jackets wanted me, and then the Blue Jackets didn't want me. The only difference was that Slava only went through it once. For me, the Columbus organization basically just hit the "repeat" button.

At the conclusion of training camp I was sent to Syracuse in the American Hockey League. "Hello AHL, it's been a couple years, did you miss me?" My disappointment at getting the tap for the fiftieth time in my career was tempered by the fact that GM Doug MacLean told me I'd be back up in no time. Of course I didn't believe him, but at least he made the effort to try to give me some hope. As it turned out, he *really* wasn't lying. He meant I'd be back and back and back....

I was sent down (and hence recalled) seven times. Yes, you read that correctly—seven times! I don't know if people can appreciate what happens when players are called up to the NHL. It's a lot more than just getting your name in the transaction section of the newspaper. Sure, sometimes the timing is perfect. You've had a couple of days between games; you're well rested with no bumps and bruises. But more often than not, the AHL and NHL schedules don't mesh that well. When your phone rings and the coach says you're getting called up, it's go time. Management doesn't care if you've just finished your third game in three nights on the farm. You have to answer the bell, because if you don't any number of other guys will jump at the opportunity, and that'll be the last time your phone rings. Basically, you take your chance when you get it.

For instance, I was in Syracuse (Columbus's AHL affiliate) and we were playing at home. For some strange reason I got in the way of a slapshot and it nailed me right in the foot. I iced it after the game, but when I woke up the next day my foot was still killing me. The swelling never went down, so I was sent to the hospital for X-rays. While I was sitting in the waiting room to get the tests my phone rang. It was Gary Agnew, my head coach with the Syracuse Crunch.

"Sean, Columbus just called. They want to bring you up. I told them your foot may be broken and you were at the hospital getting an X-ray. Did you get the results yet?"

I didn't know what to do. Basically, I had two options. One was to tell them that I hadn't had the X-ray yet. Although going that route I ran the risk of my foot actually being broken, which would terminate the call-up. The other option was to say that everything was OK and just pray that the foot wasn't broken.

What would you have done?

Yeah, me too. I walked out of the waiting room.

"Gary, I had my X-ray, it's all good. What time's my flight?"

As it turned out, my flight out of Syracuse was only a few days before my flight back to Syracuse. And no, my foot wasn't broken.

As much as the odd call-up to the NHL can be challenging, let's be honest—the real challenge is the re-assignment to the minors. Let's see if I can sum it up in one long run-on sentence. You go from the Big Apple to the crab apple, from a first-class seat on a charter to one seat removed from the urinal on the Greyhound, from the Phoenician Resort to the Ramada Resort, from Morton's to Chili's, and—perhaps most importantly—from an NHL salary to minor league pay. Of course, there's a big adjustment on the ice as well. Instead of playing five minutes a night, it's suddenly twenty minutes of ice time. And with that comes the expectation that you're going to do a little more than just warm up the backup goalie at the end of the morning skate. There is a bit of a re-entry period for players who have been in the NHL for a while and then get sent back to the minors. Many times these players are depressed because of the demotion and then go out and play without their hearts or their heads in the game. I've even known coaches in the AHL who have scratched a returning player in his first game back because they knew they wouldn't get a good performance from the guy. The whole re-assignment process can definitely be a big mindbender for the player because of the culture shock of going from first class to no class. I can't begin to tell you all of the differences between life in the NHL and life in the minors. The gap is so wide in so many areas that it's not even funny. Well, maybe it's a little funny.

Travel is at the top of the list. Once you experience first class in "the show," the charter flights alone should be motivation enough to never get sent down again. In the AHL the preferred mode of transportation is what's commonly referred to as the "iron lung." That's right, first class on Air Greyhound. And if you're a rookie, well, you get to sit next to your favourite six-foot-four Western Leaguer who thinks he's riding a Harley-Davidson. Thankfully, I was a slight six-foot-three centreman who loved to travel with his knees in his chest and listen to the sweet sound of some farm boy snoring in my ear for six short hours. What's even more awesome when you're a rookie? Well, at the end of each road trip guess who gets to clean the bus? I'll let you in on a little secret: hockey players are not that neat and tidy. After a week on the ol' bone-rattler you find discarded food, congealed pop, half-eaten candy, flat beer, well-chewed tobacco, and a whole lot of other disgusting crap. Once the bus is cleaned, the rooks get the privilege of unloading all of the wonderfully aromatic hockey gear that was seasoning under the bus for a handful of hours.

Don't get me wrong; travelling in the NHL has its difficulties for rookies too. I mean, you have to hang up the veterans' coats on all of the charter flights. And it's never easy cramming yourself into a first-class seat. The real work begins when the flight lands—there's the difficulty of carrying your designer bags down a flight of stairs before handing them off to a bus driver who makes you walk at least twelve paces to get to the bus. Then there's the hardship of your equipment finding its way to the arena and hanging itself up.

And then there's the issue of food. The Rangers plane was by far my favourite. Ground service (yes, they feed you before take-off) consisted of shrimp cocktail, smoked salmon, filet mignon sliders, cheese and crackers, a selection of fruit, and countless other bits and bites. Once in the air the hot meal would be served, always with a choice of three items. You know the drill: steak, chicken, or an awesome fish dish. And dessert could be warm apple pie topped with ice cream or a warm chocolate brownie topped with ice cream or several warm chocolate chip cookies topped with ice cream. Hell, you could have ice cream topped with ice cream.

Things aren't so "fat and happy" in the minors. Each player is given a per diem; when I played it was $38 to $40 a day. (In the NHL per diem is $85 to $90 a day. Players get an envelope with their cash in it at the start of the trip, which is highly convenient when you're looking for gambling money on the first flight.) Because you're not getting served a meal on a flight after the game you have to place your order with the trainers before the puck is dropped. On a table in the locker room will be a menu. Think local pizza joint or mom-and-pop diner with pub food. There's a cup in the middle of the table where you leave your money to pay for the feast. Whatever the total of your order, it's customary to round up and add two bucks. I can tell you that in my ten years of playing, we somehow came up short *every single time*. I'm pretty sure some of the Euros thought it was an ATM.

Now keep in mind that nutrition is probably even more important in the minors than it is in the NHL. If you're on the road in the minors that often means three games in two and a half days. Throw in the lack of proper rest because of the mode of transportation used, and you can see why eating well would be so key to maintaining a high energy level. The problem is, it's not easy to eat well on the farm so you have to eat smart. If you were a rookie, I'd bet my last dollar that a "Ray Ferraro" would be your choice. (Ferraro is synonymous with chicken parmesan, because that's all he ate at the ESPN cafeteria when he worked at the network as an analyst. Ferraro ate the meal so many days in a row it earned him the nickname "Chicken Parm.") Not smart. The kids forget that the order is placed five to six hours before the meal is going to be consumed. Plus, the order is being placed with a restaurant that probably has some association with the home team, so it's probable the Iron (Lung) Chefs won't go out of their way to make sure your food is warm. Or cooked. It's not easy trying to eat cold chicken parm on your lap with a plastic knife and fork on a bus doing 70 mph. Here's some advice for the rookies: order what the veterans order. A smart vet will order pizza. Simple to eat, relatively neat, and good hot or cold. Another veteran move is to order a couple of turkey subs. He'll eat one right after the game and save the other for about the four-hour mark of the trip. And then there's the grizzled vet who orders his turkey subs with the condiments on the side so his sandwich doesn't get soggy. Hey, we're not all ass and biceps in the minors. We have brains too.

Travel and food are not the only differences between the two leagues. I'm sure this comes as no surprise, but the hotel chains are at opposite ends of the Star Rating System. In the East Coast League think Super 8 and Days Inn. In the American League it's Ramada and lower-end Marriotts. And in the NHL, you get to stay in the Ritz-Carlton or Four Seasons. My favourite hotel was the Pan Pacific in Vancouver. Not only is it a great hotel in a great location, but the pre-game meal is unbelievable. To go along with the usual chicken and steak, they offered beautifully cooked fresh salmon. It makes my mouth water just thinking about it.

I mentioned proper rest a couple of paragraphs back. That's crucial no matter what league you're playing in. And to be honest, you can get worn down even if you're flying first class and staying in five-star hotels. Back-to-back games can be tough. (At least that's what I'm told. I averaged five minutes a game in the NHL, so I probably could have played forty nights in a row and not been physically tired.) The flight to the next city leaves after the game, and depending what conference you're in that means anywhere from a midnight to 4 a.m. arrival at the hotel. The worst cities are Edmonton and Denver, because you have to tack on a forty-five-minute bus ride to or from the airport. Yes, those two cities are in the Western Conference, and having played in both the East and the West there's no question which conference takes more of a toll on your body.

On the second half of back-to-back games, the coach will usually make the morning skate optional, since he doesn't want his regulars wearing themselves out. For a bubble boy like I was, there was no such thing as an optional practice. My fellow journeymen and I refer to those skates as "mandatory optional." You're always free to skip practice if you don't mind being sent down.

In the minors, road trips are far more taxing. Since the owners of the teams try to maximize their gate, the majority of games are on Thursday, Friday, Saturday, or Sunday. Which, to be honest, I kind of enjoyed when we were at home. On the road? Not so much. Let me offer a couple of examples from my time in Winnipeg.

Since Winnipeg is so far removed from all of the other minor-league cities, travel was challenging at best. During my second stint with them we had a game on a Thursday night in Cleveland.

Our next game, on Friday, was in Rochester. So, after the game in Cleveland, we bussed five hours to Rochester. That had us tucked into our hotel beds sometime shortly before 4 a.m. On Friday night, we played our game in Rochester and then got back on the bus. *Hello, Cleveland!* Can you believe that? Another five-hour bus ride right back to where we came from. I wonder how many cocktails deep the schedule makers were when they put that weekend together. To top it all off, Cleveland was having some sort of promotion on Saturday to attract more fans, so the start time had been moved back to noon. I'm going to take a flyer here and suggest that the promotion was conjured up sometime after the powers-that-be in Cleveland's organization saw our schedule. I remember getting to my hotel room at 3:30 a.m. and setting the alarm for 8 o'clock. There I was, trying to count on my fingers exactly how many hours of sleep I could get if I was able to fall asleep right away. Of course I couldn't. I stared at the ceiling with images of the rink burning down during the night so we wouldn't have to play later that day. I thought about the scene in *Bull Durham* where Crash Davis managed to create a rainout when the boys were having a tough time on the road. That's what the Moose needed that Saturday. A rainout—or, better yet, a burndown. If I'd had the energy to get out of bed, take a cab to the rink, douse the barn with gas, and light a match—well, I still wouldn't have. But I did think about it. And when I was done running though all that nonsense in my head it was sometime after 5 a.m. Perfect. Less than three hours' sleep before the third of three games in just over two days.

Another consideration: What exactly are you supposed to eat for a noon game? Trying to shove chicken and pasta down your neck at 8:30 in the morning is not easy. The buffet that day had oatmeal, cereal, toast, eggs, bacon, hash browns, spaghetti, and chicken. It all looked disgusting, so I settled for a coffee and donut.

As if it was going to matter. I was tired physically, out of it mentally, and sleep deprived. I kept thinking, "I'm too old for this crap." As for the game: try to picture an entire team taking twenty-second shifts. I'm sure the other coach figured we were trying to get away from his line matchups. We must've come close to setting a record for icings and pucks in the stands. Whatever we could do to slow down the game, we did. It must have gone on for four and a half hours. That's what they get for making us play at noon. I believe we lost the game 2–0. I call that a victory in my books. In the condition we were in they should've spanked us by at least a touchdown. Thankfully, only a handful of people were in the stands to witness that sorry display, and I'm pretty sure they wouldn't be coming back for another. Great marketing job, Cleveland!

One more Moose road story for you. On the schedule was a home-and-home series with Utah. Yes, that Utah. Salt Lake City is not exactly Minneapolis in its proximity to Winnipeg. But since there were only eleven teams in the league at that time, we had to travel there often—just never before for a back-to-back. Like any good rivalry, familiarity breeds contempt. So after a very physical game to start the home-and-home in Utah, we knew the game in Winnipeg was going to be really nasty. Since there were no charters in the IHL, we spent the night in Salt Lake City and headed to the airport for our commercial flight back home. Well, as you might have guessed by now, we weren't the only team that needed to get to Winnipeg that day. And if you did guess that, you're smarter than we were because we were very surprised to see our opponents from the night before sitting at the gate when we arrived. After slashing, hacking, battling, and fighting it out with the Grizzlies just ten hours prior, we would share the same aircraft to Manitoba. Since the Grizzlies got to the airport before we did they scooped up all the window and aisle seats when they checked in. And sure enough, all of us Moose players parked ourselves in the middle seats. Fortunately, the flight attendants didn't have to hand out any major penalties in the air. I think everyone was too busy laughing to think about taking a swing at someone.

As a final example of just how steep the drop-off can be, let's talk about green rooms. For those unfamiliar with a green room, it's basically where the wives, girlfriends, and families of the players go between periods and post-game. Once the game is over the players head to the green room to meet up with everyone and have a beverage or three. At Madison Square Garden the green room was unreal—you never knew who would show up for a drink. I shared a brew and a conversation with Donald Trump following one game with the Rangers.

To go from that to the boiler room at War Memorial in Syracuse is almost comical. I remember standing with my wife in the boiler room (yes it actually was the rink's boiler room, and we were standing because there were no seats) after one game with the Crunch and asking her, "Weren't we having a martini with Tim Robbins at MSG a couple of years ago?"

So, let's steer the bone-rattler back toward my first year in Columbus. Excuse me—my first year *with* Columbus. My contract with the Blue Jackets that season was a two-way deal. It paid me $400,000 at the NHL level and $125,000 in the minors, with a guarantee of $150,000 overall. Basically, I would make $125K while I was playing in Syracuse. If I didn't get called up at all to Columbus, the Blue Jackets would write me a cheque for $25K to make up for the guarantee. A clause like that helps motivate the big club to at least call you up a few times to make you earn your extra twenty-five thousand prunes.

By March 2002, I had been called up and sent down six times

that season. After some careful calculations with the abacus, I knew that I had already earned my $25,000 bonus, so any more time spent with the Blue Jackets would be gravy.

But while it had been a somewhat up and down season for me, I had nothing on my wife. She was eight months into a difficult and complicated pregnancy and had spent a good portion of the latter part of it confined to bed rest. I knew that if the phone rang that March I could be gone anywhere from a day to a month. Not a good situation to be in when your wife is a day to a month away from giving birth. Sure enough, one night the phone rang. And since it was midnight, I knew who was calling. This wasn't my first rodeo. I remember it like it was yesterday, mainly because my wife was puking while the phone was ringing.

"I'm not going to answer it."

"Sean, answer the phone."

"No. I know who it is. I don't want to go and leave you like this."

"I'm fine. Just answer the phone."

Finally, the ringing stopped. And when I checked the message, sure enough it was from my coach, Gary Agnew. Just as I thought, he said they needed me to take the first flight out of Syracuse to get to Edmonton.

I was torn. I did not want to leave my wife in a bad situation, but I also knew it would likely be my last call-up of the season. The Blue Jackets were aware of my circumstances and sympathetic to them, but they also needed a body in the lineup the next night. After some soul searching, and a little convincing from my wife that she would be all right, we decided to accept the call. We also knew that with a new member of the family on the way we could use the extra cash. Once I called Gary back at 12:30 a.m., the fun really began. I knew the routine because I had done it once before earlier in the season. It would be a 6 a.m. flight from Syracuse to Detroit. Then I'd have a two-hour layover before the flight from Detroit to Edmonton. Arrival time in Edmonton would be 3 p.m., which would give me just enough time to grab my gear and take a cab to the hotel to meet the team before the bus to the rink. Remember what I said earlier about the timing of a call-up rarely being perfect? The only decision I had to make before the AHL version of *Planes, Trains and Automobiles* was whether to sleep and pick up my gear on the way to the airport or go to the rink, pick up my gear, and try to catch a few winks before my departure. Believe me when I say it's not easy falling asleep when you know you're leaving behind an eight-months-pregnant wife. It's even tougher when that eight-months-pregnant wife can't see you to the door because she is in the bathroom hurling.

In the end, I made my way to Edmonton without incident. But the whole time I was sitting in the dressing room prior to the game all I could think about was whether I'd made the right decision. Add the fact that I was running on fumes because of the travel and about an hour of sleep, and it's shocking that I actually played a pretty solid game that night. In fact, I played so well from there on in that the Blue Jackets kept me up with the big club for the remainder of the season. Baby definitely got a new pair of shoes!

It felt good to make it to the end of a season with the same organization, regardless of the circumstances. After our final game, most of the team began the annual post-season bender at a restaurant inside the arena. However, for a handful of us the season wasn't really over. The Syracuse Crunch was just about ready to commence its playoffs in the AHL and we were being shipped in. This was the one time that season I didn't mind getting sent down. First off, the Blue Jackets flew us back on the team jet. Second, and more importantly, I was excited to keep playing. The Crunch was a great team with a legitimate shot at a championship. And while I was a low-minute grinder in Columbus, I was captain of the Crunch, was on the ice for the power play and penalty kill, and was generally part of the flow of the game in a way I seldom was in the NHL. I enjoyed playing there and I was eager to get back playing with guys I hadn't seen in a month. And I was excited to get back and re-unite with my wife. Because she was so far along in her pregnancy she wasn't able to fly to Columbus to see me. She was more than seven months pregnant and had been stranded in Syracuse for the past month. What can I say except she's a warrior and it takes a special woman to put up with the life of a journeyman.

The first round of the playoffs went according to plan. We swept the Philadelphia Phantoms in three straight games. Besides the sweep, the best part of that series was that I signed a new contract after game three. And when I say after game three I mean IN the locker room after the game before we hopped on the bus to head back to Syracuse. Another first. It was a two-year, two-way deal and I was happy to get it done before the summer and the start of round two.

In round two we were up against the Chicago Wolves, a team I was very familiar with. The year prior, when I was with the Moose, we must have played them fifteen or sixteen times. They were a good team that was very well coached. We jumped out to a 2–0 series lead after winning both of our home games. On a sour note, I injured my wrist with about five minutes to play in game two. X-rays were negative, but something was seriously wrong with it. For game three in Chicago I had the trainer tape a makeshift cast on my arm. Faceoffs were out of the question, shots were painful, and passing the puck was possible. Not ideal, but I didn't want to be pulled from the series. Besides, we were playing with confidence and seemed to be firing on all cylinders. But as any hockey player or fan knows, things can change awfully quickly in the playoffs and unfortunately for us, they did. The Crunch dropped games three and four to the Wolves, and since the series was a 2-3-2, game five was in Chicago as well. We needed to wrestle away momentum from the Wolves in game five but we didn't. A series we were once in control of was slipping away. And if the Crunch were to turn it around, it would have to be without my services. Game five was my last of the series. I got tripped in the third period and blew out my collarbone when I crashed into the boards. And I wasn't the only one on the shelf. Blake Bellefeuille and Kent McDonell joined me (that's three of our top nine forwards) in the press box for game six. The boys showed a lot of heart in game six and blew out the Wolves 6–0 to force a game seven. The tank must have been empty after that one, however, because the Wolves, led by Rob Brown, Steve Maltais, and Pasi Nurminen, would not be denied in game seven. Our season was done. If you lose in the playoffs you always want to lose to the eventual champions, and that season we can say we did.

Let's take a moment to reflect on the last twelve months. I was claimed off waivers as I was drunk and running around the eighteenth green doing the bull dance. I signed an NHL contract with organization number six. I managed to claw my way back to the show. I was called up and sent down seven times. I was named captain of the Syracuse Crunch and helped them to a record-setting regular season, winning both our division and conference. I signed a new two-year contract *before* the season ended. As far as the elder Pronger boy goes, that all adds up to a highly successful season. And the year was about to get much better, as I could focus solely on the birth of our first child. Icing on the cake to say the least.

Our original due date was May 11. I'm not sure how the hell

they can pin down the exact date, but then again I never went to gynecology school. Well, we passed our due date—going into overtime, so to speak. Our OB thought the baby had been in the nest long enough and recommended we get induced. We checked into the hospital on Monday, May 13. This felt kind of weird. In the movies, whenever I saw people about to have a child they were always frantically looking for their overnight bag they forgot to pack while scrambling to find the car keys so they could get to the hospital in time for the birth. This was more businesslike and definitely more surreal. As we were walking into the hospital it occurred to me that the next time I walked through those doors I would be a father. That was the plan, at least.

We had a C-section scheduled for the morning of Tuesday, May 14. Since we had to spend Monday night at the hospital, I had some time to kill. Luckily the NHL playoffs took my mind off things for a few hours. I watched Colorado force a game seven in their series with the Sharks while I waited for our lives to change. I had set up a couple chairs in the hospital room as a makeshift bed. I wasn't planning on sleeping that much, but I wanted at least the option to catch some winks. I'm not sure what time I dozed off, but the night nurse woke me a little past midnight. She came in quietly to check the fetal heart monitor. For some reason it was showing that the baby's heart rate was dropping. She was looking to see if maybe the monitor had slipped off my wife's belly. She seemed so calm that I wasn't alarmed. After she realized the monitor was in place, she made a quick phone call and instantly our hospital room was filled with people. I still wasn't alarmed. This was my first kid, my first birth. I figured this was just how it's done. I remember standing next to my wife when the doctor informed us that this baby was coming out *now*. She said the baby had dropped on the umbilical cord and we needed to get the baby out right away. Awesome! Let's do this, I still wasn't alarmed. Everyone seemed so calm. The doctors wheeled my wife out of the room and were running down the hall with her. Somehow, I still wasn't worried. I remember thinking to myself, "These guys don't mess around." I was impressed. It wasn't until they were about to wheel my wife into surgery that I realized something was wrong. In one of the few childbirth classes that I had been able to attend, the instructor explained to us that if there's ever an emergency they remove the father from the room. They don't want any distractions. As I was about to enter the emergency room, a nurse put her hand on my chest and said "You'll have to wait out here." My heart was in my throat. I looked at my wife and saw a tear roll down her cheek. Now I was panicked. It was 1 a.m. and there was absolutely no one around. All hands were on deck. Even the nurse at the front desk was gone. I raced back to our room to call my in-laws, who were at our house. I told them the baby's coming now so they better find their way to the hospital in a hurry. I didn't know what to say other than that—or perhaps I was just afraid to tell them there may be complications.

My wife was in the emergency room for sixteen minutes. Those minutes were like hours. No one was coming out. No one was telling me what the hell was going on. I was sitting out there with no idea what was happening in that emergency room. Finally, the desk nurse came out. And she walked right past me. I could barely hold it together.

"What is going on in there? Is everything all right?"

She calmly said, "Your wife is fine."

"And…?" I shouted.

"The doctor will speak with you in a minute," was all she said.

I was so freaked out and so pissed off I nearly grabbed her by the jacket. As I was trying to figure out what to do one of the doctors came out and pulled me aside.

"Sean, your wife is fine but your daughter—well, we did the best we could, but she was without oxygen for fifteen minutes. Again, we did the best we could."

I couldn't process what she was saying to me. I didn't know if the news she was delivering was the worst possible.

"What are you saying? Is she alive?"

"Sean, she was without oxygen for too long. We have the best surgical team in the area. They got your daughter out in less than fourteen minutes. She's still alive, but ... I don't know how to say this ... it might be best if she doesn't make it."

"What are you saying? There's no chance? She has a chance? Tell me there's a chance."

"Sean, she's alive, but since she was without oxygen for so long I fear she will be severely brain damaged."

"Is that for certain? Are you saying she has no chance of being a normal kid?"

In a matter of minutes, my little family had been whisked from the contented excitement of the hours before a scheduled C-section to a nightmare in which I was faced with only two possible outcomes: a dead child, or a child who would never grow to experience all the things I had hoped for her. I couldn't believe there was no third possibility.

"I don't know. She's going to be taken up to the NICU, the neonatal intensive care unit. They'll monitor her there."

As I was about to say something in reply, they wheeled out my daughter in an incubator. She looked so perfect. She looked so healthy. She looked like I had imagined. I just couldn't believe that she might not make it. And then it occurred to me that my wife had no idea what had just happened. Since it was an emergency surgery they had to knock her out, and now she was just coming to. Try telling your wife that the child she's been carrying around for the past ten months is more than likely going to die—and if she doesn't die, she's going to be brain damaged.

They put my wife in a recovery room as I watched the nurses take my daughter up to NICU. How was I going to tell her? How do I explain where our daughter is? Isn't the baby supposed to be resting comfortably with her mother?

My wife was still pretty much out of it when I walked into her room. She looked at me and tried to lift her head and smile, but she was still too drugged and too tired. I explained to her what happened. She was in no condition to comprehend what was going on. All she kept saying was, "I don't understand, I don't understand." I decided to leave it alone until she was properly rested. I was so beside myself I started to think of the weirdest things. I kept thinking about what I would tell people. All our friends and family knew we were having the baby today. Usually when you go in for a childbirth you end up with a child. That's just the way it works. I didn't know what I was going to tell them.

"Hi … we had a daughter but she didn't make it." I wasn't going to do that to people. I couldn't bring myself to accept that possibility.

Originally, I was going to wait to go see Kaia (that's what we named her) with my wife, but after sitting around going out of my mind I decided to go see for myself.

Walking into an NICU is not for the faint of heart. It is a heart-wrenching place to be and even worse if your child is in there. There were kids (and parents) who had spent months in there. I found a nurse and asked where the Pronger baby was. She directed me to the area that's for the most at-risk babies. I walked over and introduced myself to the nurse. Then I saw my beautiful daughter. She had a ventilator down her throat and both hands were strapped down so she couldn't tug on the ventilator. It was all I could do to not break down right there. She was so tiny, so perfect, and looked so incredibly normal. After I composed myself, I looked the nurse square in the eye and asked her, "What are the chances of our baby surviving? And if she survives, is there any chance she won't have brain damage?"

"Mr. Pronger, we don't know what's going to happen. We need to take this one hour at a time. We need her to get through the first twenty-four hours without having a seizure. If she has a seizure that's an indication there is something wrong."

"And if she doesn't have a seizure?"

"Then we'll try to get through the next twenty-four hours."

"OK. I need you to be completely honest with me and tell me exactly how she's progressing. Don't sugarcoat anything."

"Mr. Pronger, we can't give any false hope up here. We'll tell it to you exactly how it is."

Even though nothing had changed, I felt a little better about her chances. We were just going to take it one day at a time. The old hockey cliché. My wife felt better in the morning, so I wheeled her up to see her daughter for the first time. I didn't think I had any tears left but cried like a baby at that reunion. I was emotionally spent and it had only been twelve hours since the birth.

Over the next several days Kaia made remarkable progress. In the morning after her birth, the nurses removed one of the straps on her wrist and she immediately tried to pull out the ventilator. So they took that out. My wife had to take it easy because she'd just had major surgery, so I was back and forth from NICU to her recovery room checking on both my girls.

On day four of Kaia's time in NICU we were informed that the doctor who had delivered her was going to do an evaluation. Since she was progressing rapidly, they told us that if she passed these tests there was a good chance we could take her home in a couple days. The doctor performed what are called "innate" tests; they measure the things that all babies should be able to do at birth. Rub her cheek and she should turn her head toward your hand, that sort of thing. My wife and I nervously watched the doctor perform a number of these tests. After she was finished, she looked at us and said, "Mr. and Mrs. Pronger, if I wasn't the one who pulled your daughter out I would never believe this was the same kid. I think she's going to be fine and you can take her home tomorrow."

To go from the deepest, darkest place I've ever been in my life to a feeling of such utter relief and joy was almost too much to handle. All the Stanley Cup championships in the world couldn't possibly have held a candle to that day. It was, by far, the greatest day of my life. To be that close to losing a child and then told that all is good and she's in the clear is the most magical feeling in the world.

I sometimes think about how close we came to losing our daughter. So many things had to happen for her to be with us today. If we weren't already in the hospital when my wife's water broke and Kaia's head came down on the umbilical cord (just like stepping on a garden hose), there's no way she would have made it. If we weren't at Crouse Hospital—a facility equipped for high-risk births—there is no way she would have made it because no surgical team would have been on site. I don't think she would have made it. I'm happy to report that at the time of writing this chapter, Kaia is a beautiful, bright, and happy ten-year-old and we haven't had one indication that there was or ever will be an issue with her brain activity.

Prior to Kaia's birth, as you've read, I was always a stress case when it came to my hockey career. But that experience changed me. I realized what's important and what's not. My career was important, but it wasn't the only thing in my life and I knew that I had something more important waiting for me at home. I had a beautiful wife and a happy, healthy daughter who didn't care if I was scratched, benched, or waived. She was just glad to see Daddy—and man, was I glad to see her.

"The world rewards those who show up." It's my favourite saying, and there is no more appropriate slogan for the journeymen of hockey. If you hang in there long enough, good things will happen. Mind you, it may only be for a day or three.

Take my second camp with the Blue Jackets, for instance. I had played twenty-six games with the organization the year before, putting up a grand total of four points. It's never a good thing when your point total with a team is three fewer than the number of times you're sent down to its minor league affiliate.

For the first part of training camp, being away from the rink meant hanging in Summerside, Prince Edward Island. That's right, baby—the Blue Jackets took their show on the road! Doug MacLean, our general manager and fearless leader at the time, grew up in Summerside. So he decided to bring the entire team to the Island for the week. Why? Well, call it a form of Maritime nepotism. We had a mitt full of Prince Edward Islanders in the Blue Jackets organization. The assistant GM, Jim Clark, was a childhood friend of MacLean's. Gerard Gallant, the assistant coach, was from PEI. Ditto our PR man, Jim Rankin. And yes, our broadcast team, too. One player, David Ling, was from the Island. Another, Grant Marshall, now lives there. If I knew then what I know now, I would have moved to PEI in the summer, which would have made me a shoo-in to be named captain. But you know what? I can hardly blame MacLean. If I were a GM of a team and had the use of a private jet, every training camp for my team would take place in Dryden, Ontario.

So there we were in PEI. Might as well experience my annual disappointment in a new part of the world. I'd never been humiliated in the Maritimes before.

Now, you should realize that not all players share my view of training camp.

For instance, training camp for my brother and players of his ilk? That is, guys with roster spots long ago sewn up? That's what I never got to experience. A decent skate in the morning followed by a relaxing off-ice workout at noon. Maybe a conversation with other millionaire teammates about how the season is shaping up. Then maybe play some golf with a few teammates before a nice steak and a bottle of grape. Go to bed. Get up and repeat. Not much stress on the body or the mind.

It's a little different for the high draft pick or good prospect. I'm not saying they aren't nervous or there isn't pressure on them. In fact, I'm sure that for an eighteen-year-old kid just out of junior, going from playing against boys to suiting up against grown men, life at camp may seem hard. But I'm here to tell you it's not. Most have a mid- to high-six-figure signing bonus burning a hole in their pocket. Most are going to get the benefit of the doubt at camp, play in almost all of the pre-season games, and have every opportunity to make the team. Sure, they sweat. Sure, they may have to read uncharitable things written about them in the papers. Sure, they may have butterflies in their guts when they hit the ice. But what they don't see are all the doors management is quietly keeping open for them behind the scenes.

You see, the thinkers who draft these guys are the same people who decide whether they make the team. They *want* them to succeed. General managers want to prove that they picked the right guy. How could a GM possibly be objective in training camp about a kid he picked a couple of months ago at the draft? He already thinks the kid is great—otherwise he wouldn't have picked him. And the moment he picked him, he staked his own reputation, with the fans and with his own boss, on the promise that the kid can deliver. So you can bet he's going to give the kid every opportunity to deliver.

And he'd prefer if the kid were ready to play now. Remember, the worst teams pick the best players. So it only makes sense that a GM (whose butt may be on the line) wants to see his team improve as quickly as possible. He is well aware that a young star and an improving team can bring fans to the gate. In other words, he won't just look good if the kid does well and does well soon, he'll also make money. That's plenty of incentive to rush young guys into action before they're ready. Any GM will tell you that guys fresh out of junior shouldn't be playing in the NHL. And the same guys will tell you that their eighteen-year-old is an exception. It generally does no good for the individual or the team—the minors and the European leagues are full of first-round picks who didn't work out, many of them because they were rushed into the NHL and lost their confidence. The trainers' rooms are full of spindly eighteen-year-olds worn out from being tossed around by bigger, stronger veterans who make a living coming out of the corner with the puck. Forcing young, high draft picks into the starting roster is just a terrible idea. But if there's one thing you can count on every autumn, it's a GM forcing a high draft pick into the starting roster.

It also doesn't help the journeyman who's being pushed aside to make room for the kid. The grinder on the two-way contract has been working his tail off all summer so that he can show up at camp in mid-season form in the slim hope there's even a mathematical possibility of making the team. He's ready to play. He's ready to fight for a spot.

So to see that spot handed to an eighteen-year-old millionaire is a real kick in the groin.

Maybe I'm just bitter, but it was tough year after year to get clipped sometime during camp because a team wanted to showcase its golden boy even though Goldie wasn't ready for prime time yet.

As camp began, I was doing my usual training camp math.

Three returning fourth-liners
+
Two free-agent signings
+
Four prospects with a chance
+
Two draft picks
=
Not great odds for me

Especially since Columbus had the number one overall draft pick that summer. You may have heard of him—a Southern Ontario kid by the name of Rick Nash. Great, I thought. The team is going to waste a roster spot on this spoiled brat.

Well, I was right about one thing. Nash was going to get a roster spot. But I was wrong to assume he wouldn't deserve it. And wrong to think he was a brat. After watching Rick in his first practice I could tell this kid wasn't going anywhere.

As much as I wanted to hate him and all his talent, it was impossible not to like him. He acted the way every young player should when they come to their first training camp. He was quiet, respectful, and let his game do the talking. We were doing a shootout drill at the end of one practice and it was Nash's turn. He came down and instead of deking the goalie with a classic forehand to backhand move he added a little variation. While he had the puck on his forehand he rolled his wrists so that the puck was on the back part of the blade and dragged across his body so that now he had the puck on his backhand and then roofed it. He did it so effortlessly that the move looked easy. I looked up in the stands at GM MacLean; he looked like a proud father as he was high-fiving his scouting staff. After everyone left the ice and management were out of the stands I tried to do the "Nash" move. I will say it's not as easy as he made it look and leave it at that.

Adding to my woes that September was the fact that MacLean brought in a big centreman from Finland by the name of Lasse Pirjeta. He looked like the real deal from the get-go. There went another spot. The odds of me starting the season in Syracuse were getting better by the minute and training camp had just begun.

Making matters worse was the fact that there wasn't much to do in Summerside but stress over my predicament. Don't get me wrong. The people of Prince Edward Island are great. However, you know that saying "I spent a month of my life there that week"? That's what it felt like to me. There wasn't much to do but drink and fish. Granted, those are two of my favourite pastimes, but I try to keep the fishing to a minimum during training camp.

The pre-season was relatively uneventful, with the exception being I got into a pretty good dust-up in Nashville with Clark Wilm. I didn't know him personally but I'd played against him before. He was a solid role player. He was responsible defensively, good on faceoffs, a strong penalty killer, and wasn't afraid to drop the mitts every now and then. Now, no one ever accused me of being president of the Mensa club, Columbus Chapter, but I knew the best time to attempt to beat someone up is late in camp. That way the tilt is fresh on everyone's mind when decisions have to be made. Guess where the Nashville game was on the pre-season schedule?

Yep. Final game. Before the game started I had no premeditated plans of dropping the gloves that night. If it happened, so be it. But in warm-up, as we were skating around I glanced over at Nashville's side and happened to lock eyes with Wilm. We stared at each other a little longer than normal and then went about our warm-up. The seed must've been planted, because during the game, as luck would have it, we ended up battling for the puck in the corner. One thing led to another and away we went. It seemed so natural. Nothing was said but the gloves just flew off at the same time. Now that I think of it, he may have had to send the same statement to his team. As a journeyman, dropping the gloves once in a while is something you need to be willing to do. You need to bring something to the table that the coaching staff can see. Lord knows I wasn't going to impress a coach with my offensive prowess. But I was by no means a fighter. It was hard for me. Unlike my ill-tempered brother, it just wasn't in my nature. I wasn't one of those guys who could just go out and fight someone for no good reason. For me to throw down, the guy had to do something nasty to a teammate or I had to have been in an ugly mood. I'm not sure why, but I got in more fights after my daughter was born. Perhaps I wasn't as scared to get filled in. On this occasion, however, I was just trying to make a solid impression on the organization.

We had the day off after our last game. There were a few of us left that were cutting-room-floor material, so we hit a local establishment for some lunch and a few cups to take our minds off what we felt would be the inevitable "tap" the next morning. Matt Davidson, Radim Bicanek, and I sat there for most of the afternoon drinking and crunching the numbers to see if there was any way we could all make it. Deep down, we knew better. At the very most one of us would make it. More than likely, we would be seeing each other in Crunch uniforms.

Here's the heart-wrenching thing about being a journeyman. Competing for that one (maybe) spot are all the guys you played with in the minors the year before. The guys you battled with, fought for, drank beside, and took twelve-hour bus rides with. The fellas you kept in touch with all summer long to talk about who signed where, who got hurt, and who retired. Your teammates. And unless you're able to go out and grab that one (maybe) elusive spot, they would be your teammates again. These are your friends in the game and now you have to go out and kick the shit out of them to try to fight for a spot that probably wasn't there. Awesome. But that's the way it is. A guy who slew-foots me in an intra-squad game one day will be jumping someone who does that to me the next day. Think of it this way—the guy you want on your team is the last guy you want to battle for the last spot on your team.

I have to say it was a weird feeling sitting there hoping I would stick, knowing full well if that happened the two guys I was having brews with would be shot and sent down. I mean, I hoped they played well, and I hoped they made the team, just so long as they didn't take my spot! It's not easy dealing with the reality of the situation. I guess that's why we needed the liquid companionship to go with the human companionship.

I realize it all sounds like a game when I talk about it this way. But understand that this was our life. The decision could mean the difference between 75 grand and 450 grand. That's nearly half a million dollars riding on the way someone feels about the way you played in camp. That's huge dough for anyone—it's a fortune for guys who've been riding the buses. The future of your family is literally in someone else's hands at that moment. And that guy is not thinking about what's best for your family; he's thinking about what's best for the team. It's not just stressful waiting to see whether you made the team. It's also humbling.

And it's not only the money. The decision you're waiting for makes a huge impact on where you would be setting up camp with your family. Where a player's kids go to school may not be something fans or management care about, but players are like any other parents—imagine it's the middle of September and you can't tell your kids what school they're going to. Bottom line, it was a big deal. A huge deal.

We finished our lunch around 7 p.m. and decided the best decision we could make was to go back to the hotel and get some rest. After all, there were no direct flights from Columbus to Syracuse.

Cut day can be a weird day. And it's made even more bizarre if it's combined with a practice day. I remember wondering if I should put on the gear or just sit and wait for the news. If I put on my equipment I was running the risk of having to take it all off if I got called in to see the coach. That wouldn't be embarrassing at all.

Before I could make my decision I noticed that one by one the "hotel boys" were getting the tap. Everyone in the room pretended not to notice the procession to and from the coach's room. It can be very uncomfortable to catch the eye of a guy who just got his dream crushed. Believe me, I've gotten the sympathy look a million times after taking the bullet.

As I was wasting time wandering around the room sweating, Matt Davidson made his way out of the executioner's room.

"How'd it go in there, Davy?"

"The usual, you had a good camp stuff, but blah blah blah."

"Sorry buddy. Maybe I should just go in there and get it over with?"

"I don't think so."

"Why?"

"I saw the lines for practice on the board and you're on one."

211

I'm not sure if there's a face you can make that combines "I'm sorry" and "I'm ecstatic." But if there is, my mug was contorted into it at that moment. I was starting the season at the NHL level. Miracles do happen.

For only the second time in my career I got to participate in all that goes on prior to the opening of the NHL season. Silly, I know, but I was jacked. All the stuff that guys took for granted I got to do. I had to get my picture taken for the program, record a video spot for the JumboTron, tape sound bites for the radio, and conduct interviews with the various television and print outlets. I felt like someone who belonged.

The on-ice preparations continued as well. Line combinations were being solidified and our power-play and penalty-killing units were being formed. The intensity level certainly picked up after training camp ended and the season drew near. The coaching staff set their expectations for the season. For C-Bus that year it was certainly not "Stanley Cup or bust." We were still a relatively new team in the league, so our Stanley Cup dream was qualifying for the playoffs.

The beginning of the season carries a lot of hope for a lot of teams. It also carries a lot of hope for players. Some of us are trying to re-establish ourselves in the league, while others are trying to prove that they belong. For Rick Nash, it was about proving to everyone he was worthy of being a first-overall draft pick. Personally, I had given up on trying not to like him for taking up a roster spot I had pegged for myself. As I got to know him and saw how he carried himself I realized that he wasn't taking one of my spots. It was his spot. It was always his spot. And it was going to be his spot for a long, long time. Over the course of his rookie season I got to know Rick pretty well. My wife and I would have him over for dinner at least once a week. He was only eighteen at the time; I remember what I was capable of when I was his age, and it wasn't much. Rick and I also sat beside each other in the locker room *and* on the plane. I'm surprised he didn't turn out to be an angry young man after all those hours sitting beside a jaded journeyman!

An eighteen-year-old superstar in the making is just the kind of player who every thug and pest and fourth-liner wants to take a run at. Apart from running their goalie, taking liberties with the other team's prized wonderboy is about the easiest way to get them off their game. Plus, it may be a little more fun to drop the boom on a top draft pick than just about anyone else. If the golden boy is on your team, of course, the opposite is true. Nash was exactly the player you don't want anyone taking advantage of. In any case, with a guy like that around, it's easy to predict how trouble starts.

We were playing in Columbus against the Minnesota Wild. There must have been a line change, because I found myself centring Nash. He was playing left wing and was set up to receive a breakout pass just below our blue line. I was the centre cutting through the middle to pick up a pass or a chip off the boards. Nash got the puck and immediately chipped it up the boards as I was streaking down the ice. As I was looking for the puck, out of the corner of my eye I picked up a Wild player flying in Nash's direction. I heard the distinctive dull thud of a crushing hit and then what seemed like an angry groan from the crowd. I stopped, turned around to assess the damage, and see who in their right mind thought they could get away with running our franchise player.

Jamie Allison was already on the scene and looked like he was ready to seek justice from the Wild player. The trouble was, the Minnesota player was six-foot-four and 225 pounds of Brad Brown. This wasn't good for a couple reasons: 1) He's a monster and is quite capable of handling himself (and well, I might add), and 2) he is best buds with Jamie Allison (not that it mattered, as I'd seen many good friends punch each other in the face, but still). I quickly made the decision to fall on the grenade and go after Brown. I'd let Ally fight one for me another time.

So there I went, lunging into the path of a bus. The trouble was, while I had devoted some thought to the question of whether to fight Brown, I forgot to consider exactly how I was going to go about it. I went flying in against a bigger and more experienced fighter without a plan. What you want to do is square off, maintain your balance, get a good grip on a handful of sweater, tuck in your chin to protect it from harm, and keep your body twisted away from your opponent in order to present the smallest possible target. Get all that right, and you stand a chance. Deviate from that, and you're likely to get filled in.

Well, despite the fact that I was dropping my gloves with one of the toughest guys in the league, I ignored just about everything I knew, and led with my chin. I grabbed Brown with both hands, as if I were about to give him a stern talking-to rather than the beating I had in mind. I could hardly have made it easier for him. He smoked me twice in the temple and that was about it. As I stumbled to the penalty box I had to laugh at myself for being such an idiot. I sure hope Brown's hands were OK. That's how guys get hurt. You're welcome, Nasher, that should send a message around the league that you're not to be messed with.

Still, it was never my job to go out there and intimidate guys. I just had to make smart, simple plays, chip the puck out of our end, and hopefully keep it deep in the other zone. Finish my checks. Above all, avoid being scored on. And that's what I did. Barely.

Making the team out of camp didn't exactly mean that the season was going to be a cakewalk for me. In fact, it was more like an eighty-two-game tryout.

To me, there was only one thing worse than being scratched, and that was getting waived. Who the hell came up with the idea of a waiver wire anyway? What a great concept. Basically, it announces to the rest of the hockey world, "Can someone please take this bum's contract off our hands? Please?" Not exactly a boost of confidence for the player in question. The team you've been playing your guts out for is telling you that they'll dump you for nothing if someone will just pay your salary.

"Really, we don't want anything back! Just don't try to return the damaged goods we just sucked you into taking from us."

When a team waives a player it is either hoping to send said player to its minor league affiliate, or it's hoping that someone takes the player off its hands.

Take it from an expert—it's a very awkward feeling to walk around the dressing room after being waived. Believe me, it's never a secret to the other players what has happened. They know who is unwanted. They smell the stink of undesirability. Some guys get it because they've been there before. I liked those guys. They were sympathetic and always had their own waiver wire tales to make you feel a little more comfortable with the whole situation. It worked. Sometimes.

In the pre-season Doug MacLean pulled me aside and told me he didn't protect me in the waiver draft, but still wasn't sure what he was going to do with me if I didn't get claimed. He just wanted the ability to send me to my death in the minors if no one plucked me off the wire. I'm sure glad he was able to keep his options open. I felt like I was part of a macabre game show. There were three doors in front of me, none of which led to a very desirable place, and I still didn't get to pick which one I walked through.

"Ladies and gentlemen, within seventy-two short hours Mr. Pronger will find out his fate! Behind door number one is an NHL team that believes Sean can somehow help their cause. At least the Blue Jackets hope there is a team behind that door! Behind door number two is a trip to the AHL with an annual salary worth a quarter of what he was hoping to make this season. And door number three really leads to nowhere! It just keeps him here in purgatory with a team that clearly doesn't believe he fits into their plans! Don't hold your breath, Mr. Pronger!"

As tough as the situation was, I have to say that I appreciated MacLean for being upfront and honest with me. As a guy who was never a "sure thing," I always wanted to know exactly where I stood and MacLean never tried to sugarcoat things. You'd be surprised how many GMs or coaches don't let you know what is going on. I don't know how many times I had players come up to me and break the news—players do love a scoop.

(On the other hand, there is such a thing as too much honesty. At one point that year I tried the same tactic I'd used with Sather in New York. I wasn't playing much and wanted to find out what I needed to do to get more games and ice time. After a practice I skated over to Dave King, our head coach. The guy had coached—and succeeded—at every level. He was a member of the Order of Canada, for that matter. Surely he'd have some advice for a hard-working player like me.

"Kinger, can I talk to you for a second?"

"Sure, what's up?"

"I want to know what I can do to play more."

"Well, Prongs, I think you have good hockey sense. You understand the game and what we are trying to do. But I have to say that you're a very, very, very, very, very average skater."

Thanks for your professional opinion, Coach King. Sometimes to keep what little confidence you have, it's best not to speak with the coach.

As we were skating off the ice, I looked at him and said, half jokingly, "Kinger, would you mind going over that last part of our conversation with me? It was a little unclear."

At least he was trying to be honest with me. And there's no way I could have sued him for slander.)

I cleared waivers in the pre-season but stuck with the Blue Jackets, and that was a sign of things to come. That season was an emotional rollercoaster. Although it was great to get back in the show, it wasn't as if I could enjoy it. I felt as though I couldn't take a breath or let my guard down. After celebrating Halloween in the Residence Inn I finally had to ask if we could move out of our "home" in a hotel. Just so I wouldn't get too comfortable, Doug MacLean said it was OK if I found a place to live just so long as the lease was "month to month." Thanks, Doug, I won't buy any green bananas either. Thinking about it could drive a person insane. You could be one bad shift from the minors—which obviously shouldn't have been a big deal for me, but it was. When you have a wife and small child to cart around it can be downright maddening.

In spite of the mental abuse I was suffering through, I was playing pretty well. I had solidified myself on the fourth line and was killing penalties. For a player like me, to have a defined role on the team meant everything. As for the team, we were killing it on home ice but were probably the worst road team in the league. No wonder Dave King had grey hair.

I would have taken grey hair instead of a kick in the balls, but unfortunately that wasn't my choice. And that boot came just before the roster freeze at Christmas. We were in Phoenix and I was getting off the bus when Assistant GM Jim Clark pulled me aside to inform me that they had put me on waivers again. "We're not sure we're going to send you down, but we want to have the option." Awesome. Thanks Jim. I was starting to think maybe it would be better to not know. I guess that's why they blindfold guys when they put them in front of the firing squad!

Well, luckily for me the firing squad fired blanks. As mentioned, I was placed on waivers a few times that season and each time no one picked me up. Nice to know that all twenty-nine other teams in the league felt the same way about me as my own team did. So the Blue Jackets were willing to let me go three times. And twenty-nine other teams passed on me on three separate occasions. That means that ninety times in ONE season a GM said, "Who? Sean Pronger? No, we have no use for him."

The only good thing I can say is that all three times I cleared waivers I managed to dodge the bullet. And by dodging the bullet I mean that Doug MacLean didn't send me down to the minors even though he had the option to. That was the best situation I could have hoped for. Sure, getting claimed by another team can feel good, because it means someone thinks you can help out. However, the good feeling usually doesn't last long because most teams that pursue the waiver wire for players are just looking to fill a short-term need because of an injury to one of their regulars. Once that player comes back (and it was always much sooner than I would have liked), your days are numbered. I've seen players get picked off waivers four times in one month. Anyone remember the name Jarrod Skalde?

Doug MacLean and the Blue Jackets were the model franchise for handling my time on the waiver wire. Remember what I said about honesty? How MacLean always gave me the heads up when he was about to waive me? Seemed like a pretty common courtesy to me. It couldn't have been fun for MacLean to break the news, but he did it because it was the right thing to do. However, by the end it was more of a wink and a nod than a spoken word. Now I know that organizations don't have to tell you what's going on, and yes I understand hockey is a business and we're all big boys that play the game. But that said, it doesn't seem like it would be that hard to warn a player (or his agent) if his career was about to be altered.

Whining aside, it's time to brace yourself: I spent the entirety of 2002–03 in the National Hockey League. I was back, baby! I developed a role on the team that I could see lasting longer than one season. I was a fourth-line checker, strong on faceoffs, and could kill penalties. And believe it or not, I was able to mix in a goal every now and then! When you score only a couple goals a season they're real easy to remember. My best from that season was not a bank job off my behind. This one would've made Jari Kurri proud. We were playing against Chicago in the United Center. I was the high man rolling off a cycle and banked it down to David Vyborny. As Vyborny was about to kick it down to our low man he spotted me all alone in the slot with my stick cocked for a one-timer. He slid it over to me and I hammered a one-timer over the glove of Jocelyn Thibault. All of my teammates had a look of shock on their faces when I returned to the bench. It was like they had never seen such a goal. Of course their shock was due to the fact that they had never seen *me* score such a goal. Another fine memory for me was a fight I had near the start of the season with the Coyotes' Kelly Buchberger. To me, however, he was still Edmonton's Kelly Buchberger. Remember, I was a huge Oilers fan as a kid, and I watched with envy when a young Buchberger skated around Northlands Coliseum with the Stanley Cup over his head. Now I was trying to take off his head. He challenged me to a fight in our rink, and although I didn't want to get beat up I really didn't have a choice but to accept his challenge. After circling each other for a few moments I landed a lucky haymaker on his temple, which sent him to the ground. Obviously he didn't care that he'd been dropped, because he'd been in a hundred fights and lost a few along the way. As for me? It just didn't feel right. I didn't get a lot of satisfaction from my lucky one punch. But I got over it pretty quickly. Especially since the next time we played he challenged me to a rematch. And I won't tell you how that one went.

All in all, it was a great season for me. I had no doubt that my status as a member of the Blue Jackets organization had been solidified. The summer of '03 was going to be the new Summer of Sean. I was going to train my ass off and get my NHL strut back!

11

THE COLUMBUS STRAITJACKETS

If high points weren't followed by low points, you wouldn't recognize them as high points. In training camp at the beginning of my third season with the Blue Jackets, I knew something was up. The "list" was posted showing the lineup for the training camp scrimmages. The good news was that I was in my usual centre position. The bad news was that I was flanked by a "heavyweight" from the ECHL and a defenceman. That's pretty much the formula for a one-way ticket to Syracuse right there. I checked the other line combinations. Nothing was as blatant as the three stray dogs that made up my line. I knew right then that my chances of making the Blue Jackets were a lot slimmer than they had been three minutes prior. I've learned over my career that doesn't just happen when the bingo balls are yanked out. Something was up.

When you're a journeyman you develop a sixth sense for detecting when things are going sideways. Mind you, in that case it didn't require a rocket surgeon to read the tea leaves. As training camp went along I was getting more and more agitated. I thought, "What do I have to do to earn the benefit of the doubt around here?" I would've been all right with what was happening had it been the result of playing poorly. But to be written off before camp really even started pissed me off. I just played an entire season with the Jackets and thought I had re-established myself as an NHLer. Obviously the organization didn't feel that way.

Remember, the Blue Jackets had never been to the playoffs, so status quo wasn't good enough. People at the top felt changes needed to be made. And let's face it—I would be an easy change to make. I certainly didn't have the upside of a younger player. I was a known commodity, sure, but it wasn't like I was going to have a breakout season and blow everyone's doors off. They knew they could count on me to play a certain role, fit in with the game plan, and not be a distraction if they needed to put me in the press box for a few games. I was that guy they could rely on if they had to, but I had limited upside and wasn't about to take the team to the next level.

It was so frustrating to see it happening, to *feel* it happening, and yet not be able to do anything about it. It was especially maddening because I was already set up in Columbus. Since I'd played the entire season before I kept my place, so my family was nice and cozy in our townhouse. I couldn't bring myself to have to pack them up again for a trek back to Syracuse. Do they even have children's car seats for U-Hauls?

Hey, I can see where the franchise was coming from. I'm not the only one in the history of the game this ever happened to. The AHL is littered with guys who just couldn't get a break from the big club. How many times have you seen a guy not get a sniff with one team and then excel with another?

The only thing I could do was to keep showing up to practice, work my ass off, and let the chips fall where they may. All I thought was that they hadn't got rid of me yet. Maybe another miracle would happen!

As camp went along my situation didn't change. I busted my ass, and passed every test that was put in front of me, but getting D's and C's is not going to get you onto the Dean's List. So I figured I'd go back to the strategy that seemed to have worked the year before. One of our last exhibition games of the pre-season was against Pittsburgh. I was playing on a line with Tim Jackman and he was being roughed up by none other than Reid Simpson. That is, a guy who retired with nearly 1,000 penalty minutes in the NHL and considerably more than that if you add up all the time he spent in the penalty boxes of several leagues (he racked up more than 500 in only two seasons in the KHL). In other words, a guy it would be wise to avoid fighting.

To this day I still don't know what I was thinking. It was as though I could see myself from above, looking down, saying "What the hell are you *doing*?" What I was doing was squaring off with Simpson at centre ice. I vividly remember the look on his face. Not anger; definitely not fear. More like incredulity.

He certainly wasn't expecting me to drop the gloves with him. Usually it's the heavyweights who fight the heavyweights. But if something has to be done, someone has to jump in there and there's no time to do a round of rock-paper-scissors with your teammate to see who it's going to be. If you're close enough, and you're big enough, then you have to answer the bell. You've got to do what you've got to do, and it's true I wanted to make an impression. But still, it was unfortunate that the guy I ended up dancing with at centre ice was so much better at what we were about to do than I was.

As we were working our way around each other looking for a way to engage I managed to quickly get a hold of him and land a solid one. I think I surprised both of us. Maybe I was going to get through this.

Not quite. Within seconds Simpson had me tangled up, and if I hadn't spun out of the way he would have put his fist right through my face. Still, I ended up on my knees and facing the other way. I had him right where I wanted him. Thankfully, the linesman jumped to the rescue before things got uglier. Since it was near the end of the period I went immediately to the dressing room. When the boys came in after the period they gave me the "Nice job, Prongs," but most of them couldn't contain their laughter when I asked if they thought Simpson was going to be all right. You're welcome, Jackman—anything for a teammate.

Somehow, I survived training camp by the skin of my teeth. But by no means was I out of the woods. I was a healthy scratch for the first game of the season. A couple young guys, Dan Fritsche and Andrej Nedorost, had decent camps so I knew the brass wanted to keep them around to give them a longer look. I know Doug MacLean and company were especially pleased with the play of Fritsche. As much as I hated to admit it, he did look pretty good. It didn't hurt that he was from Ohio. Having local lads on the team could sell tickets, and there were not many Ohio-born players in the league. The other guy, Nedorost, I was more familiar with. I had played with him my first year in Syracuse. He had a strong camp and a decent skill set but I didn't think he was ready for the Big Show yet. I thought he needed more seasoning, or at least that's what I daydreamed. I presumed he'd stumble during the first couple of regular season games and be sent down, enabling me to slide back into the bottom two forward group. With my track record I had to play mind games with myself, otherwise it would have been too depressing. My mind games didn't last long, however, because Nedorost scored in our first game of the season. I started to get that old feeling again ... the feeling you get when you need to organize air travel and moving trucks.

The axe fell during a morning skate. Doug MacLean, serving double duty at the time as GM and head coach, gave me the tap and told me to meet him by the sideboards. It was a one-sided conversation that consisted of him telling me I was being re-assigned to Syracuse. I wasn't surprised, but I was a little pissed off. Cutting me while we were on the ice for a game-day skate? Didn't he know I still had my stick in my hand? I had busted my ass for that organization for better than two years and I didn't even get an office-visit pink slip. I bolted off the ice, got undressed as fast as I could, and left the rink. I left my equipment in my stall and didn't speak a word to anyone. When I got home I broke the news to my wife, who wasn't blindsided at all because obviously I had shared my suspicions with her throughout camp.

Our situation had changed a lot since the last time we were in Syracuse. We now had a baby girl and my wife was pregnant with baby number two. Our last pregnancy was a challenge, to put it very mildly. Mrs. Journeyman had to be on bed rest for a good chunk of it. And the birth—well, that was something I prayed we'd never go through again. With that in mind, I had to wonder if Syracuse was the best place for us. In Syracuse, we didn't have any family or support close by. What if I was on the road, or called back up to Columbus, and something went wrong with the pregnancy this time? All those thoughts went into a decision to call my agent.

"Pat, I want a trade. And I only want to go to one team."

"Sean, calm down. I know it stings right now, but give it some time and you'll be back in no time."

My mind was made up. I needed and wanted to get myself traded back to Winnipeg. I thought it would be as simple as trading my minor league rights. No dice. Pat told me it would be very difficult to pull off because we were basically tying Doug MacLean's hands. How could he possibly pry something from Winnipeg for me if Craig Heisinger (Moose GM) knew that's the only place I wanted to go?

"Pat, we're not talking about a first-round pick here. One minor leaguer for another; we can do this."

"I'll see what I can do."

It wasn't until a couple of days later that I finally spoke with the Blue Jackets. I talked to the assistant GM, Jim Clark, to let him know what I wanted.

"Sean, I don't know if we can accommodate you. The owner in Syracuse doesn't want to trade you and the coach wants you in the lineup. Is there anything else we can do to help the situation?"

"I'll tell you what, as a sign of good faith, I'll report to Syracuse and play for the Crunch. But I want to be moved to Manitoba if at all possible. It would be the best possible situation for my family."

Now, I had nothing against Syracuse. I loved playing there, and I always played pretty well when I was with the Crunch. The decision had nothing to do with the organization or the city. It had everything to do with my pregnant wife and our child.

Gary Agnew, the coach of the Crunch, was a great guy and I could talk things through with him throughout the whole ordeal. We had always got along well, and true to form he was very blunt with me.

"Sean, I want to be upfront. If I was the GM of this team, there is no way in the world I'd trade you unless we got something of greater value in return. And that isn't going to happen when we can only deal with one team. I spoke with the owner and he wants to know if there is anything we can do to help you with your situation. Can we have a doctor on call for your wife during the times you are not at home?"

Gary was there when our daughter was born, so he knew firsthand the complications we went through.

"Gary, you know I appreciate everything this organization has done for me and my family. And I appreciate the fact that Howard [the owner of the Crunch] is willing to try to help. I want to thank you for all you've done as well. But I have to do this. I'll play as hard as I can while I'm with you guys, but I want and expect to be traded."

I was never one to make demands over the course of my career, but at the time I just knew that Winnipeg was where we needed to be for peace of mind.

Seven games into the Crunch season the club was about to embark on a road trip when Coach Agnew approached me at the airport.

"It looks like you may get your wish after all. We should know something by the time we land."

That was a weird feeling. I flew with the Crunch knowing that when the plane landed I was most likely going to be a member of the Moose. And sure enough, it happened. The Blue Jackets went above and beyond by trading me to the Canucks for Zenith Komarniski.

I made a point of calling Jim Clark to thank him for getting something done and I'll never forget what he said to me.

"Sean, this was a family decision, not a hockey one. Thanks for all you've done. Good luck."

I don't know if there has ever been a hockey player that happy to be headed to Winnipeg.

Before we got traded to Winnipeg I told my wife that this may not be a good idea, hockey-wise. She knew that I loved playing in the 'Peg but didn't really understand that things had changed since our last tour. First, it was no longer in the IHL. The Moose was now a member of the American Hockey League. Second, and probably the biggest difference, was they were now affiliated with the Vancouver Canucks. The last time we played in Winnipeg the Moose were independent. Meaning they had complete control over who was on the team and in the lineup. Vancouver would have some say on who was in Winnipeg. In Syracuse, I knew the players, coaching staff, and management. In Winnipeg, I knew one player and the GM. There was a lot we didn't know about the team. She told me that she could handle one more year in Syracuse; if it meant it would make my hockey life easier, she could do it. Even though I appreciated her lying to me I had my mind made up. It was time to start doing what was in the best interest of our family. I met my new team on the road in Houston. (That's NHL organization number seven and team number fourteen. But who's counting?)

I spoke with Zinger by phone after I heard the news, one to thank him for making it happen, and two to get a feel for the team. All he said was "it's different from the last time you were here." Zinger was a man of few words and king of the understatement. It was obvious right away this was not the same team I left two and a half years ago. Everyone was so young. This was now a developmental league. A lot of the old IHL players were sent to pasture, or they made the trek overseas. In the American Hockey League, in order to promote the development of young players teams are allowed to dress only a certain number of veteran players. These are players with 260+ pro games under their belts. Two such players on this particular squad were our grisly captain Dallas Eakins and fan favourite Jimmy Roy. I had played against Eakins many times and we had some mutual friends we both had played with. I played with Jimmy my last stint with the Moose. I found out pretty fast why the fans loved him. He was from Sioux Lookout, Ontario, which is not far from Winnipeg. So, you could consider him a local. But it was more about the way he played. He ran around hitting everything that moved and chirped every player on the other team all game. It was exhausting just listening to him. He was the only holdover from the Moose and the IHL days.

Within the first few weeks it became apparent that a lot of the guys on the "new Moose" were in it for themselves. Granted, everyone's goal, in the end, is to get to the next level. However, it is my belief that there is the right way and the wrong way to do it. The right way is to work your ass off and play your ass off for your team. The end result is more playing time. More playing time equals more chances to do good things. More good things mean your name is at the top of the list when the Big Club comes calling. The wrong way is to play only for you. On the Moose we had a few of the second type of player. I hate to throw people under the bus, but it's public knowledge so what the hell....

One such player was Fedor Fedorov. Before you ask, yes, Fedor is the younger brother of Sergei (like me, a brother of a surefire Hockey Hall of Famer). When I first saw him play I was stunned. I couldn't figure out why a guy like that was not in the NHL. He was the total package. He was six-foot-three and weighed in at a cool 230 pounds. To go along with height and weight he also had speed. He could fly. As well as height, weight, and speed, he had NHL skill. I'm not talking third- or fourth-line skill—I'm talking about top-six skill.

At this point you must be asking yourself why you never saw him dominating in the NHL. Alas, a million-dollar question I finally have an answer for. Fedor looked like Sergei, skated like Sergei, and had many of the same God-given talents as his elder sibling. The only problem was that Fedor thought he should be treated like Sergei. And the last time I checked, Fedor was a Hart Trophy short, a couple of Selkes shy, and a few Cups away from being Sergei. Bottom line, Fedor was all about Fedor. He had what some may call a million-dollar runway with no control tower. Or, more simply, he had all the tools but no toolbox. He didn't know HOW to play the game. To him, every time he touched the puck the game turned into a 1–1 contest. The problem was not beating one guy; that he could do. The problem was that he tried to beat all five. Even in the AHL that's not going to happen. For some reason, in order to get to the NHL he figured he needed to do it all by himself. This drove our coach, Stan Smyl, crazy and made the rest of my teammates insane too. I don't know if he was trying to live up to his brother (Lord knows I know how that feels), or he honestly didn't understand that it was a team game, but he was frustrating to watch and to play with. I, along with Brandon Reid, played on his line for a couple months and it was painful. He would get the puck in our end and skate a hundred miles an hour and turn it over at the top of circles in the other team's end. He would skate so fast that I was always behind him. The guys on the team used to bug me because I was always the third man high. Not by choice, but because I couldn't keep up. Just as I was catching up he'd turn it over and the other team would go back the other way. And then I'd trail the play again. I felt like that kid who just started playing and always seemed to be going the wrong way. It was almost comical.

He certainly didn't make many friends away from the rink either. I don't know if it was the Hummer he drove or the beaver fur coat he sported, but he's certainly not someone I would have classified as a team guy. Maybe he thought his time in the 'Peg would be brief. And it almost was.

We had a game in December just before we were about to get four whole days off for Christmas. Just so you know, four days off is unheard of. Obviously, the boys were fired up to play well so we could feel like we earned our time off. The icing on the jelly donut was that the game was at noon. That made it almost five days!

I remember walking around with my third Tim Hortons coffee when Fedor came rolling in to the locker room a little later than his usual lateness. I remember looking at him as he walked in and he had a funny kind of glassy look to him.

Well, I guess four-almost-five days off for Fedor wasn't quite enough so he started the Christmas festivities a little early. Yep, he was still shitfaced from the night before (or that morning, depending on when he decided to pass out).

When Stan found out about it, and it wasn't because someone ratted him out, he blew a gasket. It was inexcusable. After we came back from Christmas break Stan called a team meeting. He informed us that Fedor had been suspended indefinitely and if it was up to him he would never play for the Moose again.

Indefinitely turned out to be ten games. During his "time off" the Canucks were trying to trade him. Or at least that's the story. I was told that they were asking for a first-round draft pick. With his skill set that certainly wasn't out of the question. However, with his character in question, no one was willing to take that chance. I think the Canucks were a little afraid that they'd trade Fedor to some team for an eighth-rounder and he'd go out and score fifty goals and make them look bad. As for me, I was just hoping the kid was traded to anywhere or that he got what he deserved. And I got my wish.

It was the spring of 2004 and the Manitoba Moose were on the verge of missing the playoffs. Fedor aside, the Moose had a number of character guys playing for them that season, and a bunch of characters as well. I'm not sure which of those two groups I fit into, but I know for a fact that Fedor was in the latter.

It was a Sunday and the Moose had just finished an afternoon game, so naturally the lads decided to hit the local watering hole for a few cups. Somehow dinner turned into midnight and a vast majority of the crew remained for a nightcap or four. One member of the crew was a new guy who had just finished his career at Bowling Green. His name? Kevin Bieksa. And he was on an amateur tryout contract with Manitoba. For those of you not literate in contract-speak, an amateur tryout means you are literally day to day. If you play well, you get the opportunity to play another game. If not, beat it. Bieksa had been with the team for only two or three days and had yet to see any game action. Basically, he was just practising with the team and getting to know his teammates better. Believe me, that's just one of many reasons why this story is so great.

I'm not sure what time it was, but the carriage had long since turned into a pumpkin, and the fellas were winding down. Fedor was sitting at a table with his billets (a father and his son who was in his twenties) and Bieksa. The other member of the table, Kirill Koltsov, was at the bar getting another cocktail. And this is where things heat up.

Bieksa was playing with the straw in his drink. Somehow, he lost control of said straw and it catapulted across the bar and landed on Koltsov's shoulder. Koltsov turned to see where the straw had come from and spotted Bieksa chuckling. As it turns out, Koltsov didn't see the humour in the situation and was going to let the new guy know how he felt about it. If you ask me, Koltsov shouldn't have been beaking anyone. He was still a freaking rookie himself. Koltsov was small and couldn't move very well on the ice but he had tonnes of skill and somehow got the job done. One thing he was not, however, was a tough guy—so he probably shouldn't have been playing the part with an unknown quantity. It's not like Bieksa is a small guy.

Koltsov: "What the fuck are you laughing at?"

Bieksa: "Sorry man, it was an accident."

Koltsov: "I said, what the fuck are you laughing at?"

Bieksa: "Relax dude, I just flicked the straw and it happened to hit you."

Koltsov: "Don't tell me to fuckin' relax."

Bieksa, not smiling anymore: "Get out of my face before I kick the shit out of you!"

And this is when Fedor got involved. Koltsov was one of his few friends on the team and he was going to stick up for him. So Fedor put his hand on Bieksa's arm and let him know that if he had a problem with Koltsov then he had a problem with both of them. Well, Bieksa's fuse was long since lit so he let Fedor know that if he didn't take his hand off his arm then Koltsov may not be the only one getting filled in.

Fedor: "It's time to settle this outside!"

That was it. The Manitoba Moose team-building session was ON.

Fedor got up and stormed out of the bar. Koltsov followed him outside, while Bieksa stayed and contemplated his next move. Here is a kid who just signed his first tryout contract, and on his first night out was about to fight one of his new teammates. Not a great career move, right? More on that later.

The billets were trying to convince Bieksa to stay put and just ride it out until everyone cooled down. But there are some guys who can't just stay inside when there is a scrap waiting on the outside, and I guess Bieksa is one of them.

At this point in the proceedings the rest of the team was starting to become aware of what was going on.

Someone said, "Hey, the new guy just went outside to fight Fedor."

To which Dallas Eakins, our captain, replied, "I gotta go take a leak." Eaks was such a solid guy. Like myself, he'd had to pack his bag a few times in a few different cities but he never lost his love for the game. I never had a chance to play with Eakins until I was traded to Manitoba, and I was better for the experience. He was all about the game. He was great for the young guys. To see a grizzled veteran like him who still had the passion was fantastic. He played sixteen years of professional hockey, and during that time appeared in only 120 NHL games. In any case, I guess he figured that team captains shouldn't be standing around watching teammates fight. And he may not have wanted to deprive anyone of the opportunity to punch Fedorov in the face. So he calmly got off his chair and strolled to the bathroom.

I'm sorry to say that I had no interest in heading out into the cold to watch a fight between a guy I didn't know and a guy I didn't like. Luckily, what happened outside was witnessed by two teammates who saw it while breaking for a cigarette. (I will leave them unnamed entities because I want to protect their integrity as athletes.)

Here's the story they told when they got back inside. Fedor came out of the bar and disrobed to a white T-shirt (keep in mind, it's –20). Koltsov soon followed and stood by Fedor's side. Bieksa appeared a few minutes later and didn't look too surprised that he was now squaring off against two guys instead of just one. Fedor got in his best Marquess of Queensberry stance and prepared for the scrap. Bieksa turned his attention to Fedor, and while he was sizing him up Koltsov began leg kicking him. While checking the leg kicks Bieksa tried to end things with one punch by throwing a huge drunken haymaker that just missed Fedor. Fedor countered with a right that caught Bieksa just above the right eye. Meantime, Koltsov continued to cause little to no damage with his leg kicks. Bieksa reloaded for the last punch of the night. It landed flush on the right side of Fedor's mug, cutting him wide open.

Just like that, it was over.

After seeing his buddy get his faced caved in, Koltsov decided his night was done, too, and ended the charade that he actually wanted to fight.

Fedor headed to the hospital, while Bieksa headed back into the bar. He'd never played a game with the Moose but he was already my favourite teammate. And I wasn't the only one who felt that way.

As for Bieksa, he thought his career with Manitoba was done before it even started. The next morning he fielded calls from Moose GM Craig Heisinger and Canucks exec. Steve Tambellini and was asked to give his side of the story. Both told him that the organization couldn't have teammates fighting each other outside of bars. Bieksa was also told to sit tight while a decision was made about his future with the Moose.

As for us players, we needed a story to tell the media. And yes, this was the one and only time we ever lied to the ink-stained wretches. Anyhow, the company line was that a stick in practice clipped Bieksa and Fedor tripped and cut his face open. Simple enough.

While we were coming up with that story Bieksa was summoned to the head coach's office. The coach was Stan Smyl; you'll remember he had already suspended Fedor earlier in the season. And if you're not familiar with Stan "Steamer" Smyl, well, let's just say as a player he was the anti-Fedor. What he lacked in skill he more than made up for in heart and try. He could score, hit, agitate, fight, and flat-out play. He was one of those guys who played every shift as if it were his last.

I can't say that Stan was the best coach I ever had, but I can say he was one of the most intense. Having played for him I know why they called him "Steamer" and I also know that I wouldn't have wanted to play against him. I think what frustrated him most about players and probably why he had such a hard time with Fedor and Kirill was that he couldn't fathom why players didn't give a hundred percent every time they touched the ice.

I'm told Smyl gave Bieksa the same speech that Heisinger and Tambellini did. It wasn't the riot act but the message was clear that what happened between Fedor and Kevin was frowned upon. Bieksa, now almost sure he was finished in Manitoba, got up and was nearly out the door when Smyl said,

"Kevin, can I ask you one more question?"

"Sure."

"Did you get him good?"

Brilliant stuff.

Bieksa played four games with us that season and was signed in the summer. Fedorov finished up the season and never played another game with the Moose. Apparently knocking Fedor on his can was a great career move for Kevin, because when then Canucks GM Brian Burke heard the story he said, "Sign that kid right now!"

Bieksa fought twelve times in the AHL during the 2004–05 season. A pretty big number for a guy who just came out of university hockey, where fighting is not allowed. Someone once asked how he learned to scrap while playing in the NCAA. Bieksa's reply?

"You can't fight in college hockey, but you can fight in college."

All in all, my year in Winnipeg was a struggle. I loved being back there but it felt like I was swimming upstream the entire time. It was pretty much what I predicted to my wife when we decided to ask for the trade back to the Moose. On a personal level I thought things would be great, and they were. We had a lot of support from family and friends in the area. But, hockey-wise, it wasn't great. I sometimes wonder how things would've played out if I didn't ask for that trade back in October. But then, I think that things happen for a reason. If I didn't ask for the trade, everything wouldn't have come full circle. Thirteen years later I would finally get the chance to play for Vancouver, the team that drafted me in 1991. I was a little surprised when the phone rang in early March and it was Steamer.

"Prongs, you're being recalled by the Canucks. You're flying to Detroit to meet the team. Congrats, you deserve it. Good luck." Coincidentally, my wife was eight months pregnant with baby number two. But this time things were a little different. She wasn't puking beside me. She wasn't on bed rest, and she had her parents with her. There was no hesitation this time. It was off to Detroit.

12

FOURTH MAN ON THE PILE

When I left for Detroit, I shook some hands, I kissed Mrs. Journeyman goodbye, and I took a cab to the airport. It's great to be called up, but it had been a while since I'd had butterflies in my gut; I figured I'd seen it all before. It doesn't matter how many times you get called up, it still gets the juices flowing—and the nerves.

God, when I'm full of youthful exuberance, I get it wrong. And when I slip into world-weary resignation, I get it just as wrong. This time I was about to see something I'd never seen before. And experience something else I'd never see again. I couldn't know that as I headed to Joe Louis Arena to meet up with the Canucks.

And here we go again. For the fifteenth time in my career, I was about to walk into yet another NHL locker room to introduce myself to an entire team. As excited as I was to get another shot in the NHL, I'm not going to lie to you: making the rounds to say "Hi, I'm Sean Pronger, nice to meet you" was getting old. I'm not sure if the guys sensed that, or perhaps it was because I was now considered a "veteran," but they were great and went out of their way to spare me the trip around the locker room. It's funny when someone like Trevor Linden comes up to introduce himself. "Hey Sean, Trevor Linden. Nice to meet you."

As if I didn't know who he was. He may have been just a little older than me but I had memories of watching Linden battling Joel Otto of the Calgary Flames in the playoffs as an eighteen-year-old. I didn't know many of the guys on the team but there were some familiar faces. I'd played with Dan Cloutier in New York and Johan Hedberg in Manitoba, skated with Brad May a few times in the summer in Toronto, and remembered Mike Keane from some late-summer workouts in Winnipeg. That was about it.

At the time, Vancouver was battling for a division title so every game was important. I got a very businesslike feel as I walked around the room. There wasn't a lot of chit-chat. It was mostly guys going about their business getting ready for a big game against the Red Wings. These guys knew what I knew: if you were not ready to play in Detroit, it would be a long and painful evening.

The irony certainly wasn't lost on me that I was about to play my first game for the team that had drafted me thirteen years prior. I wasn't naive enough to think this stint in the show was anything more than just a warm body filling a spot for an injured regular. Artem Chubarov was hurt and my number was lucky enough to get pulled out of the bingo call-up machine. Not that I cared how or why I got the call; I was just excited to get a chance to come full circle. As I said earlier, if you hang around long enough good things happen. Even if it was thirteen years, fifteen teams, and five leagues later, I was finally going to play for the team that wanted me first.

As I was lacing up my skates, the coach, Marc Crawford, walked in. He announced the starting lineup for the game.

"Boys, tonight's starting lineup is the 'famous brother' line. Or the 'other brother' line."

Gee, I wonder if I'm starting?

"Starting at left wing, Jarkko Ruutu. Starting at right wing, Fedor Fedorov. And starting at centre, Sean Pronger."

I must admit, it was a pretty funny move by Crow.

Much like my first NHL game, my short-term goal was to play well enough to get a chance to play the next game. Which happened to be the next night in Columbus. My long-term goal was to play well enough to catch the charter back with the team to Vancouver after the Columbus game. Hey, goals are goals, and it's far easier to achieve them if they are somewhat realistic.

We ended up losing to the Red Wings 3–1. I played as well as could be expected and chipped in with an assist. I figured that since it was back-to-back games and we were playing Columbus there wouldn't be any unwelcome players from the farm team to take my spot and ruin my long-term plans.

It was Saturday night in Columbus for my first game back with the Blue Jackets since demanding a trade out of town. I was ready for the boo birds. Yeah right! I could only wish I got booed. Such pleasantries are reserved for my brother (at twenty-nine rinks a year). At least some sort of murmur would show that the fans cared. I'm 99 percent sure most of the fans had no idea I was playing for the Canucks, or that I was no longer with the Blue Jackets, or even who the hell I was for that matter.

Sean Pronger Night at Nationwide Arena ended up being a winner for the visitors and I couldn't even celebrate because I was waiting to see if I was taking a cab or the team bus to the airport I knew all too well. Thankfully, I wasn't given any cab fare. Phase two was to actually get on the plane. I'm happy to say phase two was a success. Off to Vancouver for a big tilt with the Colorado Avalanche, the division title still up for grabs.

I was thrilled to finally get the opportunity to play an NHL home game in a Canadian city. The city was buzzing for a number of reasons. The top two teams in the Northwest were about to go head to head, the trade deadline was the next day, and of course the playoffs weren't too far down the road.

That's all just hockey, though. Sports. What happened next was front-page news. I've thought long and hard about the night of March 8, 2004, and wondered if I could have missed something leading up to the game that would have given me a clue as to what would eventually happen. And you know what? There isn't anything. Sure, knowing what I do now, I could easily look back and try to read something into words that were said and connect the dots, but really that would be me trying to force a connection. The fact of the matter is that what took place is an age-old hockey equation.

Player A does something to player B. Player C does something to player A for doing something to player B.

That's it. If you don't like it, you probably don't like hockey—because that stuff is going on *all the time*. Only this one time, the result was far worse than what usually occurs. I'm not trying to say what Todd Bertuzzi did was right. And I'm not saying Steve Moore deserved what he got. I'm just pointing out that what Bert did wasn't much different from what a number of players have done over the years.

On February 16, 2004, Steve Moore delivered an open-ice hit on Markus Naslund that knocked the Canucks captain out of the lineup for three games with a concussion.

On March 8, 2004, Todd Bertuzzi tried to get Moore to fight in a game, and when the Avalanche forward wouldn't oblige Bertuzzi delivered a punch to the side of Moore's head, rendering him unconscious before falling on him on the ice and knocking him out of the lineup—and hockey—for good.

Obviously this is a very simplistic view of the events, but I'm not here to argue intent or deliver a verdict. I'm just going to tell you the way I saw the mess.

Moore's hit on Naslund is key to the whole thing for me, because as you well know by now, my ability was more Moore than Naslund (I was picked fifty-first overall in '91; Moore was picked fifty-third overall in '98). The 2003–04 season was basically Moore's first full season in the NHL (he played only thirteen AHL games that season), and he was no doubt still trying to make an impression. Moore was averaging thirteen minutes a game that season, and believe me, that's not a tonne of time to stand out. When you're a journeyman or a guy trying to make his way into the league you do what you can to get noticed.

As a forward, hard work only gets you so far with a coach; sooner or later, you need to score a goal or provide some energy with a good offensive shift or a big hit or fight. Put it this way: if I saw a guy with his head down cruising through the middle of the ice I knew I had to try to lay him out, because if I didn't the coaches would be more than happy to point out the fact that I'd passed up the hit. And if I didn't want to make that hit, then they would surely find someone who would. I'm not talking about doing anything illegal (remember, Rule 48 was not in play when I was around); it was just about finishing my check—something you're taught to do from the time you're a kid. So I'm wondering if Moore saw Naslund in a vulnerable position in the neutral zone and thought he better try to separate him from the puck, by any means, or else he may not get another chance to do so in that game.

I can guarantee you that Colorado's head coach at the time, Tony Granato, did not tell Moore to elbow Naslund and concuss him, but I'd be willing to bet that Moore was encouraged by his coaches in the AHL and NHL to finish his checks. It makes me laugh sometimes how people say the player always has a choice as to whether or not he makes a hit. It's not that easy. I'll concede that there are times when you absolutely know a guy is in a vulnerable position and you should ease up. Like when his back is to you five feet from the boards, or you come from the blindside and headhunt when the shoulder is as open as the chin. But it's not always that simple. Many times it's a split-second decision as to whether or not you're going to make that hit. Sometimes your shoulder is lined up with his shoulder and he ducks at the last minute and ends up taking it in the head. Hockey is an incredibly fast game with big humans looking to make big hits. Shit happens.

And don't forget your high school physics. When you run into a guy, he's hitting you as hard as you're hitting him. So you're going to brace yourself. And that means you're going to be as solid as you can be. That's what makes a big hit. It's not necessarily that one guy is faster than the other, or even that one guy is bigger than the other (though both things make a big hit bigger—just ask Andreas Dackell about what it's like to get between Eric Lindros and the puck). Think about it—some of the best open-ice hitters are small guys. How many guys did Mike Peca absolutely crush? And Peca is smaller than the average accountant. The biggest hit Zdeno Chara probably ever took was from little Darcy Tucker, who ran the big guy over. What I'm saying is that you can't expect guys to ease up or not hit players who aren't ready. The whole point of hitting is being more ready than the other guy. That's what bodychecking is. Plus, coaches in any contact sport will tell you the same thing: it's when you're not going 100 percent that you get hurt. In other words, easing up can be as dangerous as lowering the boom (at least for the guy doing the lowering).

Again, I can't tell you what Steve Moore intended to do on February 16, 2004, but I can make a pretty good guess, since I know what I would have done if I'd had his spot in the lineup: I'd say he was just doing what he's expected to do. As I said earlier, if you're not scoring goals or making plays, you better be doing something to help the team. And that something can be taking the body when you get a chance. And if you have a chance to lay the body on the leading scorer of the Canucks (and the league), you better take it. However, it's a double-edged sword. If you don't, Tony Granato and Rick Tocchet will surely notice. If you do, you can bet your Gretzky rookie card the Canucks will notice. In fact, after Moore ran over Naslund he seemed to have been noticed by everyone but the referees, and no penalty was called on the play. Coaches always want the calls to go their way, but this bit of officiating seems to have really struck at Marc Crawford's sense of justice. Crawford was visibly upset after the game when the cameras and the microphones were on: "It just mystifies me that this happens in this league. They talk about players not having respect for players. Do they not have respect for the leading scorer in the league? When does that come? When does that come? It could have been an obstruction call; it could have been an elbowing call. It could have been anything. Instead, they call absolutely nothing. I have no idea. It was a hard-fought game, nobody is talking about that but that was a cheap shot by a young kid on a captain, the leading scorer in the league and we get no call. We get no call. That is ridiculous. How does that happen? That's got to be answered. Why is there no respect from those referees for the leading scorer in the league? I do not understand that for the life of me. I don't care if they fine me, I really don't. That needs to be answered."

Crawford was pissed. But he was more pissed at the officials than he was at Moore. And the Canucks were upset because their captain had to be helped off the ice after a borderline play. Todd Bertuzzi and Markus Naslund were best friends and teammates, so Bert probably took it harder than most. When a rookie takes a run at a star player it's usually frowned upon by the star player's team. And by frowned upon I mean it's beating time. And if the hit is questionable AND it knocks the star player out of the game then it's time to arm yourself, because you have a war coming. This is usually how brawls start. I was actually surprised one didn't.

As everyone knows, I wasn't an intimidating presence on the ice. I was more likely to share a beer with a guy than give him the Mark Messier stare, but there are some things that I believe in. To an extent I believe in street justice. I believe if one of your star players gets drilled, whether it's legal or illegal, something should be done. The reason I say this is it needs to be made very clear, to the opposing team and the rest of the league, that it is not open season on our top players and there will be a response if it happens. You want opposing players to think twice about throwing their body around with reckless abandon. This is not to say that they'll stop doing it. Nor should they. It actually takes a lot of courage to lay a guy out when you know you'll be a wanted man. I know the feeling of having a guy lined up and having that little voice in the back of your head (call it the "self-preservation" voice) wondering if making this hit is worth it. Is it worth having the other team's goon chase you around for the rest of the night? Most of the time I ignored the voice, but it did make me take a second to think about it. The idea of making a statement is to hopefully create enough of a deterrent that your best players are free to play at their best. The last thing you need is your top guys being intimidated because certain players on the other team are trying to run them out of the building. There are a couple of different ways to send this particular message when your guy gets hammered. One is to go out and run their star player. This is effective but sometimes difficult depending on line matchups. The other is to grab the offending party and try to lay a beating on him. Ideally, whatever path you decide on, it should happen immediately. To let things linger is a recipe for disaster. Needless to say, nothing was done to Moore after he hit Naslund.

So what happened the next time the two teams matched up? Well, actually nothing. In the Canucks' next game versus the Avalanche Todd Bertuzzi had six minutes in penalties, but none against Moore. Markus Naslund had a goal and two assists in what was a 5–5 tie. And Moore played just over seven minutes recording no penalties, no shots, no hits, no takeaways, no giveaways, and was a minus-1. If payback was on the mind of the Canucks, then they clearly forgot. And don't even talk to me about Brad May's supposed bounty on the head of Moore. I'm told May said that to reporters with a smirk on his face as a reference to the cult hockey movie *Slap Shot* and wasn't serious at all. May didn't even fight that game; the only tilt was between Wade Brookbank and Peter Worrell. The game was more important than any grudge, and since the game was close no one was willing to act up or be a part of any funny business.

On March 8, however, the game was not close. And what was supposed to be an unbelievable game between two teams competing for a division title and jockeying for home ice in the playoffs turned into a blowout. It was 5–0 after the first period. This is never a good thing. It's especially bad when the two teams are division rivals. These are the kind of games where stupid things happen, messages get sent, and fireworks sometimes explode. For the record, I've never enjoyed playing in blowouts. I've been in my fair share and they're not that fun, on either side. If you're on the losing side, well, no one likes to get embarrassed. I don't care if it's a girls' soccer game, if the score gets too lopsided it's going to get chippy. If it's a bunch of supercompetitive athletes with their livelihoods on the line, there is going to be just that much more frustration to boil over. And even if your temper is under control, you may feel that it's your job to "send a message" or salvage some pride for your team by showing everyone that if you're going down, you're going down swinging.

And if you're on the winning side, you're skating with your head on a swivel, knowing that the other team has absolutely no incentive to play the puck and every incentive to run you through the glass. Not a fun way to finish a game.

I'm convinced it was the score that allowed the game to get out of hand. If the game was close, with all that was riding on it, nothing would've happened. It was not the pre-game talk by Crawford and surely not by some alleged bounty. I was in the dressing room for Crawford's pre-game talk and I don't remember anything specific at all. That's how powerful it was. If Crawford said Moore "must pay the price," he said it only after saying Joe Sakic, Milan Hejduk, Alex Tanguay, Rob Blake, Paul Kariya, Teemu Selanne, and John-Michael Liles must pay the price first. Unless some people were pulled into a secret room and given instructions I didn't see anything to lead me to believe there was some sort of conspiracy. Believe me, if there was, it wouldn't be Todd Bertuzzi getting pulled in, it would be someone more expendable, someone like yours truly.

Todd Bertuzzi wanted Steve Moore to fight for what he did to Markus Naslund. Yes, Moore fought Matt Cooke earlier in the game, but Bertuzzi obviously didn't think that throwing a few whips with Cooke settled the tab. And you know what? I didn't either. In my opinion, Moore should have just taken his medicine, accepted whatever challenge came his way, and got it over with. I remember a game a few years prior when Darius Kasparaitis drilled Eric Lindros for one of his many concussions. It was a *huge,* highlight-reel hit, and perfectly clean (in those days). The next time those two teams played, Kasparaitis fought three times. I'm sure he just figured he might as well get it over with. And that was it. He answered the bell, gained more respect from his teammates, and, almost as important, earned the respect of the Philadelphia Flyers.

I'm no hero and I'm under no illusion that I'm a tough guy, but right before Bertuzzi engaged Moore I tried to get Moore to fight. I wasn't mad at him. I actually felt bad for him since our entire team was chomping at the bit to drop the gloves with him. That's the way hockey works. I would have dropped my shoulder into Naslund if I had been Moore and caught him with his head down. And I would have fought Moore for doing something that I know I would have done myself. I've been on both sides of the equation. Remember my first game as a pro? I had to drop the gloves to defend myself after delivering a clean hit. It didn't take me long to figure out the way things work. If you do anything that takes a bit of life out of the other team, you'd better be ready for the guys on the other bench to come get a bit of their momentum back. The night in question was only my third game with the Canucks and I knew that sticking up for our captain was the right thing to do. Even though I wasn't a part of the game where Moore knocked out Markus Naslund I was prepared to do my part for the team. Again, it may not be right, but it is the culture of our sport.

Payback has been, still is, and always will be a part of the NHL. And if you don't like to think of it as revenge then you can phrase it as keeping guys accountable for their actions with physical acts. I don't care if Gary Bettman puts a second type of instigator rule in the book; guys are always going to want to make other guys pay for their misdeeds. The players want to police themselves. In a CBC/NHLPA players' poll that was released in 2010, 98 percent of the players polled said they didn't want fighting out of the game. Why is that? Is it because they like to watch fights? Is it because they like staged fights? Maybe, but it's more because they want players to think twice about doing something stupid, or else. I know it's archaic, but that's just the way it is. And yes, I am old-school—I agree with the 98 percent in that one.

The way I see it, Moore and Bertuzzi were terribly unlucky with the way things turned out. I saw hundreds of sucker punches in my career and exactly none of them had the result of that night. Watch a few junior-B or ECHL games and you'll see a couple of punches like the one Bertuzzi delivered. That doesn't make punching someone a noble deed, but it does show that when Bert went after Moore he wasn't doing something he would have thought was dangerously out of the norm. Does anyone claim to be troubled by Tie Domi's sucker punch that rang Ulf Samuelsson's bell? People loved it then and still laugh when they talk about it.

The shift I'll never forget: A Colorado defenceman (I believe it was Adam Foote) had the puck and was setting up behind his own net for a controlled breakout. I came from the bench on a line change and sprinted to the left hash mark to cover the Avalanche right-winger, who happened to be Steve Moore. When I realized it was Moore who was right in front of me, and knowing the score was 8–2, I thought I'd try to get him to fight me. I asked him to go and gave him a whack. He didn't take the bait. The Avs broke out of their end and started heading toward our end. As I was back-checking I focused on the puck but I could hear the crowd start to buzz. Out of the corner of my eye I saw someone grabbing a Colorado player. All of a sudden there was a roar from the crowd and I realized what had happened. Someone got Moore. I saw a couple of bodies hit the ice with a Canucks player on top of Moore. I started to skate over to the pileup and saw another Avalanche player, Andrei Nikolishin, jump on the back of our guy, who I realized was Bertuzzi.

So I jumped on Nikolishin's back to peel him off. As I was on top of Nikolishin I heard him screaming for us to get off. Through the pile of bodies I could make out Moore on the bottom. I noticed a pool of blood growing around his head. This isn't good. We immediately got off the pile. Moore didn't move. I was so focused on Moore that I didn't even realize the chaos going on around me. Brad May was engaged in his third fight of the night. Some of the Avalanche players were in shock and some were going nuts. The Avalanche coaching staff was going ballistic. As I was getting my bearings I noticed that Bertuzzi was nowhere to be found. Apparently, Bertuzzi was quickly removed from the pile, escorted off the ice and out of the arena. (The next time I saw Bert was four years later at a charity hockey game in Anaheim.)

An eerie silence came over the building in the aftermath. That tends to happen when someone lies on the ice for an extended period of time without moving and is taken away on a stretcher and then in an ambulance. I think if a vote had been taken the players and fans would have called the game right there. No one wants to see anyone get taken off the ice like that. I think both teams were so rattled that the remainder of the game was relatively uneventful.

It was a bizarre scene in the dressing room afterwards. There were mobs of media dying to speak to Bertuzzi and find out what exactly happened. The problem was no one knew where he was. So that left reporters having to wait until the following day to get the story. I must admit I was a tad curious myself.

Lost in the chaos was the fact that it was the trade deadline the very next day. The following morning, as I was walking into the dressing room, I was alerted to a team meeting held by General Manager Brian Burke. Burkie gave us an update on Moore and that he was still in the hospital. He gave us an update on Bert,

FOURTH MAN ON THE PILE

which wasn't much. He then informed everyone that they traded for Geoff Sanderson and Marc Bergevin. About thirty seconds after the meeting I was given the tap to go see Crawford in his office. And that was the end of my Vancouver Canucks comeback and, as it turns out, my NHL career.

I don't want this chapter to be a downer in what is otherwise a lighthearted book. However, since this incident occurred during my final game in the league, I felt it had to be addressed.

I'll finish things with this story. A few years after the night in question I went to watch the Ducks versus the Wild in Anaheim. My brother was a teammate of Bertuzzi's at the time and Steve Moore's brother Dominic was a member of the Wild. I spent the entire night with my own personal "iso" camera on Moore wondering if he would ever try to do something to Bertuzzi. And you know what? He never went near him. Never tried to slash him, hit him, or rub him out along the boards. Maybe that was Dominic's way of saying he didn't agree with the NHL's general acceptance of frontier justice, and wouldn't be a part of it.

I've had many years to try to make sense of what happened that night. One player never stepped on the ice again, and the other never returned to the player he once was. On one side you have a player whose career was cut short by an ugly attack and on the other side you have someone who made a devastating split-second decision in defence of his friend and teammate that went horribly wrong. I'm not sure how this will all play out in the courts. Not that it matters to Moore or his family, but one thing I do know is that if Todd Bertuzzi could go back in time there isn't a doubt in my mind he would just let go of Moore's jersey and skate away.

After I arrived back in the 'Peg I was greeted by the whole Moose team asking whether or not a bounty was actually placed on Moore's head. Apparently, the fellas were reading too much of the *National Enquirer*. While I attempted to make up a couple far-fetched stories about the incident, no one believed me. Apparently I'm not that good at fiction. But someone else thought he was.

Dallas Eakins had a software program that allowed him to manipulate news stories on the Internet and make them look authentic. He found an article about the Steve Moore/Todd Bertuzzi incident that he liked and made some changes to the story. He was able to change the whole context of the article to make it look like Moore was injured when I jumped on the pile. He tried to get me to bite on the story. And he may have got me, except he just couldn't keep his poker face long enough and he cracked. However, since he did such a masterful job I didn't want it to go to waste. I knew just where to send it. Big Jim is always looking out for his boys, which makes him a perfect target. I emailed him the story and waited for his response. A couple hours later I got it: "Sean, I think you need to get a lawyer."

Hook, line, and sinker!

The Manitoba Moose's season came to an end and we didn't qualify for the playoffs. There's nothing worse than a long summer for a hockey player. The good news for me was that I had a new addition to the family. Vann Atticus Pronger was born April 2, 2004. Interestingly, this was the same date as my last goal in North America. His delivery was a cakewalk compared to his sister's, so I was able to be at the hospital for his birth in the morning, make sure everyone was OK, and still be able to make it for the game that night. I'm sure you've heard of players putting money on the board when they play one of their old teams; imagine how much you have to put up when you have a kid that day! Ouch!

If you're ever going to miss the playoffs, having a newborn is a great way to help you remember what is truly important in life.

Since the Vancouver Canucks qualified for the playoffs there was an outside chance that I could be called up. The Canucks were aware that I had a brand new baby so they didn't want to pull me away from my family unless they absolutely had to. So, they proposed that I remain in Winnipeg but skate on my own. As great as that sounds, it's difficult to try to stay ready for NHL playoff action when you're skating by yourself. So I recruited some people to skate with me. In goal was our fifty-plus-year-old medical trainer, Ross Hodgkinson; up front was *Winnipeg Sun* journalist Ken Wiebe; and anchoring our blue line was Vaughn Hockey equipment rep Jorg Achenbach. What a lineup! This collection of Black Aces was trying to help me stay in game shape in case Vancouver needed someone to shut down Jarome Iginla and company. I guess that made me the Ace of the Black Aces! As it turns out, it was all for naught. The Canucks were eliminated in seven games by the Calgary Flames and I was spared the embarrassment of trying to keep up with NHLers after skating with my new men's league team.

13

GERMANY: NEIN DANKE!

You know those music videos where they show the band on the tour bus, looking exhausted and forlorn, just staring out the window? That's exactly how I felt when I was riding the iron lung in my final year in the minors. I was in my early thirties, had spent the better part of the previous decade on the wrong side of the NHL equator, and wondered if there wasn't something better to do with my time.

I was wrapping up my second tour with the Manitoba Moose, and we were not going to make the playoffs. I was in a foul mood. It didn't matter what league I was in, missing the playoffs always drove me nuts. Missing the post-season in Canada made it even worse. Minors or not, playoff hockey in Canada is awesome and I was sour that I wouldn't be experiencing it. I guess it was a fitting end to a long, tiring year.

I had started the season with the Blue Jackets but was quickly dispatched to Syracuse. It was then that I asked for the trade to Manitoba. Thankfully, Columbus GM Doug MacLean was able to accommodate me and luckily Winnipeg GM Craig Heisinger (along with then Canucks GM Brian Burke) was willing to take me. When I arrived the Moose roster looked nothing like the group that I had left three years prior. There were a lot of young players. It was one of those years where nothing seemed to flow. It felt like we were swimming upstream the entire season. I remember speaking with Heisinger at the end of the year. He wanted me to come back but wasn't sure if the Canucks would want that. I loved playing in Winnipeg. But I didn't know if I could handle another season like the one that had just finished. I told him I was considering Europe. He told me to keep him in the loop.

Europe just seemed like the right move at the time. Mrs. Journeyman and I wanted an entire season where we would live in the same city. Our daughter had just turned two and our son had just been born. Given my history with trades/waivers/re-calls and so on, the kids likely wouldn't have seen a lot of Daddy if I'd remained in North America. We also knew that the longer we waited the harder it would be to uproot the entire family. We decided to try hockey on the other side of the pond. This was not a decision that was taken lightly. At that stage of my career I knew that if we went to Europe there would be no turning back. We'd be blowing up the bridge back to North America as soon as we crossed the Atlantic. Still, it felt like the right thing to do.

We had offers from a few teams but decided on the Frankfurt Lions. I checked to see who was going to be playing for Frankfurt in the upcoming season and there were one or two familiar names on the roster. Frankfurt offered us 70,000 euros, which wasn't bad dough but not as much as I was expecting. The financial blow was softened somewhat because the club took care of our apartment, car, and health insurance. And to be honest, money wasn't the reason we decided on Europe. It was a consideration but not *the* consideration. Our motivation was to be together as a family and have a little bit of an adventure late in my career.

255

I knew very little about the Deutsche Eishockey Liga (DEL) other than the fact that teams were allowed to carry up to twelve imports. That was a huge factor for us because we felt there would be a few other English-speaking couples that we could hang out with a bit. That was what we expected, anyway. More on that false assumption later.

The first sign things were not going to be as rosy as we expected them to be came in early August. We were a week away from flying overseas and we still didn't have confirmation from the team as to where we were going to live. Keep in mind we signed our deal in May and asked Frankfurt to provide us with the address of our residence as soon as they could. Now, perhaps we were a little at fault for not following up enough during what was a hectic summer; however, we thought that one week before arrival we should have had some sort of heads up. Ultimately we didn't get too worked up because our experience with North American teams was that things always got worked out pretty quickly upon arrival to the city especially when there were children involved. Why would teams in Germany be any different?

My wife and I were excited and anxious to begin the next phase of our lives and my career. I was just thirty-one years old and figured I still had a lot of good hockey left in me. What better way to wrap up a career than head to Europe for a couple of years and see the world while I played some hockey? During the packing process, I must have asked my wife a dozen times, "Why didn't we do this sooner?"

Since we had two small children we decided to pack more than we needed. Better to be safe than sorry, as the old saying goes. Well let me tell you, safe can sometimes be a real pain in the ass. When the packing was done we had eight huge hockey bags zipped up full. The bags were jam-packed with clothes, toys, strollers, Baby

Bjorns, bottles, sterilizers, playpens, compact discs, and a number of other things I can't remember. You name it and we packed it. Since the flights that leave Dryden aren't exactly the size of 747s, we had to ship four of the bags to Thunder Bay a day before we left on our journey to Europe.

Travelling with two young kids to anywhere can be challenging at best. Travelling with two young kids from Dryden, Ontario, to Frankfurt, Germany, is a multi-day circus act. Starting on Tuesday, August 10, 2004, our travel days went something like this:

The family flew from Dryden to Thunder Bay. We then picked up our extra bags that were shipped earlier and enjoyed a four-hour layover in the bustling Thunder Bay International Airport. Next, we flew from Thunder Bay to Toronto. Collected all eight hockey bags, loaded them on three luggage carts, and wheeled them to airport storage. Checked into a Toronto hotel and tried to keep two young kids entertained for a day and a half, until the flight to Frankfurt that left the following evening at 10 p.m.

All that was left was a seven-hour flight with two rambunctious kids to a non-English-speaking country to begin the next phase of our lives. I thought the trip from Dryden to Frankfurt was going to be the toughest part of the whole transition from North America to Europe. But when the kids slept six of the seven hours on that flight, the air travel turned out to be the only thing that really went smoothly.

When we landed in Frankfurt we experienced a bit of a culture shock. Hearing a foreign language is obviously something you brace for, but realizing that we needed to pick up at least a little German to survive was another. It had also been a while since I saw people smoking out in the open at an airport. Usually you find those people in the designated glass jail cells. Apparently, it's mandatory for all adults to light up because I didn't see one person not smoking.

Once we made our way to baggage claim we were greeted by my new coach, Rich Chernomaz, and new general manager, Lance Netherly. They helped us load up our eight hockey bags and two screaming kids. Thankfully, I rode with Chernomaz and my wife and kids rode with Lance. My wife told me later that night that both kids screamed for the entire forty-minute drive. Who knew those kids had a sixth sense? Cherno and Lance chauffeured us to our new place (which was the first time we ever learned the address of it, by the way), and I could tell by the looks on their faces that the first time we saw our new house was the first time they saw it too. It was, for lack of a better term, a dump. I would find out later that the team had found the place for us only days before our arrival. Before we left for Germany I recall the team asking if we needed anything specific. I distinctly remember asking for two cribs. For some reason I wasn't shocked that there was only one. What better time than then to introduce a two-year-old to the differences between a bed and a crib? Throw in jet lag, a new home, and a new room, and I'm sure she was feeling about as lost as I was. Did I mention that her bedroom door was hanging off its hinges? That made it really easy for her to run into our room every single hour for the first three weeks of our stay. I was forced to lie on the floor next to her at the beginning of each night so she would stay in her bed. Lucky for us it only took the team handyman two months to fix the door problem.

Our new residence was close to Frankfurt the way that Long Island is close to Manhattan. It was a fifty-minute commute in stop-and-go traffic for me to get to the rink. The icing on the cake was that we were the only family from the team living in the town of Lammerspiel. The rest of the import players and their families lived close to each other, while we were about an hour away from my nearest English-speaking teammate. The season hadn't even started and I was already frustrated on a number of levels.

Team medicals were just another reason for my blood to boil. Since I didn't have a clue where I was going, I was lucky that one of the German players, Marty Reichel, offered to give me a ride. Upon arrival at the doctor's office we noticed that Marty was scheduled for a 9 a.m. physical while I was slotted for 2:30 p.m. So much for my ride home. There was no way I was going to ask my new teammate to hang around for six hours while I waited to take my physical. I checked to see who had the 9:30 booking and it was our backup goalie Boris. Boris was a German and knew his way around, so I politely asked him if he would change time slots with me so I could grab a ride back to Lammerspiel with Marty. Boris didn't have a problem with it, but he was the only one.

When the nurse called for Boris I explained my situation and told her Boris was OK with the switch. She reluctantly led me into the doctor's office and then whispered something into the doctor's ear. After quickly dismissing her, he unloaded on me.

"This is not your correct time. Please come back at your scheduled time."

"It's OK. I switched with Boris, so he'll take my time at 2:30. Marty just finished and he's my ride. I don't want to keep him waiting too long."

"I'm sorry. That will not work. You must come at your scheduled time."

"What does it matter? I'm here now. Someone will be here at 2:30. This won't screw up the schedule. Let's get on with this."

"No, I'm not changing the schedule."

"Are you kidding me? As long as I'm on time, what does it matter who comes in?"

"It matters because you Americans always think you can come in here and do whatever you want. We have rules here for a reason. If I let you change your time, then the next player changes his time, at some point we'll fall behind schedule."

"Are you out of your mind? First of all, I'm Canadian. Secondly, I'm not changing the time; I merely switched spots with a teammate so I could help out another teammate. What is wrong with that?"

I'd like to say I got my way. But I didn't. I had to wait until 2:30 to get my medical. Marty went home and then came all the way back to get me. I had been in Germany for all of four days and I was just about ready to blow my stack. I told myself that once hockey started it would all seem a little more normal.

When I received my training camp schedule everything looked pretty standard. There was an off-ice workout in the morning followed by an on-ice session in the afternoon. Perfect. That is, until I found out how far I needed to travel to get to each of the workouts. For three weeks straight, I spent as much time on the road as I did at my profession. And that's not an indictment on my commitment level at the time. I would drive one hour to the gym, work out for an hour and a half, and then drive one hour back to Pronger Haus. I would get approximately an hour with the family before having to drive another seventy-five minutes to the rink for practice. Once the hour and a half of practice was up it was back into the Volkswagen for the trek back home. Yes, *volks,* I spent close to five hours of my day commuting. And that's a conservative number. Add traffic, and the minutes piled up dramatically. My sanity was eroding by the day.

As bad as it was for me, it was worse for Mrs. Journeyman. At least I had people I could talk to during the day. She was stuck in a strange house, in a strange town, with two small kids who couldn't speak any language. It was like she was doing time. Our romantic vision of seeing Europe while I played out my final few years in pro hockey disappeared within a month.

Our only saving grace during that training camp was due to a couple of pit stops I would make on my way home from practice. I would stop at a deli and pick up a variety of meats and cheeses. I would then drop in to our favourite wine store, otherwise known as the gas station, to grab a nice $3 bottle of grape. I can't say many good things about our European hockey experience, but I must say the gas station wine was fantastic. Once we got the kids to bed we would sit in silence, enjoy our food, and drink our wine. That was how I envisioned our year when we decided to turn our backs on North America. I figured we would enjoy some hockey, good food, and old-world wine. Yet after three weeks I'm sure Mrs. Journeyman was thinking the exact same thing that I was: Is there any way to get out of this? I guess we were just too stubborn to quit.

When you live in a foreign country there are certain things you realize you've always taken for granted. One of them was the ability to communicate on the most basic level. Looking back, it probably wouldn't have been a bad idea to try to learn just a few German phrases, or at the very least a couple of words. I don't know how many times I tried to use my vast knowledge of hand signals when asking for directions or ordering food for the family. Just another ignorant North American figuring everyone everywhere else should speak our language. One more thing we'd taken for granted was the grocery stores or Walmarts back home. In Canada or the States we're accustomed to having someone bag our groceries after they scan them at the register. That didn't happen in Germany. For the record, it wasn't a problem at our local grocery mart, where we bought only enough perishables for a couple of days. (Note to future DELers: refrigerators are very small in Europe so they can only hold so much. However, since we had just arrived, we needed to stock up on diapers, formula, beer, and so on. So we made a Walmart run. After hauling our jet-lagged kids around the store for the better part of two hours it was finally time to check out. I watched the girl at the register scan our supplies while they all piled up at the end of the conveyor. In the back of my mind I was thinking, "Someone should really bag those." I was right. Someone should've bagged those, and that someone was me. After purchasing more than $400 of "stuff" I had to bag all of it while the lady kept ringing up other people. Their crap was running into our crap and all the while I was getting the hairy eyeball from every customer that came through. The things we take for granted.

Fast-forward three months (which felt like three decades). I was playing terribly, we still lived in the dump, both kids had been sick since the moment we touched down in Germany, and I still had to commute anywhere from two and a half to five hours a day. I was losing my mind on a daily basis. One particular day I was in an especially bad mood on my daily pilgrimage to the rink. As per usual I got honked at and flipped off by a local on the roads for apparently doing something wrong. That was the proverbial straw that broke the Pronger's back. Twelve weeks of frustration finally got to me. I drove up beside the guy and made every gesture I could think of to get him to pull over. It was go time! Fortunately, he never did. But I was still fuming. The remainder of the drive did not calm me down. When I got to the rink, I stormed into the locker room and challenged every one of my German teammates.

"Any of you f—ing Germans want to go?" I yelled. "I am sick of you people and today is the day I do something about it!"

The room went quiet, as I'm sure most guys were trying to figure out if I was kidding or not. I can only assume that my meltdown wasn't the first from an import rookie to the DEL, because everyone just looked at me for a second and then went about their business. My rage was not satisfied.

"I'm serious! Someone stand up right now!"

"OK," came the response from behind me.

I was somewhat surprised to hear someone pipe up, and when I turned around I wasn't entirely happy that someone did.

I was eye to eye with our six-foot-three German trainer who was built like a truck. Word was that he was also a boxer. Oh well, in for a penny, in for a pound(ing).

"All right then, let's go."

I didn't know if he was serious or if he thought I was serious. After yelling at people my blood had gone from a full boil to just a simmer. At that point I wasn't sure if I was into a fight anymore but things had gone too far to turn back. I squared off with this very large German boxer who did not look like he was getting ready for his first dance. Right then I decided I had just been kidding. My plan was to throw a couple shadow punches to make it look good and call it a day. Unfortunately, when I loaded up and threw my first jab he leaned in. BOOM! Right hand to the left eye socket and our trainer went down to one knee. I helped him up and gave him a hug.

"Thanks, I needed that," I told him.

I was praying he wasn't pissed because he surely would have killed me.

"No problem," was all he said.

I don't know if it ever felt better to hit someone. Luckily, he wasn't hurt (just a little mouse under his eye), and luckily he decided not to hurt me.

That year was by far the most frustrating of my career. I started in a rut and could never get out of it. I remember our coach calling me into his office about five games into the season to see how everything was going. I didn't want to lie to him so I let him know that things were terrible both on and off the ice. He told me not to worry and tried to reassure me that almost all the North Americans had a tough time at first. He even told me of a story from the season prior about a player who struggled mightily out of the gate. The import he spoke of went thirty-three games into the season before he scored his first goal. Then he went on a tear for the second half of the season and helped his club win the championship. I hardly listened to the coach as he tried to cheer me up, and thought to myself that if I went the first thirty-three games of the season without scoring I would shoot myself.

It didn't take me thirty-three games to score my first goal. It took me thirty-*six* games. Fortunately, I didn't own a gun. When I finally scored, I got a standing ovation from the fans of Frankfurt. Although I appreciated the gesture I was still pissed off about my whole predicament. It was such a weak goal. Not that it mattered but I was trying to shoot high glove, fanned on it, and it went in low blocker. Unbelievable! Why couldn't it have come thirty games before? I never thought that I would struggle to score goals in what I thought would be a much weaker league than the NHL. I even thought going in that it might be an inferior league to the AHL. Of course I was wrong about that. I felt like a five-handicap in golf struggling to break 100. And the European rules! For the life of me I couldn't get a handle on them. A little heads up from the boys on the team would've been nice. Maybe since none of them were six-foot-three they didn't experience similar problems. I'm not sure if it was because I was fairly tall for a player over there but it seemed like every time I hit someone it resulted in a penalty. Two minutes for being too big, Mr. Pronger. One game I absolutely destroyed a guy with one of the biggest open-ice hits of my career and I got two minutes for roughing and another ten minutes for a hit to the head. I snapped at the German referee. "Where am I supposed to hit the guy if he's prancing through the neutral zone with his head down?" I screamed. That got me another two minutes in the box. Perhaps it was the ref who was lucky I didn't own a gun.

Every time I moved on the ice it seemed like I did something wrong. Early in the season we were on a power play and I went to forecheck the defender after the puck was dumped in. What are we taught early on about forechecking? First man takes the body and second man takes the puck. Well, I took the body. Another great hit, or so I thought. Apparently, I hit him a little too hard for the ref's liking. That was another two-minute penalty for finishing my check. Which pretty much finished my days on the power play.

With my frustration building there were a few moments on the ice that made me laugh. Our captain, Jason Young, had played in Germany for the better part of a decade. He played for one or two years in the American Hockey League before he took his talents to Germany. He had put together an impressive résumé, winning two championships with Cologne and one with Frankfurt. He was a good player and a good captain who was passionate about winning. He was also very impressed with himself and his DEL accomplishments. One game, we were playing the Iserlohn Roosters on the road. Mike York, who played for a number of years in the NHL for a number of teams, was playing for the Roosters during the lockout. I was already in the penalty box when York and Young started mixing it up together. They both got roughing minors and headed to the penalty box. While Young was in the penalty box he continued to taunt York.

"Hey York, how many championships do you got?"

To which York replied, "Hey Younger, I don't even play in this league!"

Young was my captain and teammate, but I couldn't help but laugh out loud at that zinger!

As I was struggling to find my way on the ice, the off-ice situation didn't get any better. After seeing where the other players and their families lived I had told the team that we needed to move. This request took place near the end of August. I had been told in early October that they had a new place lined up for us. Yet somehow in the middle of November we were still living in the dump. I don't know if they couldn't find a place, didn't think I was serious, or just didn't care, but nothing happened. So I decided to go for the low blow. A little white lie. I told them that my wife and kids were going to go back to Canada for the remainder of the season if our living arrangements didn't change. Oddly enough, the tactic worked. Within a week we had a new place.

Our new place was great. It was a huge townhouse at the end of a complex so it only had one common wall. We had a backyard for the kids and all the doors were still on their hinges. It was only ten minutes down the freeway to the rink. We also had teammate Dwayne Norris and his family only five minutes away. The Newf had seen many a North American lose it their first year. He said to be patient. Things seemed to be turning around. We moved in the week before Christmas and I was pretty sure that the season could still be salvaged. I should have known better.

Shortly after we took possession of our new townhouse, Mrs. Journeyman had some of the wives and girlfriends over on a Sunday while we played an afternoon game on the road. The sun was shining so the kids in attendance were outside playing in the backyard, a backyard we shared with our neighbours. They were a young couple with no kids. We never really introduced ourselves to them but they seemed nice. Oh, how looks can be deceiving.

I remember sitting in my usual spot on the bus neck-deep in a game of Texas Hold'em when one of my teammates' wives called. All I heard was:

"Prong's wife did what? No way."

Apparently, the kids were playing ball hockey in the backyard and every so often the ball would go over to our neighbour's side. The kids would go get it and keep playing. This happened a few times. The last time it went over the kids decided they'd had enough and went inside. Before Tracy Norris (teammate Dwayne Norris's wife) went over to grab the tennis ball, our neighbour came out of her house and picked it up. Tracy thought she was going to hand it to her, but instead our neighbour threw it, hit Tracy in the chest, and then walked back into her house. Tracy came in from outside and told the rest of the women what happened. With months of frustration built up, that was Mrs. Journeyman's snapping point. She went out and started pounding on our neighbour's front door. The neighbour opened it and my wife laid into her. Our neighbour didn't want to hear it so she tried to slam the door shut, but my wife stuck her foot in the doorway and then kicked the door in. Mrs. Journeyman continued her verbal assault on our next-door neighbour until the lady's husband came down the stairs to see what all the commotion was. He calmly separated the ladies, and my wife went back to our house. I'm not sure if I've ever been more proud of my wife than on that day.

Don't get the wrong idea about us. We're usually very nice people. There was just something about that period of our lives that made us act like my brother after a playoff loss. That's just what culture shock is, I guess. That, and when nothing happens the way you think it should. When all the little things that make up your day—the small courtesies and gestures you never think about, or the taste of your coffee or the smell of your fabric softener—when all of that feels wrong, suddenly you're just in a bad mood. All the time. It's strange trying to explain to someone who's not there why you're in such a rage, because as you describe your circumstances it's clear that nothing is really all that wrong. And yet, everything is wrong.

We were angry, frustrated, and constantly looking for an argument or a fight. Need further proof? Since we had such young children it was sometimes challenging to go to certain places. The mall in Frankfurt was not such a place. It had a lot of room to let them run around and, well, act like kids. The mall also had a few North American restaurants. As much as we loved the food in Germany, it was fun to head to a Pizza Hut for a change. This particular Pizza Hut had a designated kids' area. I'm not going to lie—both our kids are loud and lively, which I love. However, in Germany I was in the minority when it came to the love of noisy children. Five minutes after we sat down an elderly German couple took a seat right on the edge of the kids' section. I knew right away that trouble was a-brewing! Every time one of our kids screamed, laughed, or acted like a child we got the furry eyeball from the couple. We didn't care a single bit. The louder the kids got, the more we smiled and stared at the older couple. We were practically begging them to turn around. Can you believe it? We were silently taunting an elderly couple. Not our finest moment, to be sure, but I blame it on six months of pent-up frustration. And besides, they chose seats in the kids' section. Finally, the old lady couldn't help herself; she turned around and "shushed" us. If looks could kill, that lady would be in the ground and my wife would be locked up. Fortunately my wife had our son on her lap, because if she could have she would've walked over there. Instead, I got the "Sean, get over there and straighten them out." I wasn't exactly sure what "straighten them out" meant, but I was happy to go yell at the old couple. The six-foot-three German boxer/bodybuilder had not been a smart fight, but I knew I could handle myself against these misers. I went over to our cheery German friends and leaned on their table.

"Is there a problem?"

"No speak English."

"Kinder. Do you have a problem with the kinder?" I said, making gestures to our kids and knowing full well they could speak English.

She basically said our kids were loud.

"Then don't sit near the kids' section. And don't ever shush us again."

If that was an isolated incident we probably would have apologized for the noise and tried to keep our kids quiet. Yet with all the crap we had endured since arriving in Germany, we actually felt better for confronting the old coots. Sad, I know.

One of the bright spots in an otherwise dim season was the arrival of Doug Weight. There was another work stoppage in the NHL and this time it landed me a linemate instead of costing me a job. I had played against Doug in college and in the NHL as well. Obviously, he was a player with world-class skills. He was extremely talented and had incredible hockey sense. In other words, he was exactly the type of player I didn't get many chances to play with when I was lucky enough to be in the NHL. For the team it was great to add a player like Doug. And, selfishly, for me it was nice to have another North American around to talk to. Doug had been a member of the St. Louis Blues with my brother, so we knew each other a little before he arrived and became pretty good friends once he did.

I'm not sure why the coaching staff decided to put Doug on the same line as Sean "the anchor" Pronger, but I like to tell myself that Doug had it written into his contract. Whatever the reason,

Doug and I were linemates for most of the remainder of the season and developed decent chemistry. We didn't set any league records together, but we had our moments. Dougie had his as well. When he first came over he was without his family, so they put him in a hotel. Around the same time we hired Brad McCrimmon to be our assistant coach. Brad was a mentor for my brother, Chris, when he was a rookie in Hartford, so we shared a common bond. He basically had to undo all that I had done when Chris was growing up. Anyway, I remember Doug approaching me one day before practice.

"Prongs, I need help." I was thinking he was having a "language" problem or a "German" problem.

Excited by the possibility of another confrontation, I told him, "Who is it and let's go get him!"

"It's Beast [Brad McCrimmon]," he said.

"What? Brad's German?"

"No, you idiot. He's trying to drink me to death!"

I guess what was happening was after practice the two of them would head back to the hotel and grab lunch. While they ate lunch Brad thought it was a good idea to have a couple beers and talk hockey. Why not? The problem was that one of them was still playing and one wasn't. Apparently, this went on for the first two weeks Doug was in Germany. It was too bad my wife wouldn't let me move to the hotel—you know, to help out a teammate.

I had the privilege of playing for Brad McCrimmon for only a few months. But in that short time it was easy to see why he'd spent his entire adult life in the NHL. This guy lived and breathed hockey. I learned more from him in the three months I was with him than with any other coach I've had. While he was unbelievable on the ice, you certainly don't want him at the card table. And it's not because of his card skills. We used to play Texas Hold'em after every game on the road. We'd pick up a couple cases of beer and some pizza for the four- to five-hour bus ride back to Frankfurt. Almost on cue, Brad would come back and grab a slice and a pint. Once the beer hit his lips it was story time. I loved listening to his stories, but it was frustrating that our card games would grind to a halt because everyone was listening to him spin his next yarn. As he went from story to story he kept eating our pizza and chugging our beer. Beast was a great hockey player, a great coach, and one of the best guys I've ever met. He will be missed.

The season in the DEL is somewhat shorter than in the North American leagues. We played fifty-two regular season games before the playoffs began in early March. The Frankfurt Lions finished the season in first place and ended up playing Hamburg in the first round. When the regular season ended I kept thinking that I could still salvage the season by playing well in the post-season. If I could play like I'd expected to when I came over all would not be lost. I wish I could tell you a happy ending to this story. I wish I could say that we caught the bad guy, saved the world, *and* got the girl in the end—but, as I'm sure you've figured out, that just isn't my style. Nope, my style is to go pointless and rack up six penalty minutes before blowing out my MCL in game four of the first round. If I could have scripted my time in Europe before my time in Europe it would have gone pretty much exactly opposite to the way it did.

I stuck around to watch my teammates fall in the second round to Mannheim. And once that was done, the Pronger family couldn't get out of Germany fast enough.

Even though I played a lot better in the second half of the season, scored a few goals, spent a little more time on the ice than in the penalty box, and picked up a new BFF in Doug Weight, all of that did little to brighten my Germany experience. I knew I wasn't going to return to the DEL, and I also knew that my playing career in all likelihood was over. I didn't care at that time. I just wanted to get back to Canada before I tried to start another fight with a seventy-year-old. And I almost made it.

As easy a trip as it was with the kids on the way to Germany, it was that difficult on the way home. My son, who had just turned one, started screaming the moment we arrived at the gate. And the screaming continued as we pre-boarded the flight and took our seats in the bulkhead right behind first class. That was a perfect spot for everyone to see which kid was going to ruin their flight as they walked past to their rows. It didn't matter how loud my son screamed, I couldn't wipe the smile off my face. Sure, we tried to calm him down, but as any of you with kids know, a screaming one-year-old will do what he wants 90 percent of the time. As we sat on the runway, I closed my eyes and thought, *We're going home!* I opened my eyes to catch a man to my left who had walked up from the back of the plane. He looked into the first-class cabin and then turned toward us. To this day, I swear he said "You better shut that kid up." And then he walked back to his seat.

I sat there stunned. Did that just happen? Did I hear that right? Did he just tell me to shut my one-year-old son up? Why am I being tested again? Talk about picking the wrong door. I was raging! I took a breath and asked my wife if she heard what the man said. She wasn't sure. If I had to lay money on it, I would have bet the house he said it. By the time I convinced myself that he said what I thought he said the plane had started to taxi. The man in question was sitting with his wife about ten rows behind us. He looked to be about sixty-five years of age. A little young for my liking, but I was amped up on adrenaline. I sat there for twenty minutes stewing about what I was going to say to the man. After the year I just suffered through that guy picked the wrong time to shoot his mouth off. I wasn't exactly sure what I was going to do, but at the very least I knew a verbal attack was in order. My wife was too funny. Normally, in a situation like that, she would tell me to calm down and forget about it. But she'd been in Germany the whole year as well. She basically said "Go get him." So when the seat-belt sign turned off, away I went.

As I walked down the aisle the man's wife stood up and went to the bathroom. I was a little disappointed because I wanted her to hear what kind of husband she had. I made eye contact, leaned in, and said:

"What kind of a man tells a one-year-old to shut up?"

"Excuse me?"

"You heard me. You walked up to the front of the plane and told me I'd better shut my kid up."

"I would never do that. I would never say such a thing. I have six grandkids myself."

"Mister, I've had a tough year. Do you promise me that you didn't say anything?"

"Son, like I said, I would never say such a thing to someone with a crying kid. I've been there myself."

Yes, it was official. I was possessed. And the only thing that would rid me of the demon was to get back on Canadian soil.

Ashamed, I apologized to the man.

"I don't know what to say other than I'm sorry, sir. I was out of line for coming back here. Enjoy the flight."

Completely rattled, I walked back to my seat, sat down, and whispered to my wife, "We need to hurry up and get into North American airspace before someone gets hurt."

It was the shortest twenty hours of travel in my life. We did it all in one day. Frankfurt to Toronto to Thunder Bay to Dryden. Much of the way back I thought about my future as a hockey player. I definitely did not want to suffer another nightmare like the one I had just had. If my agent had greeted me in Dryden with a fresh contract from the DEL it would have earned him a punch in the mouth.

For months, I had been dreaming of coming home. I'd spent years moving from city to city, so by "home" I didn't mean a white picket fence or anything. But I couldn't wait to be back where everything felt right. I'm not going to get all sentimental, but there's no way around the fact that when you spend a few months on a continent far away from most of the people who've mattered most in your life, you start to figure out that what you really miss is the company of the people who see things the way you do. And that means friends and family.

I know people say that time heals all wounds, but every time I think about our European hockey experience my cuts open right back up.

I often wonder how many more years of hockey I would have played if I hadn't gone to Europe.

14
———

SEAN'S BROTHER

Sean is writing a book? I think that is so nice that
Sean would write a book about Chris.
—FAMILY FRIEND, DECEMBER 2010

I'm sure a lot of people had the same thought when they heard that I was attempting to write a book about hockey. And while this book isn't about Chris, it wouldn't be my story if he didn't get his own chapter. My brother, Chris, plays for the Philadelphia Flyers. In all fairness, it can't be easy to be referred to as Sean's brother all the time. I mean, I was the first in the family to be drafted in the NHL and I was the first to be elected to the Hall of Fame. Yes, you read that correctly. I was a 2009 inductee into the Northwestern Ontario Sports Hall of Fame. I'm in the process of having my name legally changed from "Sean Pronger" to "Hall of Famer Sean Pronger." Stay tuned.

Although I was the first one in the family to be drafted, and even though my name has already been immortalized in a Hall of Fame, I'm sure it's been a long time since Chris was referred to as Sean's brother. In fact, it's more likely that people don't even know

Chris has a brother. And for the ones who do, let's just say I'm an afterthought to the majority of them. Countless times I've been referred to as "Chris" or "Chris's brother." Forget "Hall of Famer Sean Pronger"—I might as well change my name to "Rodney Pronger" or "Sean Dangerfield" with the amount of respect I get. Take for instance one beautiful sunny day when I was walking with Mrs. Journeyman down the street in our hometown of Dryden, Ontario. A friend of the family, whom I knew fairly well, stopped us to say hello. This is not uncommon in our town since everyone knows everyone. So, there I am, standing with my wife, when our friend says hi to my wife and then says to me:

"Hey Chris, you had a great season last year. Good luck next year. Make sure you say hi to Sean for me." And then he walked away.

I looked at my wife completely stunned and said, "Did he just call me Chris and ask me to say hi to myself?" If I weren't so lazy, I would've chased that old man down and given him a knuckle sandwich. As you know, I'm not afraid to throw down with a geezer. I mean, what could've been going through his head? I was walking with my wife and the old man knew she was my wife, yet instead of making the assumption I was Sean he blurts out Chris's name. I've been called Chris or Chris's brother a million times and on most occasions I couldn't care less. But for some reason the stupidity of that guy pissed me off.

Now, I will admit that we do look a little similar. I can see how those who don't know us very well or haven't seen us in a while make the mistake of calling me Chris. I'm tall, he's tall. We both have a ridiculously shaped nose. I get it. However, there were times when it should have been impossible to refer to me by my brother's name. When I played in the minors it was a common occurrence that an official would call me Chris. Usually it was just a slip of the tongue after seeing the nameplate on the back of my jersey. But on one occasion a linesman messed it up so many times I had to call him on it. The dude in question was already closing in on double digits in the wrong-name-calling department when I got ready to take a faceoff in the third period.

"Chris! Get your stick down! I don't want to have to say it again."

"Buddy, are you kidding me or yourself? You know this isn't the NHL don't you?"

"Yes Prongs, I do."

"Then can you explain to me why the fuck you keep calling me Chris?"

"Sorry, it won't happen again."

"Right."

I just don't get how it would happen on a daily basis. How could someone involved in the game make that mistake? Chris is a six-foot-six all-star defenceman who couldn't even name a minor-league city, and I'm a six-foot-three minor league journeyman centre. Let's not forget my first training camp with the Mighty Ducks. You may recall something about a missing medical folder. As it turned out it wasn't missing, it was just misspelled. Instead of spelling it S-E-A-N they spelled it the Canadian way, C-H-R-I-S. I guess it was just wishful thinking on the Ducks' part.

It's a good thing I don't take myself too seriously or I would have surely killed someone. The funny thing is people don't even realize they're being jackasses when they introduce me as "Chris Pronger's brother, Sean." It wouldn't be so annoying if they actually knew Chris, but more often than not they don't. Somehow they think it's a compliment to me to have my identity tied to my baby brother. And I guess in some instances they are right.

You may think I have an inferiority complex when it comes

to my superstar brother, but my therapist would say otherwise. After all, I'm smart enough, I'm strong enough, and gosh darn it, people like me. Besides, who do you think created the angry beast anyway? That's right. He may not admit it, but those of us on the inside know who should get some of the credit for the unbecoming way he carries himself on the ice. I'm sure he'll give me a great big thank-you at his Hall of Fame induction. I can't wait until I get my well-deserved fifteen minutes of fame for being an asshole big brother to him as a kid.

Like most little brothers with their older siblings, Chris was pretty much in my hip pocket when we were younger. Wherever I went, he went. And that was usually to a rink of some kind. I showed him how to shoot. I showed him how to pass. I kicked the crap out of him every second day (at least up until the day I thought I might not win the fight). Now, I can't take all the credit. I certainly didn't teach him to be six-foot-six. And I'm sure he'd say that there were some good hockey coaches along the way who helped him become the player he is. But this is my book, so I say he got where he is because of the countless pickup games we played as kids. Every day after school and on weekends the same group of buddies would come over to our house to play street hockey. And every day, Chris and I would be captains of opposite teams. Since we were the two best players they'd split us up. That set-up would usually last for about half the game. It was almost a certainty that at some point the other players would have to rearrange the teams so Chris and I would be on the same team. It wasn't because one team was destroying the other. It was due to the frequent stoppages in play to break up the fighting. Chris and I would go at it tooth and nail until someone decided to put us on the same team. And then it was like we were Gretzky and Kurri. Growing up we had an interesting relationship; we could be locked in a death match one minute and best buds the next.

I don't know how many fights we got into but it had to be somewhere in the thousands. And that is no joke. We would get after it a couple of times a day. Sometimes it was just a little jab and some hair pulling but most of the time it was the real deal. And it didn't matter where we were or who was around. If we couldn't play hockey on the street or at our local outdoor rink we would usually play in our basement. I was always the forward and he was always the defenceman. I'm certain this is where he perfected his signature "slash, slash, cross-check, can-opener" combination. Like most kids, we could make a rink out of any room. Our "basement rink" consisted of couches and oversize pillows. The way we had the net situated gave us the opportunity to hit each other into the couch (one side) or into a wall (the other side). The game would always start out nice and easy. I'd make a couple moves; sometimes I'd beat him, but most of the time I wouldn't. The layout of our basement certainly gave the advantage to the defenceman. Even as a young kid you could see Chris taking everything in. If I beat him one way one time, he would process what I did and then make sure it didn't happen again. On one particular day Chris kept closing the gap on me in the basement (yes, even as a ten-year-old he understood what it meant to take away time and space). As the game progressed he closed the gap tighter and tighter until I had no choice but to dump it into the corner of the basement, the side without the couch. I sprinted around him and tucked the ball into the goal. Chris was not pleased. So the next time he loosened his gap a bit as to not get beaten to the wall and slashed me across the hands for good measure. I was not pleased. The next time I dumped it in and let him beat me to the ball and then hammered him into our basement wall. As I scooped up the ball to score Chris delivered a large lumberjack two-handed chop to the back of my legs. Sound familiar? While I was on the ground screaming he ran past me to go find a safe place to hide. He decided to make a break for the stairs. I chased after him and caught up with him just as he reached the top of the stairs. I still remember the rage I felt. I grabbed him by the neck, had him stretched out with my right hand ready to fill him in. The whole time this was going on I was screaming language at him that no ten-year-old should have in his vocabulary. I was just about to deliver my first punch when someone interrupted the process by grabbing my wrist.

"What the hell?"

Sure enough, my mom had a hold of my arm so I wouldn't hurt her little baby.

"Sean, what are you doing?" she whispered.

"He slashed me!"

"Sean, would you shut your mouth." Again whispering.

And then I saw why. I guess it was bridge day at the Pronger household and about twenty ladies were just about to witness a domestic.

Just like that, the situation was resolved. And with no supplemental discipline to boot.

About a block and a half from our house was an outdoor rink, Milestone Rink. As soon as the ice was in we were on it. It was awesome. It felt like our personal arena. Sometimes we would skate there after school but mostly we would skate on the weekends. And when I say weekends, I mean the entire weekend. Looking back from a parent's perspective I have to think we must have been fairly easy kids to manage (I mean, outside of the fighting and swearing). We would be outside playing hockey for hours on end. Anyway, one night Chris and I were playing at Milestone Rink. As usual, we were on opposite teams. Even when we played against the older kids they'd separate us. Maybe it was because they wanted to see us kill each other. On one of the plays I undressed him and went in and scored. I may have taunted him afterward, but the details surrounding that are fuzzy so I can't be sure. The next time I came down, I went by him and then felt my right leg give out. It was another slash across the back of the legs. Are you kidding me? Does anyone see a pattern developing here? I got up immediately to see him skating off the ice.

"You're dead!" I screamed at him as I started the chase.

I was wondering where he was planning on going, because he made a left turn as he exited the rink. The shack where we put our boots was to the right. The only thing to the left was the dark alley that led back to our house. Wait a minute. He isn't planning on running home with his skates on, is he? Nope. He was planning on *skating* home. As I finally got out of the rink I could see him skating down the alley. For those unfamiliar with the winter conditions in Dryden, let's just say it gets a little chilly in the winter. Somewhere between −20 and −40 is the norm. This makes it cold enough to skate home on the road. I tried to chase him down but he beat me there. If that wasn't enough, to piss me off more he locked the door and stood on the other side beaming at me through the window. (And you thought stealing pucks at the end of Stanley Cup final games was annoying.) I stood at our back door screaming my head off at him. He sat in the window taunting me. He put his face right up next to the glass. I figured this was the closest I was going to get to give him a shot in the head. So I wound up and punched the window. As luck would have it, since it was so cold, the window cracked. As I was assessing the damage my dad walked around the corner to see what all the commotion was about. He took one look at the door, shook his head, and sent me to my room. As he escorted me down the hall I kept telling him, "Dad, he slashed me!" As usual, the referee only saw the retaliation.

Because we were two years apart we never really had the opportunity to play together during a season. I would play on one all-star team (or travel team) and he would play on the all-star team the age group below. However, one season the minor hockey association changed the age groups, which allowed me to play on the Peewee all-star team along with Chris. That was my first glimpse at the player Chris was becoming. Don't get me wrong, there's a long way to go between Peewee hockey and the National Hockey League, but you could tell there was something special about the kid. And he played the game then as he does now, fast and hard. One game we were playing in a regional tournament in Thunder Bay. It consisted of the best players in our area for our age group. Chris was by far the youngest, but that certainly didn't stop him from playing his game. As a defenceman he played a tight gap even back then. But he didn't always skate backwards with the opposing forward trying to drive around him. Sometimes Chris would just tomahawk the guy around the knees. The refs called it most of the time, but Chris understood they couldn't call it all of the time. And it didn't take long for the other kids to lose their desire to try to get around Chris. Remember, this was a nine-year-old playing against older and bigger boys. He wasn't six-foot-six yet, but he sure played like it.

In the fall before I was to enter Grade 12 I moved to Thunder Bay, Ontario, to play tier 2 Junior "A" hockey with the Thunder Bay Flyers. When I left Dryden in August I was about two inches taller than Chris. He was entering Grade 10. Chris and my parents came to visit me in October. We had a game that night. I remember walking out of the locker room after the game to see my brother towering over my parents. I figured he was standing on something.

I walked over to him and found myself staring at his mouth. He had grown about four inches in two and a half months. It was freaky. I knew I would never be looking down at my little brother again.

After my season in Thunder Bay was done I headed home for a weekend in May. Chris was playing in a high school hockey tournament in Fort Frances, Ontario. Throughout the year I heard from my parents that Chris was making quite a name for himself and he was starting to get a lot of attention. Since I hadn't seen him play at all that year, I decided to make the two-hour drive to Fort Frances to watch. What I saw was complete domination. Chris was the real deal. After growing more than a foot in six months, Chris somehow didn't skate or play with any awkwardness. He was tall and super thin yet there was no Bambi effect on the ice. I think that was the first time I was really proud of my brother. The first time I was proud to be his brother. I had no doubt he was going places, but I wasn't sure yet just how far he could go.

Since we grew up in Dryden we were fairly isolated from any big-city hockey talent. When you live in a remote area you think there's always going to be kids in the big cities that are better. It's not until you get to play against them that you realize those guys aren't better than you. I believe Chris had this figured out all along. For me, it was a constant struggle to convince myself that I was good enough.

As you can imagine, there were and are some perks to having a superstar brother in the NHL. One of them was that I got to have a superstar agent in Pat Morris. Do you think there would have been any way he would have represented me if Chris wasn't one of his clients? Picture Ari Gold from *Entourage* having to take on Johnny Drama because Vince said so. Same thing. Pat would no doubt argue this until he was blue in the face, but there was no way a player of my calibre should have had an agent of Pat's calibre.

Without Chris, I wouldn't have gotten a behind-the-scenes experience of Canada's dramatic gold-medal-winning performance at the 2010 Olympic Games in Vancouver. I'm about as patriotic as they come, and to share that moment with my children was one of the most memorable experiences of my life. Because of Chris, I also got to experience the Stanley Cup finals on three different occasions, including a game-seven loss as well as a game-five series-clinching win. I got the opportunity to take part in a Stanley Cup celebration. Although it was a celebration that almost didn't happen for me. Chris had to get twelve tickets—for our parents, numerous friends, and me—for game five of the 2007 final versus the Senators. Being such a large party, we had to sit a little higher in the stands than normal. At the end of the game we made our descent down to the locker room. On the way, we ran into a few of Chris's celebrity buddies. So Cuba Gooding Jr. (Rod Tidwell himself!) and Michael Rosenbaum (aka Lex Luthor) joined the crew and were at the front of the line to lead us all into the dressing room. I figured once we got to the team locker room I would flash my "I'm Chris's brother" badge and have security allow Cuba, Michael, and the rest of our posse in. As Cuba and Michael approached the security guard at the door I tried to yell at them to wait so I could take care of things. I don't even know if they broke stride as they were ushered straight into the Ducks locker room. As the door closed behind the "celebs" I went to open it. Instantly, I was stopped by security and received the hairy eyeball from the large doorman.

"Sorry sir, you're not allowed in here."

"It's OK. I'm with the team. I'm Chris Pronger's brother, and these are his parents."

"I'm sorry; you'll have to wait until they give me a list of who's allowed into the dressing room."

"Are you kidding me? We're family! Why did you let those other guys in?"

"They said they were friends of Chris."

Just before I was about to go off on a self-entitled rant to the nice security dude, Cuba poked his head back out of the door.

"It's OK. They're with us," he said.

"OK, Cuba. Thanks. Go ahead everyone."

I was too happy to get mad. After all, Chris had just won the Stanley Cup and it was party time. I still remember walking into the packed room with the plastic on the walls and the champagne flowing. And this was before the players had even made their way in from the ice! I saw GM Brian Burke out of the corner of my eye, walked over to give him a congratulatory handshake, and before I could extend my hand he bear-hugged me. That was one of the few times in my life I saw the big Irishman crack a smile.

It was a great night. The locker room was rocking and guys were going off like they should in a moment like that. But, to be honest, it was a little weird for me. It was when Teemu Selanne stood on the top of a table screaming his head off, guzzling champagne, that I realized I was never going to get to experience that feeling. I knew that I was never going to get a chance to win a Stanley Cup as a player. It was a sobering thought. But it was also about the only sobering thing of the night. I was ecstatic for Chris. He deserved it. Since I had witnessed the heartbreak of a game-seven loss the year before, I knew how badly he wanted it. I was especially happy for my parents. They certainly deserved it. It was great to watch them drink out of the Cup. For me, it felt strange to drink out of it. It wouldn't have been that awkward if I hadn't played in the NHL, but since I did I felt like I shouldn't be doing it. In the end I did hold the Cup, I did drink out of it, and I did get some great pictures with it. But I couldn't bring myself to hoist it over my head. That's what you do when you win it.

One question I get asked a lot is if I'm jealous of my brother. And you know what? It is definitely a legitimate question. The simple answer to the question is no. To be honest, if he was only a marginally better player than I was then perhaps there would have been more of a sibling rivalry in our professional years. There may have been sticking points and reasons for jealousy. But since our skill levels were so vastly different from the age of sixteen on, I never thought it made any sense for me to be jealous. Now that I think about it, maybe his success is a reason why I never packed it in. That's another talking point to bring up with my therapist. I'm not jealous of the fame he has. Not even when he won the Hart and Norris trophies. When they called out his name for the Hart Trophy at the 2000 NHL Awards in Toronto I remember thinking of him and me playing on an outdoor rink back in Dryden. And that somehow I had a small part in him standing up there accepting the trophy from Mark Messier. I certainly don't envy the fact that he's public enemy number one in virtually every city he goes to. The fine fans of Detroit booed Chris for his 1,000th game. It actually made me smile in the stands, although I'm not sure my folks enjoyed it that much. (I understood; I played against the guy.)

Personally, I take that as the ultimate compliment. I could only wish people cared enough to boo me! That said, I'm not jealous that no one has held an event to burn my rental furniture. Sure his bank account would be nice, but that by no means would make me happier than I am. What I can say I am jealous of is the way he plays hockey. I love the way he plays the game. He is a highly intelligent hockey player. I think people lose sight of that and focus on the slashes, cross-checks, elbows, and stomps. When I watch him play it's like he sees the game from the press box. Maybe it's because he's so tall, but he sees the ice and everyone on it at almost all times. As a former player I can tell you it's not that easy. When I was on the ice it felt like there were twenty people out there. Chris plays like its three-on-three. I remember playing against him in an exhibition game. I was playing for Boston and he was playing for St. Louis. I felt like the little engine that couldn't. It took every ounce of energy I had to keep up with the best players. I was sitting on the bench during that game, gasping for air, when Chris calmly skated backwards with the puck and sent a six-foot-high saucer pass up the middle for a breakaway chance. He's always made it look so easy. For him, the game is in slow motion. For me, the game was in fast forward. I got to witness up close the making of a Hart Trophy winner, Norris Trophy winner, Stanley Cup champion, two-time Olympic gold medallist, and a surefire first-ballot Hall of Famer. The way I see it is that people should probably be jealous of me for getting to go along for the ride.

Anyway, I'm not going to make the mistake that everyone else makes, and treat this chapter as though it's all about my brother. He's a good guy and all, but there's a lot more to the story.

What kind of book would this be if I didn't mention "the boys"? The childhood friends I grew up with. Everyone has a group of lifelong friends. You know, the ones who stick with you throughout the years. The ones you can go months without talking to and then pick up the conversation like it was only a day or two. The kind of friends who can't bail you out of jail because they're sitting there next to you.

All those hockey games Chris and I played in front of our house (161 St. Charles St.), all the games we played at Milestone Rink, and all the games we played for real, these guys were always there. Our wolf pack was not made of a lone wolf. No, we were a six-man wolf pack. In the pack were Darcy Mitani (Mit), Steve Roll

(Rock), John Cummings (Hummer), Chris Hancock (Herbie), Chris Pronger (Weasel), and yours truly.

I wish I would've videotaped our street hockey games. You want to talk about passion? All we knew was hockey. In the book *Outliers,* Malcolm Gladwell enlightens us on the amount of work it takes to become an expert: 10,000 hours. We probably had expert status in hockey by the time we were twelve years old. We played after school, and then after dinner. On the weekends, as soon as everyone was up it was Game On. Our games weren't about trying fancy new moves. No way. Our games were life or death. It wasn't considered a game until someone was bleeding. And that would happen often. If anyone watched us play they would've thought we were crazy. Since it was so cold when we played, we had to wear ski mitts. And the ski mitts we wore had puffy padding on the front, so when you hit something with your fist it was cushioned. As we got older we started to perfect our fighting skills on each other. We had a couple guys with braces on their teeth. As I'm sure most of the brace-face community can attest, getting punched in the face while wearing braces is a messy proposition. It looked like a crime scene after some of our games. There was blood on the snow, on mitts, on jackets, and for some of the fellas, on faces. I remember coming in one evening after one of our usual games when Eila (Mom) saw my snowsuit in the light.

"Oh my goodness, Sean, what happened to you?"

"What are you talking about Mom? I'm fine." And then I checked myself out. I had blood all over my jacket and my mitts. And I don't mean a little, I mean a lot.

"It's OK, Mom. It's not mine."

Once in a while, a new kid would want to play with us. After he passed the required background check we'd let him know the time and place. One time we invited one of these kids to play with us. He wasn't entirely new, as we had played with him years before. Unfortunately for this kid, he hadn't played in our game for a long time. I don't think he got the memo that the game had progressed a little from the last time he participated. He was a decent player, but once things got physical he had second thoughts about joining our politically incorrect version of street hockey. To make matters worse, he got into an altercation with one of the boys and went home crying (and bleeding), never to return. What can I say; our game wasn't for everybody.

As we got older our road hockey games got a lot more physical. Once the snowbanks on the streets were high enough it was time to work on our hip checks. We'd set up the "gauntlet." All but one of us would line up beside the snowbank along the road. The lone runner's job was to try to run down the road and get through the gauntlet without getting hit. Things started out innocent enough, but as you can imagine it escalated quickly. It went from just getting a piece of the guy to trying to flip him over the snowbank. By the end of it the guys that were doing the hitting would work together to set up the runner for the last guy to absolutely CRUSH him. Of course this led to more fisticuffs and more bloodshed. Keep in mind all this is happening on the street outside my house. If my folks ever opened the door to listen to the language getting thrown around and witness the abuse they'd have signed Chris and I up for synchronized swimming in a heartbeat. I recall after one of our gauntlet sessions we had two or three guys bleeding while the rest of us were picking up sticks just as an elderly lady was driving by. I'll never forget the look of horror on her face when she got close enough to see our faces. There we were, laughing and bleeding, while this poor lady was trying to comprehend what she just saw.

Needless to say, with all of our hitting practice we couldn't wait to be able to use these skills in a real game. Mit, Herbie, Hummer,

Roll, and I all played on the same travel team, while little baby brother had to play on a travel team an age group below. One year, I think we were eleven or twelve years old (and still not allowed to hit), we were going to play in a tournament in Duluth and were told that body contact would be allowed.

"What? We finally get to hit for real!"

"This is going to be awesome!"

"We better start practising again."

So, for two weeks prior to the tournament, the six of us had mandatory hitting practice in the snowbanks outside 161 St. Charles St.

You can't even imagine our excitement in the locker room before the first game. And when the puck dropped, it was like a scene out of *Slap Shot* with the Hanson brothers running around like lunatics. We must have got seven or eight penalties before our coach finally asked the ref what his problem was.

"There's no hitting in this tournament."

"What the &%$#!"

Even now I'm still not sure who told us there was hitting allowed, but man it was fun for those first ten minutes.

As we entered high school the games became less and less frequent. Some of us started playing on a Midget travel team based out of Kenora, Ontario, and some played high school hockey. We were always tight in school but our years of playing together were coming to an end. As much as I would've liked, the band just couldn't stay together forever. Once in a while, scheduling would allow us to get together again. One particular game stands out: imagine a cold, crisp, clear afternoon on a lake in northwestern Ontario where the wind has blown all the snow off and the ice looks like sheer glass. That was the backdrop of one of our epic pick-up games. It was a scene out of a movie. We were out in front of Herbie's parents' place on Wabigoon Lake. I can't remember how many guys we had, but it was the six of us plus a few stragglers. Picture the biggest ice surface you've ever played on and multiply it by ten, and you get the idea of our sheet of ice on that day. We must've put the nets 300 feet apart. We played for hours. The temperature was at least 30 below but none of us cared. It may have been the greatest game of hockey we ever played. Did it ever get any better than that? No, it did not.

I still look back to those games in front of my house, at Milestone, on the lake, and wish I was a kid again. We didn't play because we were trying to make the NHL. Even though we dreamed of playing in the NHL we never thought it was possible for a bunch of small-town kids to make it to the big time. We played for the absolute love of the game. It's all we thought of and all we wanted to do. And boy did we ever play. I love telling my kids stories of what I did when I was their age. It makes me a little sad sometimes knowing my kids won't get to experience that feeling of freedom that comes from skating down a mile-long rink and the feeling of beating the shit out of their buddies in 40-below weather.

What's funny is that all the guys in our six-man wolf pack moved away from Dryden and have become successful in their own way:

John Cummings (aka Hummer) lives with his wife, Sandra (from Dryden), and two daughters (Kendall and Kate) in Guelph, Ontario. And he has found his new passion, ping-pong.

Steve Roll (aka Rock) lives with his wife, Cindy (from Dryden) and two kids (Ayla and Jack) in Calgary, Alberta. Steve spends most of his time trying to get back a six-pack (I don't mean beer) that he never had.

Darcy Mitani (aka Mit) just retired from playing professional hockey in the Asian League. And yes, he is Asian. And yes, they do have pro hockey in Asia. And yes, he is one of the most decorated players to ever lace them up there. He now lives in Winnipeg with his wife, Colleen (a police officer from Gimley), and two kids (Sam and Maggie), where he'll spend his time looking for his tacos and the cops.

Chris Hancock (aka Herbie) went on to play college hockey at Union and now lives with his wife, Natalia (from Vermont), in New York City, where he is relentlessly trying to perfect the optimal amount of vodka a human should consume on a nightly basis.

Chris Pronger (aka Weasel) lives with his wife, Lauren (from St. Louis), and three kids (Jack, George, and Lilah) in sunny Philadelphia where he is still coming to terms with the fact that he is the second-best golfer and third-best fisherman in the family. To his credit, he is the best defenceman in our family. Big Jim is a close second with a sneaky snap shot.

15

MY FAREWELL TOUR—OR NOT

I always thought that when I retired it would have been planned at the start of my final season or even the summer leading up to that season. I envisioned having my entire family on hand to witness my last game. I would be able to address the crowd in each of the sixteen cities I played in and thank them for all their loyal support. Perhaps I might even shed a tear. Nope. Instead, my career ended pretty much like it began. That is to say, very unspectacularly.

During our prison sentence that was the DEL in Germany, my wife and I decided to rent a house in Newport Beach, California, for the months of May and June. One reason for this was that it had snowed in our hometown of Dryden in the middle of May the year prior so we were looking to avoid any early-summer snow flurries. It also gave us a chance to see some friends we hadn't seen since our days with the Anaheim Mighty Ducks. But mostly it gave us a chance to try to forget about a forgettable year, decompress, and figure out our next move.

I didn't know if I was ready to call it a career yet. I kept thinking to myself that this is no way to go out. Not like this. I can't let Germany beat me. But, the one thing I did realize was the end was near. I decided to keep my options open. I was going to continue to train as if I was going to keep playing, but I also needed to be realistic and start figuring out what I wanted to do with the next phase of my life.

I knew I wanted to stay in the game somehow. If I couldn't play then coaching was an obvious choice to continue in the business. But coaching wasn't going to bring me any more time with the family. I knew it would also likely mean dragging my family from town to town AGAIN if I was going to try to climb up the rungs of the coaching ladder. There was no way that conversation would have gone over with the wife.

"Honey, I've decided to retire…."

"Fantastic, it's about time! I've enjoyed our whole hockey experience, but I can't wait to settle down and plant some roots in a community. As much as I have loved our travels, I think it's time to give the kids some stability. I'm so excited!"

"No, honey, I've decided to retire from playing hockey but not hockey itself. What I meant to say was I've decided to pursue a coaching career."

That wasn't going to fly. Starting off as a coach is pretty much like starting off as a player. You have to start at the bottom and work your way up. Mrs. Journeyman wasn't prepared to begin another journey like that, so I needed to figure out something else to do.

A friend of mine, Monique Lugli, recommended I contact Career Joy to speak with them about helping me "find myself." It wasn't cheap, but I needed help. And there was no way the family would live long off the wooden nickels I had saved during my lucrative career. Don't get me wrong; the ability to make a good living in professional hockey is there. But when 90 percent of your career is spent in the minors there's no pot of gold at the end of the rainbow.

Since I still hadn't *officially* called it a career, I wanted to keep all of my options open. That meant working with my new career counsellor and working out in the gym as well. I wanted to train as if I was going to be attending a camp in the fall. Be ready just in case someone called looking for that final piece of the puzzle. (Yeah, right.) Anyway, I hooked up with a former teammate of mine, Jason Marshall. He was still playing in the NHL so he was a motivated training partner. We would spend a few hours at the gym in the morning and then after lunch I worked on the next phase of my life.

For eight weeks, life was great. I trained hard, completed all of my career assignments online, and spent a lot of time with the family at home and on the beach. If making Germany a distant memory was indeed a goal, then mission accomplished. The only problem was that after those two months I still didn't know where my life was headed. On one hand I wanted to keep playing, if only for lack of a better option. But I knew that I couldn't put the family through another year like we had just endured.

After our two-month beach vacation, Mrs. Journeyman and the kids flew back to Dryden and I hopped in the truck and drove the U-Haul back. That gave me three days of alone time to try to figure stuff out. Yet even after all that time by my lonesome I was no closer to making a decision on the future. Being between jobs is a precarious position. I was definitely feeling the pressure of the situation.

I left Newport Beach on a Friday and arrived in Dryden late Sunday evening. After driving for three consecutive days I was in much need of a workout. No decision had come to me, but I knew I needed to keep training. Little did I know that the workout was about to provide an answer for me. I stepped into the squat rack, and about five minutes later I limped out of the gym with a pulled muscle in my back. Apparently, putting a couple hundred pounds on your back after sitting in a car for seventy-two hours is not good for you. Who knew? That was it for the workouts for a week.

The following Monday I went back to the gym. That time I wasn't going to do anything to compromise my back. I wasn't going to do any weights. I did a fifteen-minute warm-up on the bike and then started some plyometrics to get the legs going again. During my first set of squat jumps I felt my hamstring give. I mean, are you kidding me? One week, two brief workouts, and two injuries. Was it a glimpse into the future if I ultimately decided to give hockey another go? I wasn't prepared to take that chance.

I can still remember where I was the moment I decided to call it quits. Since the gym was only a five-second walk from our house, I limped home *again,* grabbed an ice pack, walked upstairs, and lay down in our bedroom loft. I was staring out at the lake when I yelled down to Mrs. Journeyman, "That's it. We're done."

And just like that, the professional hockey career of Sean Pronger was over. It was a weird feeling. I was expecting the thought of not playing to hurt a little. I figured maybe I'd experience a small bout of depression. But I didn't feel a thing. I wasn't sad or mad. I was just kind of … indifferent. Maybe it was because the decision came in the summer, when there wasn't any hockey to be missed. But I don't think so. I just don't think there was any more blood to squeeze from the stone. I gave all I could to the game and I had nothing left. I really believed my time had come. And to be honest, there was no one left to fool! I mean, sixteen teams in eleven years in five different leagues. The jig was up, and I was at peace with that.

For most players, retirement doesn't happen that quickly. And before that not-so-fateful day in July I figured someone would have to cut off my skates to get me to stop playing. I envisioned playing till I was at least forty. Sometimes I think I may have been able to keep playing if I hadn't decided to head overseas, but that's a moot point. I would have just been delaying the inevitable. You see, at some point, we all have to retire. Since journeymen typically don't make life-changing money, we need to find employment. For whatever reason, that is a shocker to some people. The summer after I played for the Manitoba Moose I went back to Winnipeg for a charity golf tournament. I took a cab to the golf course and the driver recognized me. That, my friends, is a big hockey fan! He asked me what my post-playing day plans were. I can still picture the puzzled look on his face when I told him that I didn't know what I was going to do, but I had to do something. He figured since I played in the NHL I was set for life. No sir Mr. Cabbie, you've got the wrong brother.

A lot of players are terrified of retirement. And, really, can you blame them? Hockey is all they know. From an early age every minute of every day was spent focusing on making it to the NHL. And once they do, all their time and energy is spent on trying to stay there. There's not a lot of time for guys to find another craft they may be good enough at to earn a living. That's why some guys hang on and play for a couple years past their best-before date. What the hell else are they going to do? Retirement is tough even on the elite players. I know what you're thinking: "Cry me a river about another millionaire athlete who can't let go of the game." And you may have a point. But the challenge is mental, not financial. These guys have been identified as "Joe Smith, star hockey player" their whole lives, and when that turns into plain old "Joe Smith" it can be tough on the ego. Hockey defines them. It's their identity. And once these guys retire it's like their identity erodes a little bit day by day. Obviously, I was not a star in the game, but I'm guessing it takes a pretty balanced individual to make a seamless transition from pro hockey life to everyday life.

I don't know. Maybe being well-balanced is overrated. Maybe seamlessness is not all it's cracked up to be. I'm thinking this way because I realize that at the moment of retirement I was pondering the same things I was that day back at the farmhouse, during my first season as a pro, when I was tempted to pack it in. What I was thinking then was that I had to go on, because Sean Pronger was a hockey player. So what else was he going to do?

I'm glad I came to the decision I did, because if I had chosen poorly back then I would never have had the chance to live the dream that dominated my whole youth. Yeah, there were some tough years, but I got to do what I set out to do. I scored some big goals, laid a few hits, dropped the gloves in front of 18,000 fans once or twice. It doesn't make me a Hall of Fame candidate (not counting the NWO Hall of Fame, that is), but I'm sure glad I didn't blow my chance to do those things. When I was a kid playing road hockey in Dryden, I would have given anything to face off against a Doug Gilmour or a Steve Yzerman. And I got what I wanted. (And won the draw, too, as I recall.)

So I'm glad I made the decision I did. But I see now that I was wrong about one thing. I didn't make that decision just because I was a hockey player and I couldn't do anything else. I probably did what I did for the challenge. Maybe I did what I did because the good things in life are the tough things to achieve. That's what I think now, anyway.

Maybe the journeymen out there learn better than others how to value what comes through great difficulty. I'd like to think that we probably prize the precious things in life a little more highly than others do, because in many cases we worked harder than others to achieve them. I'm thinking that now because, as tough as a career in hockey was, being a parent is even tougher.

Which reminds me. Now that I'm a parent, I have a much

clearer sense of what my parents did for me. Not just growing up, but throughout my career, when they would trek to the outposts of civilization to see me ply my trade. Young men may take this sort of thing for granted, but now that I'm a father myself I realize that what I often thought of as *my* career was actually not just about me at all. That's another reason I'm glad I didn't hang up my skates in Tennessee.

It also means that retirement is not entirely about me. It means saying goodbye to something I shared with people I love. But this time around it's not giving up. There are other challenges out there, which I hope I meet with the same fortitude my parents brought to their challenges.

That's not to say that retirement is easy. It's bittersweet, and probably more bitter than sweet. But I have no doubt in my mind that I made the right decision that day. I may be the exception to the rule, but I have never, ever regretted my choice to retire. Still, there are some things I miss about being a professional hockey player. And there are a lot of things I don't miss, too.

What I don't miss:
I don't miss constantly worrying about getting sent to the minors.
I don't miss getting sent to the minors.
I don't miss not being able to make plans a few weeks in advance
    for fear of being traded or sent down.
I don't miss playing zero minutes in a game when my parents have
    travelled to see me play.
I don't miss being a healthy scratch with friends and family in the
    stands.
I don't miss leaving my family in August to find a place to skate
    for a month—oh and hopefully find a job, too.
I don't miss training camp (but you could have guessed that).

I don't miss losing streaks.

I don't miss seeing my name on the fifth line of the depth chart.

I don't miss thirty-three-game goal-scoring droughts and the feeling of wondering whether I would actually hit water if I fell out of a boat.

I don't miss being out of the playoffs in February.

I don't miss spending entire summers waiting to sign, or wondering IF I'll sign.

I don't miss playing three games in three nights in three different cities.

I don't miss playing with unbelievably talented players who have no idea that hockey is a team sport.

I don't miss missing my mom's birthday every September because I'm too wrapped up in my own world.

I don't miss having to make that phone call to my wife to tell her we got sent down.

I don't miss having only two days off at Christmas.

I don't miss Germany.

I don't miss missing my family.

What I do miss:

I miss going to the rink.

I miss being on a team.

I miss being in the locker room with the boys.

I miss being on the road.

I miss that exhausted feeling after a game.

I miss having that first beer after a victory.

I miss the feeling of scoring a goal.

I miss the feeling of losing myself in the game.

I miss having my summers off.

I miss playing down the stretch.

I miss winning streaks.

I miss the feeling of walking into the locker room for practice after playing a great game.

I miss playing the game.

I miss dreaming about winning a Stanley Cup.

APPENDIX

Pronger All-Stars

Below is MY all-star team. If there was only one person (me) stuffing the ballot box, here's what the lineup would look like. These are players I had the opportunity to play with either in the NHL, minors, or the DEL.

In order to be considered for this team, you had to be:

a) an owner, GM, or coach of a team I played for
b) a great player AND more importantly an
    awesome teammate
c) a good guy
d) a family member
e) famous enough to help sell books

For those players who received this book as a stocking stuffer, had the good fortune of playing with me, AND don't see your name, fear not—just like in training camp, I'm sure you'll be named to the second all-star team.

C

Wayne Gretzky (NYR)
Ron Francis (PIT)
Doug Weight (Frankfurt)
Mark Jannsens (ANA)

LW

Paul Kariya (ANA)
Rick Nash (CLB)
Adam Graves (NYR)
Jody Shelley (CLB)

RW

Jari Kurri (ANA)
Teemu Selanne (ANA)
Ray Whitney (CLB)
Tyler Wright (CLB)

LD

Chris Pronger (Dryden Apollos)
Brian Leetch (NYR)
Stephan Robidas (Frankfurt)

RD

Rob Blake (LAK)
Ray Bourque (BOS)
Jason Marshall (ANA)

Goalies: Johan Hedberg (Manitoba Moose), Kay Whitmore (Providence)
Scratches: Sean Pronger
Owner: Mark Chipman (Manitoba Moose)
GM: Neil Smith (NYR)
Assistant GM: Craig Heisinger (Manitoba Moose)
Coach: Craig MacTavish (NYR)

FIRST LINE

C: **Wayne Gretzky** (NYR)—Do I need to say anything?
RW: **Jari Kurri** (ANA)—How do I not play Jari and Wayne together? I idolized these two while I was growing up. I had the

opportunity to play with Jari in Anaheim. Even as his career was winding down he was still a great player and, as I found out, an unbelievable guy.

LW: **Paul Kariya** (ANA)—Paul may have been the most disciplined and committed athlete ever. And the speed with which he could make plays was incredible. He also happened to be an exceptional euchre player. I think he was the second-best Euchre player in the NHL. Of course, I was number one. As partners, we tore apart the poor Mighty Ducks charter flights. Give me a call Paul: "You can be my wingman anytime."

SECOND LINE

C: **Ron Francis** (PIT)—Another player I grew up watching. To get the chance to play with him was a thrill. Ron was one of the smartest players I ever played with and has to be top ten of all time.

LW: **Rick Nash** (CLB)—Total package even at eighteen years old. He was a great guy then and is a great guy now. I ran into Rick right after he won the gold medal at the 2010 Olympics. Still the same humble guy he was when he was a rookie. Rick was lucky enough to sit next to me in Columbus his rookie year, both on the plane and in the locker room. I'm fairly certain the coaching staff did it on purpose so Rick could see what not to do on a daily basis! However, he did learn one valuable lesson: when going out for dinner with your teammates, always over-order. A brief story: It was late in his rookie season and we had been mathematically eliminated from the playoffs a couple months earlier. It's always tough to play games when you know your season's ending before your taxes are due! Anyway, we were on the road in Washington and six of us decided to go out for a nice Italian dinner. Rick decided to join us. While most of us ordered appetizers, Rick chose to skip the appetizer portion of the meal. We ordered a couple of bottles of wine for the table since we were embracing the Italian culture. Rick ordered a Diet Coke. Since we have such a large per diem in the NHL we spared no expense when it came to dining out. And this would be no exception. Almost everyone decided to live a little and order the most expensive item on the menu. I say almost everyone because Rick decided to order the spaghetti and meat sauce. Another bottle or two of wine later the bill comes, and it's big. We split the bill evenly, six ways. Upon finding out his $20 bill wouldn't cover his share, Rick blurted out "But I only had spaghetti and a Coke!" Don't worry, Rick, you'll figure it out soon enough. Always order last and always beat the pot! Sometimes you have to pay to learn.

RW: **Teemu Selanne** (ANA)—Talk about someone who's never had a bad day. Obviously, he's an unbelievable player and a PURE goal scorer. Of all the guys I've played with, besides me, he may have the worst shot of all! Certainly the worst shot of any player in the 600-goal club! I guess when you can skate a hundred miles an hour you don't need to shoot it a hundred. One of the fondest memories of my Anaheim days was on the road in Phoenix. It was after a game and we were back at our hotel. Around midnight I found myself in a sauna, having a beer with Teemu and the Godfather of Finland, Jari Kurri. There we were: the student, the teacher, and the wannabe. What's funny is my mom was born in Finland, so, technically, I'm half Finn. What a line that would've been, the Three Finns. If the coaching staff only knew!

THIRD LINE

C: **Doug Weight** (Frankfurt)—Dougie may have been my saving grace in Germany. He allowed me the chance to NOT have to tell my kids that I pitched a zero in goals my last year of pro hockey. I only wish we'd joined forces in the NHL AND I could skate, shoot, and pass better. We would've made a deadly combination. Now that he's retired, with his passion for the game I have no doubt we'll see him behind an NHL bench in the near future.

LW: **Adam Graves** (NYR)—What more do I have to say? He was a two-time Stanley Cup champ. He was a member of the Kid Line for the '90 Oilers. Who can forget when the '94 Rangers won the Cup after fifty-four years of heartbreak, Gravey skating around hollering "Nineteen-Forty!" To have the opportunity to play with him was a thrill. To see what he was like off the ice was incredible. He may be the nicest, classiest athlete in sports.

RW: **Ray Whitney** (CLB)—"He's just a little guy," but man can he play! They don't call him "The Wizard" for nothing. And, by the way, a Stanley Cup champ. Speaking of champs, after he won the Cup with the Hurricanes in 2006 (over his hometown Oilers), he insisted that his wife refer to him as "The Champ." And he would only answer to that. Needless to say, Ray's one of the funniest guys in the National Hockey League and a great guy to have in your locker room—or, just as important, on the ice.

FOURTH LINE

C: **Mark Jannsens** (ANA)—All the guys on my fourth and fifth lines have at least one thing in common: they are warriors. Mark was the ultimate warrior as well as the ultimate professional. When you're a teammate of these guys, when you get to hang out with them and see how nice they are it's hard to picture them beating the shit out of people for a living. Mind you, Mark could do more than drop the gloves. He was a great faceoff guy and great penalty killer. And a great guy ... welcome to the team Mark.

LW: **Jody Shelley** (CLB)—I had the privilege of playing with "Shellano" (as they referred to him in Columbus) when he just broke into the NHL. He was an awesome teammate and a great linemate. We played on the same line for most of the season. It's funny how much bigger and braver you feel when you get to ride shotgun with Shellano. He's another guy you'd have a hard time picturing beating guys up for a living—until you saw his face and hands!

RW: **Tyler Wright** (CLB and PIT)—He's a gritty little man. My first encounter with Tyler was when he was playing for the Cape Breton Oilers and I was playing for the Baltimore Bandits (AHL). We were about to take a faceoff against each other and he blurts out "Nice ski-jump nose!" He must've thought long and hard to come up with that one. However, when I played with him years later, he had drastically improved his verbal game. He improved his physical one as well. He's taken on some of hockey's biggest tough guys. Pete Worrell (six-foot-six) and Sandy McCarthy (six-foot-five) are some of the ones. He's five-foot-ten and 180 pounds, maybe, but he has balls of steel. The fans loved him in Columbus.

FIRST D PAIR

LD: **Chris Pronger** (Dryden)—I think an entire chapter on the snaggletoothed monster is enough. I don't care what you think of him; you want him on your team.

RD: **Rob Blake** (LAK)—Anyone who goes to bat for an average fifth-liner like me can play on my team any day! Blakey and I actually met ten years prior when he played college hockey for Bowling Green. He and Nelson Emerson took me out to dinner on my recruiting trip and then out on the town. (I'm told I had a great time!) Not a bad career: Gold Medal, Stanley Cup, Norris Trophy.

SECOND D PAIR

LD: **Brian Leetch** (NYR)—I had the pleasure of playing with Brian for only a couple of months, but what a thrill. Sometimes a player's reputation precedes him and when you finally meet it's a little disappointing. Not with Leetchy. He is such a quiet, humble, unassuming guy you'd never know he's one of the best defencemen of our generation.

RD: **Ray Bourque** (BOS)—Please revisit the "Lame Duck" chapter (aka "Training Camp Sucks"). Ray is one of the greatest and most respected players ever. And a fantastic teammate to boot!

THIRD D PAIR

LD: **Stephan Robidas** (Frankfurt)—I got to know Robi while playing through my nightmare in Frankfurt. He is a fun player to watch and I think he came into his own over there. So much so the fans hated to see him leave, even though he never really left. Robi was playing in the DEL because of the 2004–05 NHL lockout. And for those of you who don't recall that dark period in the NHL, there were rumours the lockout was going to end two or three times. And every time it looked like the lockout was going to end and the NHL season was going to be saved Robi felt compelled to give the fans of Frankfurt a proper goodbye. After one of our games Robi was informed the lockout would end so he went out and did a lap to say thank-you and goodbye to the fans. I think there were seven or eight thousand people clapping and chanting "Au-Rev-Oir Ro-bi-das." It was pretty awesome. So awesome that he got to do that two more times that season because the lockout never ended!

RD: **Jason Marshall** (ANA, Baltimore)—aka Sheriff. If you've ever had the opportunity to meet Marshy you'd never believe he was one of the most intense players I've had the privilege of playing with. He may be the nicest guy you'll ever meet. But when he suits up and puts in his black mouthguard (aka Black Bart), look out. He wasn't an overly big man, but could he throw 'em. I loved playing with him because it was all out, all the time. That's the only way he played. I don't care what league we're playing in, Marshy will always be on my team!

GOALIES

G: **Johan Hedberg** (Manitoba)—MOOOOOOSE!! Remember the playoffs in Pittsburgh when he burst on the scene? Has anyone said anything bad about this guy? Ever? And you never will. Great goalie and a great teammate. Have I mentioned the story about our rookie dinner with the Manitoba Moose? We were playing two games in Salt Lake City with two days in between each. Is there a better opportunity for some team bonding? A coach will never give you a blatant green light for a night out, but let's just say it was a "flashing amber." We decided to make the forty-five-minute drive to Park City for our rookie dinner. The meal was great but it was the trip home I'd like to discuss. Our captain, Brian Chapman, Johan Hedberg, and I decided to call it a night and piled into a taxi van for the trek home. Upon entering the van we noticed a large speaker and microphone between the front seats. "Is that what I think it is?" I said. "Yes, it's a karaoke machine," cabby said. "No $#%&ing way!" the three of us said in unison. For the next forty-five minutes we rocked the shit out of that cab. Actually, it was more like two and a half hours, since we made the driver pull over to grab some beer and make a couple laps of the city so we could crank out a few more Neil Diamond ballads. I can say this with all honesty: I've yet to meet anyone to belt out "Under the Boardwalk" like the MOOOOOOSE!

G: **Kay Whitmore** (Providence)—Get a hit, Crash! Shut up. Whits— or, as I like to call him, "Crash"—was a well-travelled goalie, which probably is why we got along so well. As I mentioned earlier in the book, I struggled quite a bit in Providence but Whits made it a lot more manageable. We used to travel to practice together along with Keith McCambridge and host our own "Hot Stove Lounge" in his pickup. Let's just say it was a great place for some of us to "vent" our frustrations. Speaking of venting frustrations, we had just finished our game-day skate in Hershey and I asked Whits if I could take a couple shots on him after practice. He wasn't playing that night, so of course he'd stay in and get some extra work. Normally, the goalie that's not playing that night gets to enjoy some chin music by the fellas working on their high heat. I say normally because you don't fire high hard cheese at a veteran netminder like Kay. And, obviously, a veteran like myself would know this. Did I mention we were close friends? Did I mention my wife literally helped deliver his first child? Did I mention I was working on my one-timers from the top of the circle? Did I mention one got away from me? Yep, I ripped a slapshot off his forehead from about forty feet. Not a good feeling. Not a good one for him, either. I think it was twenty stitches later when the bleeding finally stopped. Fortunately, Crash had a shaved head so you could barely make out the scar from about 200 feet away. What an ass I was! And to my own buddy and fellow journeyman no less. Sorry, Crash.

Scratches: **Sean Pronger** (Everywhere)—aka Chris's Brother. Good in the room. So leave him there.

Owner: **Mark Chipman** (Manitoba)—One of the classiest people in hockey, period. I couldn't be happier for him to bring a team to the 'Peg. The NHL is lucky to have a guy like Mark. He has a genuine passion for the game and cares about his players. How many owners do you know who will run down to the medical room to check on a player that just got hurt? I know, because I was that player. I got into a fight with Tavis Hansen because I was sticking up for one of our young Russian players. Can you believe it was Kirill Kolstov? What a dummy I was! Tavis laid out Kirill with about a minute left in what would be a 5–1 victory. If it didn't happen right in front of me I couldn't have cared less. But he levelled him about two feet from me so I had to do something. So, off came the gloves and a fury of heavy rights from both of us. Details are still a little sketchy but apparently he caught me with a right on the temple and down I went. As I was lying face down on the ice the linesman was patting me on the back saying "it's OK, it's over." Like an idiot I said "What happened?" "He caught you with a right." To this day I swear the ref hit me! Anyway, as I was getting stitched up in the training room in walks Chipper. "Great job, Prongs!" I wasn't feeling that great since I just got buckled in front of my friends, family, teammates, and 7,000 people all while sticking up for someone I know certainly wouldn't do the same for me. He then walks over to me, looks me in the eye, shakes my hand, and says, "Thank you for what you did." How many owners would do that? The players on the Jets are going to love playing for him, I guarantee it.

GM: **Neil Smith** (NYR)—Even though I didn't spend much time in New York, or on the ice for that matter, my experience with Neil left a lasting impression. This guy lived and died with every win and loss. He had a star-studded lineup that was a perfect fit for the bright lights of the Big Apple. And he had no problems treating the players like royalty. All he wanted was for us to shuffle in a win every once in a while. Is that too much to ask? One moment in particular stands out. We were on the road in Phoenix. We had a couple days off, and since we had such a veteran team it almost always meant lots of golf and as little skating as possible. The season is such a grind that when you have a couple days to let the bumps and bruises heal it is a fantastic idea. Normally, this would be welcomed with open arms by this cowboy, but as you may have guessed the only bumps and bruises were on my ass along with a few slivers from riding the pine. So, instead of hitting the links I figured I might as well hit the gym. Don't worry; I was planning a steam and massage afterward. As I walked into the gym at the hotel there were only two bikes open. Naturally, I jumped on one and went to work. As I reached the third minute of my workout, the GM of the New York Rangers saddles up next to me. My first instinct was to get off my bike and go use the NordicTrack. However, this is the general manager, so it might not be that bad of an idea for him to see his star fifth-liner grind out forty-five minutes on the bike while everyone else is trying to figure where the beer cart girl is. I also figured there was a good chance Neil had no idea who I was. As the sweat was starting to pour off my nose, Neil says, "Sean, what do you think of the hotel?"

Is he talking to me? "It's great, Neil."

"Where did you guys stay when you played with Anaheim?"

He proceeded to pick my brain for the next forty minutes. We talked about different players, coaches, general managers. And it wasn't like he was trying to gossip; he was genuinely interested in how other general managers in the league behaved.

For a guy like Neil Smith to care what a scrub like me had to say was pretty cool. Our bike ride only lasted forty minutes but I'll never forget our conversation.

Assistant GM: **Craig Heisinger** (Manitoba)—aka Zinger. *Orchestrated my trade back to the 'Peg?* I've made a lot of mistakes and bad decisions in my career. And if there was one thing I would consider doing over it would be to try to stay in Winnipeg instead of signing to play in Frankfurt. I think we know how that turned out. Of all the people I've met along my journey in this game, Zinger may be my favourite. He wants nothing more than to win hockey games. He's as honest a person as you'll ever meet in the game. He wants none of the recognition and none of the glory. He just loves the game and works tirelessly behind the scenes to put a winning team on the ice. My favourite Zinger moment happened a couple years after I had retired. Zinger won an award as the top executive in the AHL. He was then interviewed in the *Winnipeg Sun.* One of the questions went as follows:

Sun: What did winning the James C. Hendy Memorial Award (as outstanding executive in the AHL) mean to you?

Zinger: Nothing.

So classic!

Coach: **Craig MacTavish** (NYR)—aka Mac T. Even though Mac T was never a head coach of mine I have a pretty good idea he's just the guy I'd want to lead my all-star team. A funny story: It's the summer of 2005 and Mac T is coaching the Edmonton Oilers. Upon hearing that the Oilers have acquired Pronger, Coach MacTavish is heard saying, "What? Why? We already have ten Sean Prongers!"

"Uh, no Craig, *Chris* Pronger."

Even with that comment you can still be my coach. And by the way, the 2006 playoff run may have been the most fun I've had as a hockey fan ever! I went up to games three and four, and I can tell you, it was *electric*.

ACKNOWLEDGMENTS

I can't believe this book made it onto bookshelves! I suddenly feel the urge to go out and buy a tweed jacket and an ascot. Let this be a lesson to everyone—if I can do it, ANYBODY can do it. That will bring an end to the motivational speech portion of the program. Obviously, writing a book doesn't just happen, and now that I've gone through the process I feel the need to thank those responsible for making this possible.

I'd like to thank my agent, Brian Wood, for taking a chance on a couple of no-name non-authors. I'd like to thank Penguin Canada for believing in the *Journeyman* story, with a special thanks to Nick Garrison, our editor at Penguin, for his unbelievable patience and understanding in helping us bring the story to light.

I want to thank my co-author, Dan Murphy, for continuously and relentlessly mocking my hockey-playing ability and for helping to illustrate the fact that I'm mentally weak. Just when I thought I couldn't put myself down any longer, Dan was there to pick up the baton. Seriously, Murph, this book wouldn't have happened without you. I would consider it an honour and a privilege if you gave me the opportunity to repay the favour and make a mockery of your life.

317

To the boys (John Cummings, Darcy Mitani, Steve Roll, Chris Hancock, and Chris Pronger), thanks for our childhood. I wouldn't change a thing. Thanks for not letting me take myself too seriously, because my illustrious career would never have happened if I did! But most of all, thank you for your friendship.

I need to thank Big Jim and Eila Pronger, aka Mom and Dad. I wish I had the words to convey my gratitude for all that you've done for me. If only I were a writer. Thank you both for all your support and for allowing me to find my way. As you both know, it wasn't always pretty!

To my beautiful children, Kaia and Vann, thank you for showing me what's truly important in life. You guys are my inspiration, and I hope this book shows you that if you find your passion, believe in yourself, and stick with it, anything is possible. However, due to adult language, you won't be reading this for a while.

Lastly, I want to thank my beautiful wife, Marnie, aka Mrs. Journeyman. You are my psychiatrist, psychologist, chef, bartender, motivational speaker, ass-kicker, moving coordinator, realtor, etc. If it weren't for you there is NO way I would've lasted as long as I did. Thank you for your unwavering support and for making our journey an adventure.

Dan Murphy

I'd like to echo much of what Sean has written by first thanking Brian Wood for telling the two of us over and over that there was definitely enough content to write a book.

"Seventy thousand f---ing words, Brian, are you crazy?"

I guess he wasn't.

Nick at Penguin, I'm sure we are responsible for any grey hairs on your head, so please pick up the phone whenever you need another supply of Just for Men. Seriously, thanks for helping us shape this story. We didn't always want to hear your ideas, but they always pushed us in the right direction.

Sean, thanks for blindly jumping into this project like the idiot you are. We didn't know what we were getting into, but the process was a blast because you made it so. You are a great friend, and of all the authors I know, you're one of them. I just wish we could have made fun of Chris more.

Thanks to my parents, Jim and Rita, for all your support.

And finally, thanks to my wonderful wife, Christy, who encouraged me from the start. Countless nights I spent more time with the computer than with you, and yet you never complained. Thanks for your love and for always having my back.